"*Collective Genius* is practical in its approach, yet deep in wisdom. It is a must-read for those who realize that innovation is the key to an organization's survival, as well as for any passionate leader who strives to build workplaces where people can create, collaborate, and ultimately deliver innovative solutions to problems that, at the outset, appear impossible to solve. The concepts and lessons found within these pages can be perfectly described as 'genius.'"

— **Khalil A. Al-Shafei**, head of Technical Services, Aramco Services Company; former interim President, King Abdullah Petroleum Studies and Research Center

"I find innovation, and companies that innovate, one of the most important things to study, because we not only learn but get inspired by true innovative leadership. *Collective Genius* does a great job of explaining why innovation—the search for better solutions—is so important in companies large and small."

— **Andy Bechtolsheim**, Chairman, Arista Networks

"*Collective Genius* goes to the heart of leading innovation in today's fast-paced world. This book is filled with evocative stories of leaders of innovation, it digs deeply into their dispositions and catalytic mind-sets, and shows how they create contexts for breakthrough innovations. An inspiring read."

— **John Seely Brown**, former Chief Scientist, Xerox Corporation, and Director of the Palo Alto Research Center (PARC)

"The leadership of innovative teams and organizations is perhaps the most confounding mystery in business today. Business leaders know they have to do it but have little idea where to start. *Collective Genius* tells the stories of those who have cracked the code. It reveals the principles by which we might unlock the collective potential of our colleagues and release the creative potential of our organizations."

— **Tim Brown**, President and CEO, IDEO

"Defines the role of the leader in innovation—not as the person with all the answers but rather as the enabler and context setter. This book provides engaging stories and examples to help leaders create an environment where their teams embrace the creative friction and trial and error needed for true innovation."

— **Amy Bunszel**, Vice President, AutoCAD Products, Autodesk, Inc.

"The authors challenge the widely accepted myth of the leader as a 'visionary' inspiring people to follow. When it comes to achieving true innovation, the process is way more complex. The book shows how the 'sausage' is made, and it should be mandatory reading for anyone aspiring to make a difference."

— **Bruno Campos**, founding partner, BCMF Arquitetos, Brazil

"Although common sense tells us innovation occurs as a 'brilliant individual, isolated idea,' *Collective Genius* tells us that innovation is built on a leadership style that allows innovation to happen from the bottom up—collectively, based on engagement and trust. I highly recommend this book for twenty-first-century leaders."

— **André Rodrigues Cano**, Executive Director, Banco Bradesco, Brazil

"*Collective Genius* offers real-world insights that will help today's business leaders challenge the status quo, drive new ideas, and create an environment where change and innovation are the norm."

— **Kenneth I. Chenault**, CEO and Chairman, American Express

"Innovation. Leadership. Motivation. Execution. What we need to do is quite obvious. And thanks to this book, we now have a guide to teach us how."

— **Clayton M. Christensen**, Kim B. Clark Professor of Business Administration, Harvard Business School; author, *The Innovator's Dilemma*

"Innovation is key to competing in today's environment. Hill, Brandeau, Truelove, and Lineback reveal the leadership practices for unlocking the 'collective genius' needed to achieve breakthrough innovation."

— **Edith W. Cooper**, Executive Vice President and Global Head of Human Capital Management, Goldman Sachs

"As the purpose of organization now tips from seeking efficient repetition to creating value through change, knowing how to lead fluid, open teams of teams has become essential. That's why *Collective Genius* is so important."

— **Bill Drayton**, founder and CEO, Ashoka: Innovators for the Public

"Innovation cannot be ordered from above but, rather, needs to be enabled and fostered through proper leadership. *Collective Genius* brilliantly tells us how, why, and when. By expertly linking leadership and innovation, this highly readable book provides superb insights into why so few companies have succeeded in sustaining an innovation culture, and then shows us what it takes to shine where it really matters."

— **Mohamed A. El-Erian**, author, *When Markets Collide*; former CEO, PIMCO

"A must-read. *Collective Genius* represents a complete transformation of what leadership means. The authors take you on a fascinating journey, revealing the art and best practice of leading for innovation. A brilliant piece of work."

— **Khaled El Gohary**, Advisor, Ministry of Cabinet Affairs, Prime Minister's Office, United Arab Emirates

"An essential read for any leader looking to tap into the latent creative talents throughout their organization, *Collective Genius* provides a clear road map of

'Innovation Island,' with modern leadership principles and incisive examples of implementation from many of today's most exciting and successful companies. The elusive task of driving innovation put in real terms."

— **Gary Ellis**, Chief Digital Officer, Hearst Magazines International

"Innovation is not the domain of one individual in an organization; it occurs where there is empowerment and teamwork. *Collective Genius* captures best practices from global leaders in a compelling and concise manner and demonstrates the opportunity to apply a common business ethos across diverse industries. Unlocking the power of the 'collective genius' is the common denominator of all great leaders."

— **Alan J. Fuerstman**, founder and CEO, Montage Hotels & Resorts

"Leaders can't make innovation happen. But the best leaders know how to create a space where it can happen, over and over. *Collective Genius* will inspire and instruct you toward leading a truly innovative organization."

— **Vijay Govindarajan**, Coxe Distinguished Professor of Management, Tuck School of Business, Dartmouth; *New York Times* and *Wall Street Journal* bestselling author, *Reverse Innovation*

"An interesting and instructive look at how leaders can create flexible corporate ecosystems to unleash individual talent in ways that lead to greater organizational innovation."

— **Reid Hoffman**, cofounder and Chairman, LinkedIn; coauthor, *The Alliance*

"Linda Hill and her coauthors argue that innovation requires a different kind of leader—someone who can create and sustain a culture that brings out the 'collective genius' of all their diverse and talented people. A great read for anyone leading a team, organization, or community."

— **Tony Hsieh**, CEO, Zappos; *New York Times* bestselling author, *Delivering Happiness*

"As someone who serves as a custodian of an institution dedicated to creativity and innovation, I found this book full of great stories and practical ideas that I believe in deeply, as well as new ideas that I can't wait to try out. A must-read for any manager or participant in an organization that requires innovation—in other words, any organization that wants to be successful in the new world of continuous massive disruptions."

— **Joi Ito**, Director, MIT Media Lab

"As every company struggles to be more innovative, *Collective Genius* provides an excellent framework that highlights each aspect required to foster an innovative environment. It is one of the few books that truly captures innovation in action and the important role—and qualities—of leaders who make it happen. I would recommend *Collective Genius* as a worthwhile read for anyone who wants to accelerate their innovation efforts."

— **Terri Kelly**, President and CEO, W. L. Gore & Associates

"*Collective Genius* illustrates the crucial differences between the qualities of conventional leaders and leaders of innovation. Inclusiveness, openness, and purposefulness create the opportunity to engage the collaborative brilliance that fuels inventive thinking. This book provides an essential framework for developing leadership that can make collective genius a reality in your business."

— **Randy Komisar**, partner, Kleiner Perkins Caufield & Byers; serial entrepreneur; and author, *The Monk and the Riddle*

"*Collective Genius* is a great read, full of important insights for anyone involved in high-impact innovation. The book shows how teams in diverse fields, from technology to design, collaborate to deliver breakthrough results. I look forward to sharing it with my colleagues."

— **Mark M. Little**, Senior Vice President, Director of Global Research, and Chief Technology Officer, General Electric

"As Nelson Mandela wrote, innovation leaders are like shepherds: they stay behind the flock, letting the most nimble go on ahead without realizing that all along they are being directed from behind. *Collective Genius* teaches us how to deal with common dilemmas in a creative business environment, such as encouraging collective thinking when faced with urgent business deadlines, or respecting the individual while leveraging the whole team. The business cases and practices in this book inspire me in my journey to build an innovative organization in the renewable energy industry."

— **Jerry Luo**, Vice President, Envision Energy, China

"*Collective Genius* shows aspiring leaders how important it is to create the context for innovation—and how to do so. It is a gem. Don't miss its in-depth case studies and insightful analysis."

— **Chunka Mui**, coauthor, *The New Killer Apps*

"Linda Hill, an unusually perceptive scholar of leadership, has turned her focus to leading innovation within organizations. She and her coauthors studied leaders as diverse as Ed Catmull of Pixar, Vineet Nayar of HCL, and Amy Schulman of Pfizer. From their experiences, the authors develop common themes and actionable advice on how leaders can unleash and simultaneously harness the collective genius in their organizations."

— **Ashish Nanda**, Director, Indian Institute of Management, Ahmedabad

"*Collective Genius* builds upon rich case studies of some of the world's most innovative companies. The authors identify essential paradoxes that lie at the heart of sustained innovation and fuel each link of the value chain, from inspiration to execution."

— **Richard Pascale**, Associate Fellow, Saïd Business School, Oxford University; author, *Surfing the Edge of Chaos*; and coauthor, *The Power of Positive Deviance*

"Hill and company have written the definitive manual for innovation to guide business leaders of the twenty-first century."

— **Milton Pedraza**, CEO, Luxury Institute, LLC

"Innovation is the driving force for our economy, yet poorly researched and understood from a leadership perspective. *Collective Genius* fills this void. It captures the essence of how leaders can foster innovation and unleash the full creative potential of their organizations."

— **U. Mark Schneider**, CEO, Fresenius Group

"*Collective Genius* provides great insights that put a fresh perspective on the subject of leadership and innovation, a potent combination for constant business regeneration and sustainability. The authors argue convincingly that those in leadership positions are not necessarily prone to lead in a way that creates an environment conducive to generating new ideas; and importantly, that leaders have to understand their role in enabling innovation to take place."

— **Isaac Shongwe**, Executive Director, Barloworld Ltd.; founder and Chairman, Africa Leadership Initiative

"Almost every leader talks about innovation, yet most are frustrated by a lack of it. This book goes to the heart of how innovation can be fostered so that it occurs naturally. It breaks traditional models of leadership and offers a practical guide to what it takes to lead an innovative culture."

— **Man Jit Singh**, President, Sony Pictures Home Entertainment

"Insightful thinking on the true meaning of leadership in an ever-changing world. A must-read for any leader aspiring to transform an organization and capture its innovative spirit."

— **James C. Smith**, President and CEO, Thomson Reuters

"We tend to think of innovation as a spark of genius. This book proves that sustainable innovation actually requires 'collective genius'—a 'jazz ensemble' or group of talented people whose leader sets the stage."

— **Dr. Shinji Tanabe**, HR Manager, Human Resources Development Center and former R&D Group Leader/Chief Engineer, Mitsubishi Electric

"Leaders—you are on notice! Linda Hill and colleagues will teach even the most experienced leaders how to rethink their approach to leading organizations that thrive on innovation. *Collective Genius* explains the paradoxes that make innovation so difficult and provides powerful lessons on how leaders can effectively collectivize the diverse slices of genius inherent in all organizations."

— **Robert Tepper**, MD, partner and cofounder, Third Rock Ventures; former President of R&D, Millennium Pharmaceuticals

"It is often difficult to overcome diversity and complexity in creating organizations that are able to innovate. This book is a great practical guide for any leader who wants to learn how his or her leadership has to change in order to establish the right climate, which is so essential for innovation."

— **Agah Uğur**, CEO, Borusan Group, Turkey

"*Collective Genius* is a terrific book for any business leader who cares about or trades in ideas. The authors have chosen a diverse and compelling set of companies— from a luxury brand in Korea to a California animation studio—to demonstrate how to build a culture of diverse thinking and innovation. The concept of 'creative abrasion,' especially, struck a chord with me, as it perfectly describes the research process we employ at Bernstein."

— **Robert van Brugge**, Chairman and CEO, Sanford C. Bernstein

"*Collective Genius* is a fascinating book about the role of leadership in creating an innovative organization. Innovation requires a different approach to leadership, and the authors tell us exactly how it works. A must-read for tomorrow's leaders of innovation."

— **Cristina Ventura**, Joyce Senior Vice President, Lane Crawford Joyce Group, Hong Kong

"Just when you thought the world didn't need yet another book on leadership or innovation, *Collective Genius* comes along, packing a disruptive punch. Hill, Brandeau, Truelove, and Lineback reveal a new area of theory and practice that challenges conventional thinking on leadership. They assiduously demonstrate the power that comes from exploring the domains of leadership and innovation through an integrated framework and, in the process, introduce us to some of the most creative, diverse, and inspiring leaders working in business today."

— **Darren Walker**, President, Ford Foundation

COLLECTIVE GENIUS

COLLECTIVE

GENIUS

THE ART AND PRACTICE
OF LEADING INNOVATION

LINDA A. HILL
HARVARD BUSINESS SCHOOL

GREG BRANDEAU
FORMER SVP TECHNOLOGY, PIXAR

EMILY TRUELOVE
MASSACHUSETTS INSTITUTE OF TECHNOLOGY

KENT LINEBACK
EXECUTIVE & BEST-SELLING AUTHOR

HARVARD BUSINESS REVIEW PRESS

BOSTON, MASSACHUSETTS

HBR Press Quantity Sales Discounts

Harvard Business Review Press titles are available at significant quantity discounts when purchased in bulk for client gifts, sales promotions, and premiums. Special editions, including books with corporate logos, customized covers, and letters from the company or CEO printed in the front matter, as well as excerpts of existing books, can also be created in large quantities for special needs.

For details and discount information for both print and ebook formats, contact booksales@harvardbusiness.org, tel. 800-988-0886, or www.hbr.org/bulksales.

Printed in the United States of America

10 9 8 7

The web addresses referenced in this book were live and correct at the time of the book's publication but may be subject to change.

ISBN: 978-1-4221-3002-5

eISBN: 978-1-4221-8759-3

Library of Congress Cataloging-in-Publication Data

Hill, Linda A. (Linda Annette), 1956-

Collective genius : the art and practice of leading innovation / Linda A. Hill, Greg Brandeau, Emily Truelove, Kent Lineback.
    Pages cm
  ISBN 978-1-4221-3002-5 (hardback)
  1. Leadership. 2. Organizational behavior. 3. Technological innovations. I. Title.
  HD57.7.H55 2014
  658.4'092--dc23   2013050672

The paper used in this publication meets the requirements of the American National Standard for Permanence of Paper for Publications and Documents in Libraries and Archives Z39.48-1992.

TABLE OF CONTENTS

CONTENTS

ACKNOWLEDGMENTS

Written by Linda A. Hill

The roots of this project go back to 1986 when I wrote a case study about Suzanne de Passe, then the president of Motown Productions, who had just won numerous awards for producing *Motown 25: Yesterday, Today, Forever*. Suzanne was gracious enough to let me shadow her as she went about her work, all the while offering her well-honed point of view about what it takes to lead talented, passionate, creative people. The lessons learned were never forgotten and I made a promise to return to the question of "leading creatives" someday. In 1999, I met Ahmed Kathrada, known by his friends as "Kathy," a South African anti-apartheid activist and former political prisoner who spent decades in a cell across from President Nelson Mandela on Robben Island. Kathy introduced me to his "comrades," who shared their experiences of what it took to lead a revolution. Many recited a passage found in Nelson Mandela's autobiography: A leader is like a shepherd. He stays behind the flock, letting the most nimble go out ahead, whereupon the others follow, not realizing that all along they are being directed from behind.

Despite their divergent circumstances and ambitions, I was struck by the commonalities between the leadership philosophies of Suzanne and Kathy—both consummate leaders of innovation who knew how to unleash *and* harness people's creativity to fulfill a collective purpose. In 1999, when asked to write an article about leadership for the new century, I titled it "Leadership as Collective Genius." Not surprisingly, I argued that building organizations that could innovate was going to be *the* critical leadership task for the foreseeable future—whether that meant creating competitive advantage in the private sector or addressing recalcitrant social ills in the public or not-for-profit sectors.

As faculty chair of the Leadership Initiative at Harvard Business School, I decided it was time for me to get serious about reexamining our image of the ideal leader and figure out what it takes to lead innovation. As in all great adventures, my coauthors and I came together in large measure through fortuitous events. We share a passion: how to develop leaders who can build organizations that can innovate time and again. For almost ten years we have been engaged in a collaborative project on leadership for innovation. We are an interdisciplinary and multigenerational team and have introduced each other to colleagues and friends in our respective worlds. We have had the privilege to work and study with individuals in organizations across industries, sectors, and the globe.

This book would not have been possible without the generosity of hundreds of people who have assisted us along the way. First and foremost, we must thank the leaders and their colleagues who have allowed us to become intimately acquainted with the inner-workings of their organizations. They have been true partners in our journey, pushing our thinking forward with their insights and incisive questions. A special thanks to our friends at Pixar, the company that came to serve as the touchstone for this project. Truly everyone at Pixar was welcoming. Ed Catmull and Lori McAdams were tireless champions of our efforts.

We are indebted to those who critiqued the manuscript allowing us to refine our argument and narrative: Robert Cohen, Rob Cook, Lorraine Delhorne, Carol Franco, Letty Garcia-Pacheco, Joline Godfrey, Paul Hemp, Barbara Hood, John Kirkman, Karim Lahkani, Ann Le Cam, Steve May, Anthony Mayo, Sunand Menon, Gautam Mukunda, Randy Nelson, Karen Paik, Anne Pia, Maurizio Travaglini, and the anonymous readers Harvard Business Review Press enlisted for us. Many of these individuals read multiple drafts and served as our community of developmental editors. It is only fitting that I dedicate this book to my research associates, my intellectual partners from data collection and writing to handling the countless details associated with the final production of a manuscript. Three in particular must be noted: Dana Teppert, Jennifer Suesse Stine, and Allison Wigen.

Others who assisted in indispensable ways include our editor at the Press, Jeff Kehoe, whose confidence in and commitment to this endeavor kept us going; Carol Franco, our agent, who inspired us to do "just one more rewrite" though we were weary, and to keep talking when discord more than collaboration seemed to be the state of affairs; and Barbara Devine, my assistant, who kept our virtual team organized. I also extend a special thanks to the Harvard Business School Division of Research for providing me with the significant resources required to complete this work.

We'd also like to acknowledge the support and sacrifices made by our families; they gave us the encouragement, time, and space to fulfill our ambitions. For me, that includes Roger Breitbart, Jonathan Hill Breitbart, Dana Hewett, and my lifelong cheerleaders, my parents Clifford and Lillian Hill. For Greg: Joan, Pinky, and Snapper. For Kent: his wife, Carol Franco. For Emily: her parents and siblings and her husband, John Truelove.

A few words from Greg: Linda and I met when I had been wondering why some companies thrived and others didn't. I had been lucky enough to work with terrific people at amazing companies who taught me which things mattered and which didn't. She and I had a number of fascinating conversations on that subject that eventually led to our work on this book. Thanks to everyone I have worked with over the years, particularly Dominique Trempont at NeXT and Lawrence Levy at Pixar, who hired me into great organizations and helped me flourish.

A few words from Emily: I would like to extend a special thanks to Doug Ready and the ICEDR team, who were not only wonderful colleagues, but incredibly patient ones as the research and writing process of this book moved along. I am also very grateful to my graduate school mentors—especially Kate Kellogg, John Van Mannen, and Lotte Bailyn—and my fellow doctoral students, who have pushed me to ask new questions and to refine my craft as a qualitative researcher.

We hope we have done justice to all those who have contributed to this effort. For any shortcomings, we collectively accept responsibility.

INTRODUCTION

Why does the world need yet another book on innovation or leadership? Haven't both been studied in great depth?

Our answer is simple: it needs this book precisely because it's *not* another book on either of those familiar topics. It is, instead, a book about a topic much less discussed or understood—leadership *and* innovation, or the role of the leader in creating a more innovative organization.

Search the literature and you'll discover what we found—volumes of research on innovation and as many or more on leadership, but almost nothing on the connection between the two.[1] Why is this so? Perhaps practicing leaders and management thinkers have simply assumed a "good" leader in all other respects would be an effective leader of innovation as well. If that's the case, however, we must report it's a deeply flawed and even dangerous assumption. Leading innovation and what is widely considered good leadership, we found, are not the same.

We know this because for more than a decade we've been studying leaders who were proven masters at fostering organizational innovation. The people they led, from small teams to vast enterprises, were able to produce innovative solutions again and again.

To understand what they did, how they thought, and who they were, we sought them out, from Silicon Valley to Europe to the United Arab Emirates to India and Korea, and we explored businesses as diverse as filmmaking, e-commerce, auto manufacturing, professional services, high-tech, and luxury goods. We spent hundreds of hours in total with them and their colleagues. In the end, we interviewed and observed sixteen and studied twelve in depth who included talented women and men of seven nationalities serving different functions at different levels in their organizations.[2] All this research, of course, was built on the foundation of the thousands of leaders and organizations the four of us have experienced, observed, and studied in our varied individual careers.

What we found in our research—confirmed, actually—was the critical role of the leader. That leadership matters to innovation should come as no surprise. Look beneath the surface of almost anything produced by an organization that is new, useful, and even moderately complex, and you'll almost certainly discover it came from multiple hands, not the genius of some solitary inventor. Innovation is a "team sport," as one leader told us, in which individual effort becomes something more. Somehow, in the language we've come to use, truly innovative groups are consistently able to elicit and then combine members' separate *slices of genius* into a single work of *collective genius*. Creating and sustaining an organization capable of doing that again and again is what we saw our leaders do.

They understood the nature of innovation and how it worked, and so they fully appreciated that they could not force it to happen or get it done on their own. Consequently, they saw themselves and their role differently. They focused their time and attention on different areas and activities. They made different choices when faced with the difficult trade-offs leadership constantly required of them. In studying these leaders, we found, above all, that leadership as it's widely understood and practiced today isn't what these leaders of innovation were doing.

The source of this discrepancy, we suspect, is that over the past few decades, the leader's role has become equated with setting out a vision and inspiring people to follow. This conception of the leader's role can work well when the solution to a problem is known and straightforward, but is counterproductive when it's not. If a problem calls for a truly original response, no one can know in advance what that response should be. By definition, then, leading innovation cannot be about creating and selling a vision to people who are somehow inspired to execute that vision. So common is this notion of the leader as visionary that many of those we studied had to rethink and recast their roles before their organizations could become truly and consistently innovative.

What we observed across all the diverse individuals and organizations we studied was a surprisingly consistent view of the leader's role in innovation, which can be expressed this way: *Instead of trying to come up with a vision and make innovation happen themselves, a leader of innovation creates a place—a context, an environment—where people are willing and able to do the hard work that innovative problem solving requires.*

One of the leaders we studied neatly summed this up by repeating a line he had heard from a CEO he admired. "My job," he said, "is to set the stage, not to perform on it."

Based on what we saw in our research, we present in *Collective Genius* a framework that you and other practicing leaders can apply to "set the stage"—that is, to create a place where people are willing and able to innovate time and again.

That framework is reflected in the flow of chapters ahead.

Why Innovation Requires a Different Kind of Leader

The first three chapters open by looking in depth at Pixar Animation Studios, a company with a formidable innovation track record. During the period we studied, Pixar was able to produce hit film after hit film, each one an innovative tour de force. Because its work is so widely known, Pixar is an ideal choice for showing what's required to transform the individual efforts of hundreds of people—all those slices of genius—into a single, coherent work of collective genius. In chapter 2, we explore the unavoidable tensions and conflicts built into the innovation process, which explain both why innovation is so rare and difficult and why it requires leadership. But what kind of leadership? In chapter 3, we paint a detailed portrait of a CEO who went far beyond the conventions of "good leadership" to turn a declining Indian computer company into an international dynamo of IT innovation.

The chapters that follow focus on what leaders of innovation actually do to foster creative genius. They are organized around the two great tasks we saw our leaders perform. In part I, chapters 4 and 5, we show what they did to create organizations *willing* to innovate. In part II, chapters 6 through 8, we show how they created organizations *able* to innovate.

What Leaders Do: They Create Organizations *Willing* to Innovate

It's tempting to believe that people and organizations are naturally eager to create something new and useful, when, in fact, they often are not. The diversity innovation thrives on, the conflict of ideas and options it requires, the patience it needs to test and learn from multiple approaches, and the courage it demands to hold options open until possibilities can be integrated in new and creative ways—all these things can make innovative problem solving feel awkward, stressful, and even unnatural. Without leadership, internal forces common to virtually all groups will stifle and discourage innovation, in spite of everyone's rhetoric about how much they want it. In part I, we show how our leaders overcame these destructive forces by creating communities whose members were bound by common purpose, shared values, and mutual rules of engagement.

What Leaders Do: They Create Organizations *Able* to Innovate

The organizational ability to innovate is equally important and, unfortunately, equally difficult. In part II, we show how the leaders we studied focused on three key aspects of the innovation process: collaboration, discovery-driven learning, and integrative decision making. Each of these aspects has already been identified and studied by others, though typically in isolation from each other. Our contribution is to show how effective leaders actually build a key organizational capability in each of these areas—*creative abrasion* for collaboration, *creative agility* for learning through discovery, and *creative resolution* for integrative decision making. These are difficult for organizations to acquire, exercise, and maintain. They require leaders who can constantly balance the tensions and paradoxes built into the innovation process.

The final section of *Collective Genius* examines two forward-looking aspects of leading innovation. In chapter 9, we outline the leadership challenge of an increasingly common approach today—the innovation ecosystem, which comprises disparate organizations and sometimes even competitors that join together for the purpose of developing something new. Given how hard innovation is within the same organization, it's easy to appreciate the supreme difficulty of crossing boundaries and getting diverse groups to collaborate creatively. In the epilogue, we look briefly at three organizations that have found effective ways of identifying and developing the leaders of innovation they will need tomorrow.

Because our goal is to provide practical and concrete guidance, we not only describe what leaders of innovation do, but we show it as well. Every chapter in *Collective Genius*, save one, is written around an in-depth portrait of one or more of the leaders we studied. In these stories and descriptions, we present both the art and practice of leading innovation by showing our leaders in action. Unless otherwise indicated, all quotations are based on our primary research, and because our leaders all believed that rhetoric matters, we have quoted them extensively. In this way, we hope to help practicing leaders bridge the knowing-doing gap between conceptual knowledge and an ability to apply that knowledge in everyday settings.

Some of our leaders worked in organizations widely considered hotbeds of innovation; others ran parts of firms rarely associated with the cutting edge. Some led start-ups; some led well-established companies trying to figure out how to sustain success, while others took over organizations that had lost their way and desperately needed rejuvenation. The innovations produced by their groups ran the gamut from new products and services to business processes, organizational structures, business models, and social enterprises. What their experience can teach us applies to organizations of all types and sizes and to leaders at all levels and in all functions.

Watching them at work, we hope, will not only inform but intrigue, challenge, and inspire you as well. These people are far from perfect and they would be the first to admit it. But they have mastered a difficult art and their examples can be highly instructive. We hope you will learn from them.

We don't claim to have cracked the code for leading innovation.[3] But we're convinced any leader can apply the lessons drawn from the experience of these accomplished leaders to make his or her group more innovative.

Leaders of Innovation in *Collective Genius**

Section	Name	Title	Company
Chapter 1	Ed Catmull	Cofounder, CEO	Pixar Animation Studios
Chapter 3	Vineet Nayar	CEO	HCL Technologies
Chapter 4	Luca de Meo	Chief marketing officer	Volkswagen
Chapter 5	Kit Hinrichs and others	Partners	Pentagram
Chapter 6	Greg Brandeau	Senior vice president, systems technology	Pixar Animation Studios
Chapter 7	Philipp Justus	Country manager, then senior vice president, Europe	eBay Germany and eBay
Chapter 8	Bill Coughran	Senior vice president, engineering, infrastructure group	Google
Chapter 9	Larry Smarr	Founder, director	Calit2
	Amy Schulman	General counsel, executive vice president, business unit leader	Pfizer
Epilogue	Steve Kloeblen	Vice president, business development	IBM
	Jacqueline Novogratz	Founder, CEO	Acumen Fund
	Sung-joo Kim	Founder, chair, chief visionary officer	Sungjoo Group

All information as of time of story.

When it comes to innovation, leadership matters, and it's not leadership as commonly conceived today.

Every person in your group, whether that's a small team or a large corporation, contains a slice of genius. Your task as leader is to create a place where all those slices can be elicited, combined, and converted into collective genius. Our goal in *Collective Genius* is to provide the insights, guidance, and real-life examples you need to do that.

WE'RE NOT JUST MAKING UP HOW TO DO COMPUTER-GENERATED MOVIES, WE'RE MAKING UP HOW TO RUN A COMPANY OF DIVERSE PEOPLE WHO CAN MAKE SOMETHING TOGETHER THAT NO ONE COULD MAKE ALONE.

—**Ed Catmull**, cofounder, Pixar, and president, Pixar and Walt Disney Animation Studios

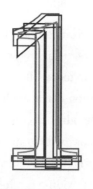

W H A T

C O L L E C T I V E

G E N I U S

L O O K S L I K E

Why are some organizations able to innovate again and again while others hardly innovate at all? How can hundreds of people at a company like Pixar Animation Studios, for example, produce blockbuster after blockbuster over nearly two decades—a record no other filmmaker has ever come close to matching? What's different about Pixar?[1]

This question is crucial. In a time of rapid change, the ability to innovate quickly and effectively, again and again, is perhaps the only enduring competitive advantage. Those firms that can innovate constantly will thrive. Those that do not or cannot will be left behind.

Pixar released *Toy Story* in 1995, the first computer-generated (CG) feature film ever produced. Since then, as we write this, it has released fourteen such movies, including *Toy Story 2* and *Toy Story 3*; *A Bug's Life*; *Monsters, Inc.*; *Finding Nemo*; *The Incredibles*; *Cars*; *Ratatouille*; *Wall-E*; *Up*; *Cars 2*; *Brave*; *and Monsters University*. Virtually all have been critical, financial, and technological successes. The winner of numerous awards, including twenty-six Academy Awards, Pixar is one of those rare studios that command the respect of filmmakers, technologists, and businesspeople alike.

CG movies are mainstream today, but Pixar's founders took two decades to realize their dream of creating a feature-length CG film. After years in academia, Ed Catmull and a handful of colleagues joined Lucasfilm, where Catmull led the effort to bring computer graphics and other digital technology into films and games. Catmull and team pushed the boundaries of what could be done, securing patents and providing producers like Steven Spielberg with the tools to create scenes like those of the dinosaurs in *Jurassic Park*. Ultimately, however, the division was too costly for George Lucas. In 1986, Steve Jobs bought it for $10 million, and Pixar Animation Studios was born.

Pixar has survived since then only because it has been consistently inventive. Every film it produced has been an innovative tour de force. But conventional wisdom about innovation cannot explain its extraordinary accomplishments. No solitary genius, no flash of inspiration, produced those movies. On the contrary, each was the product of hundreds of people, years of work, and hundreds of millions of dollars.

What has allowed Pixar to accomplish what it's done? We begin to see at least part of the answer in a personal comment by Catmull, the computer animation pioneer who cofounded and then led the studio as it produced hit after hit:

> *For 20 years, I pursued a dream of making the first computer-animated film. To be honest, after that goal was realized—when we finished* Toy Story—*I was a bit lost. But then I realized the most exciting thing I had ever done was to help create the unique environment that allowed that film to be made. My new goal became ... to build a studio that had the depth, robustness, and will to keep searching for the hard truths that preserve the confluence of forces necessary to create magic.*[2]

What Catmull discovered in making *Toy Story* was the critical role of leadership in creating an organization or context that fostered and enabled innovation. He understood innovation could not be compelled or commanded. Indeed, this most voluntary of human activities could only be, to use his word, "enabled."

To understand what Catmull and other effective leaders of innovation do, we begin by looking at what collective genius looks like. For that, there's no better example than Pixar, because most of us have seen at least one Pixar movie. So when we describe all the individual slices of genius that go into making a CG film, you will be able to appreciate the difficulty of converting those slices into the collective genius you see on the theater screen.

What Pixar does may seem different from the work of most other organizations. Certainly, the product it makes is different. But think of any other firm that offers a product or service that no individual could provide alone. Clearly, such a firm must grapple, in form though not substance, with the same kinds of challenges Pixar has had to overcome in every film it's made. Every example of innovative problem solving embodies exactly what Catmull described: hundreds and even thousands of ideas from many talented people.

How Pixar Innovates

Innovation is the creation of something both novel and useful. It can be large or small, incremental or breakthrough. It can be a new product, a new service, a new process, a new business model, a new way of organizing, or a new film made in a new way.

Whatever form innovation takes, people often think of it as a chance occurrence, a flash of insight, a brainstorm by one of those rare individuals who's "innovative" or "creative." It can be, but most often such things play no role or only minor roles, and the actual process of innovation is more complex. This becomes crystal clear when we return to Pixar and look more closely at how it works.

Making a CG movie

Some have said that creating a CG animated film is like writing a novel because both start with a blank slate. The creator can do whatever he or she can imagine. Blow up the world? No problem. Hop over the Grand Canyon? Easy. In making a CG film, however, that freedom comes with a price. Everything in the film—*everything*, down to the tiniest speck of dust or the subtle flow of a shadow across a character's face—must be consciously chosen, created, and inserted by one of the hundreds of people involved. Every piece of it must be created, invented, innovated.

To explain the process in simple terms, we use a diagram produced by Greg Brandeau based on his experience running the systems group at Pixar (see figure 1-1).

Each block in the diagram represents not only a stage in the process but a group of highly talented people who perform some essential task.

The process begins with a director who has an idea for a story. He works with people in the story department over twelve to eighteen months to flesh out the tale in words and drawings, usually through many revisions. From the idea, they create a treatment or description of the story. From that, they produce a script. Once the script is approved, they put together thousands of individual storyboards (images) that are in turn cut together to produce reels. Meanwhile, the art department begins to work on the look and feel of the characters and film in general. The film's editor works with the director to cut together the storyboards and create reels that link together the art, dialogue, and temporary music. These reels are updated, revised, and refined as the production progresses. Now the work passes into the hands of various groups of artist-technicians who use sophisticated design software to create the thousands of digital elements that compose the final film. One group creates three-dimensional digital models of the story characters. Another builds and shades the digital settings—a bedroom, a racetrack, a city—where movie scenes will be placed and "shot." Another creates and places the digital objects—tables, chairs, books, beds—that appear in every scene. The layout group—the CG equivalent of cinematographers—roughs out how characters and objects will be shot as they move through each scene. Lighting specialists specify how light appears to fall in each scene.

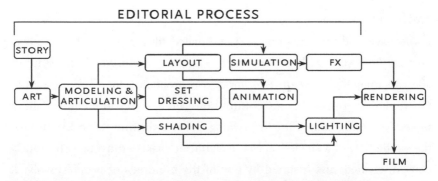

Figure 1-1 **Core Activities of the Film Production Process**

Animators specify the exact movements of characters in every scene to show not only what they do but also how they feel—happy, afraid, or angry, for example.

That's complicated enough, but there's even more. Yet another group creates the texture of surfaces, such as skin or hair, and how light interacts with the surface, which can be a major problem for a computer to recreate realistically. Simulators produce digital versions of various natural phenomena, such as hair blowing in the wind or the way a piece of loose clothing falls and drapes as a character moves. Special-effects specialists depict objects that move in complex ways, such as falling snow, wind, flames, sparks, and water. In the final step, called rendering, hundreds of computers run by systems experts use all the instructions created in earlier steps to compute each individual movie frame. At twenty-four frames per second, a feature film contains well over a hundred thousand frames, and each frame—*every one of them*—can require up to several hours of computer processing.

Reducing all this to a diagram seems to imply that producing a CG film is a simple series of steps these different groups take in a neat, sequential way. It fails to communicate how iterative and interrelated—in short, how messy—the steps of the process are, because the story can and usually does evolve throughout the making of the film. As it's being made, the thousands of digital objects in it, linked into shots and scenes, move through the production pipeline, but not in order. Different shots and scenes move through at different times and even at different rates. Some move quickly, while others take months or longer because they present difficult artistic and technical challenges, large and small, that require the joint efforts of many groups to resolve. For example, one gifted animator took six months to get ten seconds of the film *Up* right. Almost nothing is simple and straightforward.

For that reason, we often present a slightly different version of the diagram that reflects its inherent messiness. In concept, this is the same as the previous diagram except it shows all the feedback loops and multiple iterations that actually occur (see figure 1-2). No wonder CG films require so much time (years), money (hundreds of millions of dollars), and the creative exertions of so many people (200–250) to make.

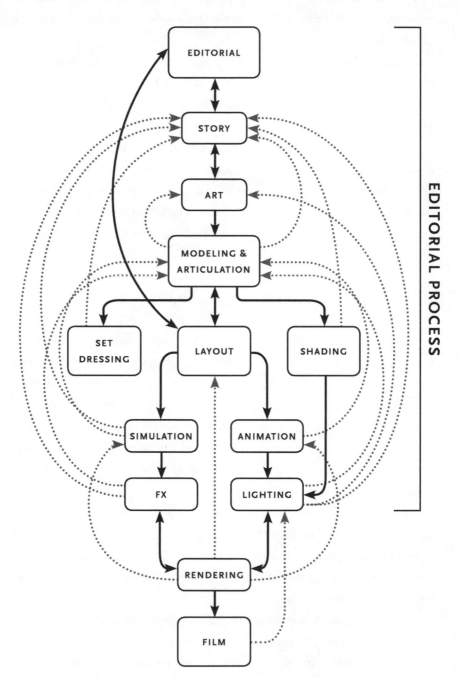

Figure 1-2 The Reality of the Film Production Process

The analogy we drew earlier between making a CG film and writing a novel is fundamentally flawed. It would only apply if a novel were written not by one author but by hundreds of people, some in charge of the story, some others in charge of nouns, some in charge of adjectives, some in charge of sentences, some in charge of paragraphs, and some in charge of chapters. Yes, every movie has a director—in effect, the master storyteller, the one with the overall creative vision for the movie—who determines what is ultimately seen and heard on the screen. But it's impossible for the director, or any other individual, to specify everything that must be invented to make a CG film. She must rely on the creativity of everyone involved.

As Catmull said, each Pixar film "contains tens of thousands of ideas."

> They're in the form of every sentence; in the performance of each line; in the design of characters, sets, and backgrounds; in the locations of the camera; in the colors, the lighting, the pacing. The director and the other creative leaders of a production do not come up with all the ideas on their own; rather, every single member of the 200- to 250-person group makes suggestions. Creativity must be present at every level of every artistic and technical part of the organization.[3]

Now, with your understanding of how Pixar makes movies, put yourself in a theater and imagine you're watching a Pixar movie—the final outcome of this long, complicated, arduous process. What do you actually see and experience? The engaging images and sounds flow by seamlessly, as though created effortlessly by a single master storyteller. Every part fits into a coherent whole. There's no indication of the process or the many disparate individuals who created what you're watching.

In this contrast between the simple coherence of the outcome and the complexity of the process that produced it, we can see the ultimate challenge of all organizational innovation: to create a coherent work of singular collective genius from the diverse slices of genius brought to the work by all the individuals involved. This is what all innovative organizations are able to do well, over and over.

Talent is critical, of course. Conventional wisdom at Pixar says that great people can turn a mediocre idea into a great movie, while mediocre people will ruin even a great idea. But the ultimate challenge of innovation extends far beyond finding creative people. Pixar does have such people; it works hard to find and keep them. Unlike most film studios, which hire talent movie by movie, Pixar hires employees who stay and work on movie after movie. But Pixar certainly doesn't employ the only talented people in the world. Any organization that wants to innovate again and again must do more than hire a few "creative individuals" because, even with the right people, there's still the huge problem of getting them to work together productively.

That is the job of leaders who seek innovation. In the way they behave and structure an organization where talented people work, leaders create the environment that somehow draws out the *slice of genius* in each individual and then leverages and melds those many slices into a single work of innovation—a new product, a new process, a new strategy, a new film—that represents *collective genius*. This is what happens when organizations innovate.

Leading Innovation

Though each of our leaders and their firms differed in key ways, all leaders paid particular attention to making sure their organizations were able to:

- Collaborate
- Engage in discovery-driven learning
- Make integrative decisions

Our leaders' uniform emphasis on fostering these three capabilities will not surprise anyone familiar with existing research on innovative problem solving. Much evidence exists for the importance of each. However, they have been most often studied separately. Because our focus was on leadership in action, we were able to observe how these three interrelated organizational skills work in concert as leaders and their groups undertake to create something novel and useful. Based on those observations, we have developed an integrated framework for understanding, describing, and prescribing how leaders build organizations capable of consistent innovation by focusing on these essential abilities.

Leaders create collaborative organizations

Lore perpetuates the myth of innovation as a solitary act, a flash of creative insight, an Aha! moment in the mind of a genius. People apparently prefer to believe in the rugged individualism of discovery, perhaps because they rarely get to see the sausage-making process behind every breakthrough innovation.

Three decades of research has clearly revealed that innovation is most often a group effort.[4] Thomas Edison, for example, is remembered as probably the greatest American inventor of the early twentieth century. From his fertile mind came the light bulb and the phonograph, along with more than a thousand other patented inventions over a sixty-year career. But he hardly worked alone. As many have observed, perhaps Edison's greatest contribution was his artisan-oriented shops—a new way of organizing for innovation he created that has evolved into today's R&D laboratory with its team-based approach.[5]

The process of innovation needs to be collaborative because innovations most often arise from the interplay of ideas that occur during the interactions of people with diverse expertise, experience, or points of view. Flashes of insight may play a role, but most often they simply build on and contribute to the collaborative work of others. Edison may get the credit for his inventions—it was his laboratory, of course—but each one typically arose from years of effort that included many others. Certainly he contributed many ideas himself, but he was equally an inventor and a leader of invention.

Collaboration was obviously a hallmark of Pixar's approach. Without the interplay and collaborative contributions of large numbers of people, it could not make a CG movie. One of Pixar's unusual features as a studio was that all three functions of the organization—art, technology, and business—were considered equal partners in the process of making great films. No one voice dominated, as often happened at other studios.

Another major shortcoming of the diagram in figure 1-1 is that it fails to convey how collaborative the process of making a CG film at Pixar actually was. Pixar instituted a number of practices that fostered collaboration among all the groups and individuals involved. Key among them was the "dailies"—gatherings of Pixar staff to watch and discuss presentations of work in progress. Such meetings occurred at other studios too, but at Pixar a wide array of those working on the production, not just a select few, attended and contributed ideas and comments regardless of their role or level. Thus, not only did individuals receive feedback and guidance on their own work, but they were also able to see the work of others and understand how that work related to their own.

The collaborative nature of innovation is what leads us to talk of slices of genius that come together to create collective genius. No individual contribution will suffice to create a final solution, especially for large, complex problems. But each contribution—through collaboration—plays its part in creating collective genius. In the right organizational context, with the right leadership, a group can amplify the diverse talents and ideas of its individual members.

Leaders foster discovery-driven learning

Innovation usually arises from an often lengthy period of conscious experimentation and repeated trial and error.[6] As intuitive as it sounds, this characteristic also contradicts yet another myth of innovation, that great new ideas spring in full and final form from the mind of the inventor, ready to be applied. Innovation rarely works that way, and that's why the innovation process is usually so messy, which is what we tried to convey in figure 1-2 of the real CG movie-making process.

Since innovation is a problem-solving process, it's really about searching for a solution by creating and testing a portfolio of ideas. It often takes time even to frame a problem in the right way, especially if it's complex. Consequently, innovation is a process of trial and error, often to embarrassing degrees, even for the most skilled innovators. Thomas Edison used a cut-and-try method—test out an idea to see if it works, reject or refine it, and try again. Hence, Edison's famous definition of genius: "1 percent inspiration; 99 percent perspiration." Missteps, dead ends, and rework are inevitable and must be accepted, even encouraged. Innovation requires a mind-set of try, learn, adjust, try again. In a conversation we had with Catmull about Pixar's enviable track record, he reminded us that "our appetite always exceeded our ability" and that they are in the "business of hitting home runs." He went on to add, however, that if Pixar had "no failures," which he defined as a "less than spectacular outcome," then that would suggest it had lost its passion for doing cutting-edge work. This is why at Pixar, no one got beat up for making a mistake or for trying something that didn't work.

Some who study innovation make much of the difference between idea generation and idea implementation. That's understandable, because ideas must be created before they can be tested or implemented. However, once experimentation begins the distinction quickly makes less sense. Ideas beget experiments and experiments beget more ideas, and any difference between ideation and implementation quickly fades. We know that none of the many innovative companies we studied made much of the difference between the two.

Pixar certainly followed the discovery-driven approach. Yes, it prepared scripts and storyboards in advance of production, but even that process was iterative. People acted out scenes and drew characters again and again, until the characters and story seemed exactly right. But after that, during production, every story element continued to be tested and to evolve based on frequent reviews of work in progress.

Leaders support and encourage integrative decision making

Leaders and their groups can resolve problems, disagreements, and conflicting solutions in one of three ways. The leader or some dominant faction can impose a solution. Or the group can find a compromise, some way of splitting the difference between opposing options and viewpoints. Unfortunately, domination or compromise often leads to less than satisfying solutions.

The third way, integrating ideas—combining option A and option B to create something new, option C, that's better than A or B—tends to produce the most innovative solutions. Making integrative choices, which often combine ideas that once seemed in opposition, is what allows difference, conflict, and learning to be embraced in the final solution.[7]

Albert Einstein hinted at the integrative nature of the process when he said, "To raise new questions, new possibilities, to regard old problems from a new angle, requires creative imagination and marks real advance in science."[8] For him, innovation was about "'combinational chemistry' ... about taking ideas, half-baked notions, competencies, concepts, and assets that already sit out there and recombining them ... What's new in many instances is the new mix."

So important is integrative decision making that innovative organizations and their leaders don't just allow it, they actively encourage it. They keep opposing options on the table as long as possible because they know fruitful integration can occur only after people have devoted sufficient time to debating options or testing them through trial and error. They also refuse to make trade-offs or accept compromises that merely produce a least-bad solution or allow people to feel good.

The CG process at Pixar was based on the use and value of integration because that process followed a simple principle: *no part of a movie is finally done until the entire movie is all done.* Anything and everything remained open to revision until the very end. People at Pixar knew that integrative decision making often involved more than simply and mechanically combining ideas.

For example, at a point midway through making a Pixar movie, an animator gave a character a sideward glance and a slightly arched eyebrow. Only a split-second long, it nonetheless hinted at some slyness or irony in the character; maybe he didn't mean exactly what he just said. It was an aspect of the character's personality that hadn't been seen before that scene. The director saw this moment in the daily review of work in progress and said, "No, no. That's out of character. This is the most innocent, straightforward guy you'd ever meet. What you see and hear is what you get. Nicely done, but it doesn't fit here. Lose it, please."

Then, two weeks later, the director came back with a different reaction. "I've been thinking about that moment, that little revelation, where we see a side of this guy we've never seen before. It makes his character richer and more interesting. In fact, it will help set up and explain some events that happen later. Let's keep it. Tone it down a notch. But put it back."

Though it was a small thing, adding that touch of irony improved the character and the story. It happened because an animator almost inadvertently added his understanding of the character, his slice of genius, in the process of animation, and that led the director to reconceive the character in a subtle but important way.

The problem, as it emerged in subsequent discussions, was that this new character twist couldn't just appear suddenly halfway through the story. The viewer would react the way the director reacted initially. So earlier scenes had to be adapted to hint at this aspect of the character so that the viewer's reaction would be, "Oh, yeah, I saw that coming," rather than,

"What!? I'm confused!" Also, of course, later scenes, which were already in various stages of production, had to be revised to take advantage of this new character element. If the story had been fixed and immutable, if the director hadn't been able to hold opposing views of the character in his mind until they could merge, none of that could have happened and the story would have been worse for it.

At Pixar, people knew the heart of a good movie was a good story, and they knew stories would get better throughout the process of making them. The stories got better through constant iteration; through trying different approaches, including approaches that at first seemed inconsistent; through the involvement of lots of talented people, like that animator; and through a willingness to wait and see what worked and what needed tightening or expanding.

When Pixar finished *Toy Story 2*, which took an incredible toll on all involved, it assembled a cross section of people to explore ways of avoiding so much pressure in making future films. One of the key suggestions was to lock the story—not allow any further changes after some point early in the process. Constant story iterations and changes are the source of much stress because they almost always have implications that ripple throughout the film and force multiple changes, as we just saw.

In that postmortem, one employee recalled that John Lasseter, director of the film and a cofounder of Pixar, responded to the idea by saying, "We need to focus on quality and that only happens by iterating. If we lock in the story, we will be disappointed. I can't do it. I know it would save us pain, but Hollywood is littered with films that refused to change." By refusing to lock a story, Pixar was able to put a variety of ideas on the table and keep them there until they began to gel, often in ways that no one could ever have anticipated.

The three characteristics reinforce our earlier point that innovation requires more than talented people. History, and not just Hollywood, is littered with star-studded teams that failed. So it's not just about talent, but it *is* about talent *in the right context*. We all know, perhaps from firsthand experience, that it's not easy to get people to collaborate on a straightforward task, let alone to create something new and useful. Almost all cultures have some version of the saying, "Too many cooks in the kitchen."[9] We know how hard it is to keep testing possibilities before choosing one. It's often easier to make an initial choice and move on. And we know how hard it is to do what that Pixar director did—keep a wrong idea in mind until it's no longer wrong. The job of the person leading innovation is to create the conditions that allow and encourage all these things to happen again and again.

Catmull and other leaders at Pixar were able to create an organization superbly able to collaborate, learn through testing and iteration, and find integrative solutions. By focusing on those aspects of the innovation process, they made Pixar a place that could take the "tens of thousands of ideas" Catmull mentioned and make of them the seamless work of art you see in a theater.

That's why, in recognition of all the individual contributions, the credits for each of Pixar's first dozen or so movies named *everyone* in the organization who played a role, including the cooks in the company cafeteria and babies born to employees during production.[10] This was no trivial matter. In the film business, credits are serious stuff, not given lightly. As Ed Martin, Pixar vice president of human resources at the time, told us:

> *Pixar has always erred on the side of having people feel like they're a part of the process. I know of very few employees who don't immediately go to the theater just to see how many people are lined up when a film first comes out. You'd be hard pressed to find that at any other business, and I would say any other studio. Imagine the receptionist going to do that. People are so engaged.*

We asked Jim Morris, then a relatively new senior executive at the studio, what he thought made it tick. Morris had joined Pixar from Lucas Digital, where as president he oversaw Industrial Light and Magic, the company that produced special effects for the *Star Wars* and *Harry Potter* films, among others. Without hesitating, he said, "Ed and John." In the remainder of *Collective Genius*, we will explore exactly what Ed Catmull, John Lasseter, and other leaders of highly innovative groups actually did, as well as the thinking behind their actions that enabled their organizations to innovate over and over. In particular, we will look at how they fostered the willingness and ability of their organizations to collaborate, learn through discovery, and make integrative decisions—the three skills that all innovative organizations possess.

MANAGING TENSIONS IN THE ORGANIZATION IS AN ONGOING ISSUE ... YOU DON'T WANT AN ORGANIZATION THAT JUST SALUTES AND DOES WHAT YOU SAY. YOU WANT AN ORGANIZATION THAT ARGUES WITH YOU. AND SO YOU WANT TO NURTURE THE BOTTOMS UP, BUT YOU'VE GOT TO BE CAREFUL YOU DON'T JUST DEGENERATE INTO CHAOS.

—**Bill Coughran**, then senior vice president, engineering, infrastructure group, Google

WHY COLLECTIVE GENIUS NEEDS LEADERSHIP: THE PARADOXES OF INNOVATION

We've described how innovative organizations need more than talented people. They also need leaders who can create and sustain a place—a context or environment—that unlocks the slice of genius in each of their people and then combines them into collective genius. And we described how leaders create that place by making sure their organizations are capable, in particular, of collaboration, discovery-driven learning, and integrative decision making.

This brings us back to the question raised at the beginning. Why aren't more organizations able to innovate again and again, like Pixar? One piece of the answer is the persistent myth that innovation requires a solo genius having an Aha! moment, and another is the misguided mind-set that leadership is primarily about vision. But even when leaders understand how innovation really happens, they will still find the challenge difficult.

Each element of leading innovation—fostering collaboration, discovery, and integration—asks organizations and leaders to act in unaccustomed or uncomfortable ways. Because each places enormous intellectual and emotional burdens on everyone involved, all three require uncommon courage and persistence.

By the end of this chapter, you'll understand why innovative problem solving is often discomforting hard work, what it requires of leaders, and why, as a consequence, it's so rare in most organizations.

Unleash *and* Harness—the Fundamental Paradox

The heart of the difficulty is a fundamental tension, a paradox, inherent in what is required for innovation to occur. A paradox is a truth that contains contradictory elements but is true nonetheless. For example, "To succeed, you must be reflective *and* action oriented" seems, on the face of it, impossible. But anyone with work and life experience knows its fundamental truth. To succeed requires the ability to manage the tension between those disparate approaches either by learning when each is appropriate or by combining them in a never-ending process of rapid doing and reviewing.[1]

The unavoidable paradox at the heart of innovation is the need to *unleash* the talents of individuals *and*, in the end, to *harness* those talents in the form of a collective innovation that is useful to the organization. Both elements are essential. *Unleash* is how ideas and options get identified or created. *Harness* is how those ideas and options are shaped into a final solution. Our definition of innovation—something new *and* useful—reflects this paradox. It's easy to think of many new ideas, but it's much more difficult to convert those ideas into something new that actually solves a problem.

Perhaps the best way to understand this central paradox and its implications for leading innovation is to break it down. Look at each of the three characteristics of the innovation process using the unleash-harness paradox and you'll find that it appears in each characteristic in slightly different but obviously related ways. In our research, we identified six paradoxes related to the core unleash-harness paradox.

The Paradoxes of Collaboration

Innovation emerges most often from the collaboration of diverse people as they generate a wide-ranging portfolio of ideas, which they then refine, improve, and even evolve into new ideas through discussion, give and take, and often-heated contention.

Obviously, then, collaboration means far more than a simple willingness to work together. Innovation requires not "get along" or "go along" cooperation but creative collaboration, which typically involves—*should* involve—passionate discussion and disagreement.

Nor is creative collaboration, this give-and-take, something an innovative organization simply accepts or allows. On the contrary, it *encourages* the heartfelt clash of ideas and alternatives by creating routines and forums where it's expected and can occur naturally. At Pixar, for example, those involved in producing a film gathered every day to present their latest work for review by colleagues and the film's director and producer.

We saw something similar in all the innovative organizations we studied. Whether it was a no-holds-barred review of work to date, a star designer who deliberately placed himself in a setting where he'd stew in the creative ideas of others, or an idea-sparring session among marketing, sales, and manufacturing in an auto company, collaboration meant embracing diverse points of view and even conflict.

Yet the friction of clashing ideas can be hard to bear. The sparks that fly in heartfelt discussions can sting. At a minimum, they can create tension and stress. Many organizations consequently dislike conflict in any form and try to discourage it.

But blanket condemnation of all strife and conflict will only stifle the free flow of ideas and rich discussions that creative collaboration needs. What's required is that the leader manage the tension in the relationship between the individual and the group as a whole, the collective. That tension appears primarily in the form of the first two paradoxes. Getting these paradoxes right is what enables an organization to generate a rich portfolio of ideas through creative collaboration.

Affirm the individual and *the group*

A rich, diverse supply of ideas will only emerge if group members are willing and eager to contribute their thoughts. The more diverse their ideas, the better. Indeed, a leader needs to *amplify* people's differences because they are what produce a richer and more robust marketplace of ideas. Thus, leaders encourage and support the individuals in their groups because they are the source of ideas that constitute the raw material of innovation.

Yet the ultimate innovation will almost always be a *collective* outcome, something devised through group interaction. Rarely will it be the result of one person's flash of insight, though several such flashes may occur along the way. Most people's ideas will be considered and discarded by the group, adopted only in part, or combined with other ideas to make something different.

Moviemaking at Pixar worked because its leaders built an organization able to focus on the whole—the film in production—while recognizing the critical contribution of the hundreds of individuals involved. People were able to feel a part of the whole without giving up their individuality. This was evident in a number of Pixar's practices:

- In the steps built into its moviemaking process like the daily review of work in progress where individual ideas and contributions were encouraged and where the contributors were clearly valued even when their contributions were rejected.
- In the company's norms about open communication—anyone could talk to anyone else about a problem without having to go through official channels; everyone at all levels and in any role could give comments to the director of a movie in production.
- In the way the studio designed and used office space to foster spontaneous interaction of people from all parts of the organization.
- In the generous bestowal of credits at the end of every film where people could be recognized both as individuals and as part of something not one of them could possibly have done alone; the films were literally both "mine" and "ours."

In addition to the extensive credits that ended each film, Pixar's ability to balance "me" and "us" was perhaps most clear in the obvious respect that existed between the artistic and systems groups. Unlike what usually happened at other studios, neither dominated, nor was either considered better or more important. Everyone was encouraged to see his or her fingerprints on each movie. "I'm not a creative person sketching storyboards or animating a character," someone in systems told us, "but it's my support and service to the artists that allows Pixar to make a film. No one can make a movie alone." As the leaders at Pixar said—words we heard quoted throughout the organization—"The art challenges the technology, and the technology inspires the art."

In every organization we studied, we saw how leaders dealt with this ongoing source of tension. They made sure the disapproval of more experienced expert members didn't smother dissension, minority viewpoints, or the fresh perspectives of the inexperienced or the newcomer. They encouraged constructive disagreement. They gave people discretionary time to pursue their particular passions. They recognized that individuals need engagement and connection, as well as intellectual and emotional space, to do their best work. In short, leaders created places where individuals were willing to contribute their best efforts because they felt not only part of the group but also valued by and valuable to the group.

Of course, this is not what happens in many organizations where differences and disagreement are discouraged; where people are told to "go along and keep the peace"; where contrarians and disrupters are ignored or driven out; where people's ideas and passions are discouraged, especially if they lead to conflict; and where ideas, when offered, are rejected in personal ways that make further contribution feel dangerous.

Support and *confrontation*

The leaders we observed allowed and encouraged confrontation as a way of fostering innovation. They knew that discouraging disagreement was unlikely to produce anything new and useful.

Yet here the job of leading can seem almost impossible. How can a leader support people in the free and full expression of their ideas while encouraging group members to challenge all ideas? Why would someone contribute an idea if the likely response is a storm of hard questions and criticism? Why would anyone expose herself in this way to the negative reaction and even implied scorn of people who disagree?

The "dailies"—the daily reviews of work in progress at Pixar that we've already mentioned—are a good example of one way the studio serves and balances both sides of the support-and-confront paradox. In one dailies session we observed, an animator jumped to his feet and acted out a moment in a scene as he thought it should go. Like many other Pixar animators, he was an actor, and his passion was obvious as he literally pranced around the room and his colleagues laughed at his antics—the exact reaction he wanted. Some suggested slight changes, and so he altered his performance—a little more head scratching, a little less prancing. But, in the end, the others—including, critically, the director—rejected his approach, and he sat down with a smile and a shrug as the group gave him an encouraging round of applause.

What happened next was illuminating. Though the group had refused his ideas, he remained engaged in the session, laughing and clapping as two others acted out their approaches, one of which was, more or less, accepted. Afterward, when asked about the group's response to his ideas, he said, "Oh, that's par for the course. Most ideas don't get adopted, but sometimes they do." He did admit it wasn't always easy to weather the countless critiques at the heart of Pixar's moviemaking process, particularly when he felt strongly about a character and a scene. But he distinguished between rejection of his idea and rejection of him as a person—a common distinction at Pixar. He had felt free and safe to make his animated suggestions, to put himself literally "out there," because he and everyone else in the room shared the same goal—to produce the best film possible—and they all knew it took a hundred ideas to find the right one.

As leaders of innovation deal with this paradox of support and confrontation, they face danger at both extremes. Confrontation can stifle the willingness of people to offer ideas. But group members can become *too* supportive as well and stop challenging each other at all. In highly cohesive groups, strong norms to preserve harmonious and friendly relationships can discourage candor. People may disagree but not speak out. They may even suppress their own thoughts and feelings, sometimes at great personal cost, for fear of violating unspoken group rules for how they should behave. Here the leader's role is to create dissonance by injecting different points of view and forcing the group to deal with them, by encouraging dissenting voices, and by bringing in new members who think differently and letting their voices be heard.[2]

Because innovation depends on the generation of many diverse ideas, the ability to innovate depends on getting these first two paradoxes right. Collaboration means group members embrace the friction, make themselves vulnerable, and allow others to ask hard questions. Still, even in the best circumstances, these debates, no matter how well intentioned and constructive, can be emotionally draining.

The Paradoxes of Discovery-Driven Learning

Leaders and organizations require performance, and results are always the ultimate test of success. Consequently, most leaders prefer to march systematically toward the outcome they want. Set a goal, they say, make a plan, work the plan, and track progress until the goal is achieved. This approach works well in many situations. So, naturally, they apply it to creating something new and useful. They set targets, make detailed plans, and assign responsibilities.

Unfortunately, this approach rarely produces anything truly innovative because, by definition, no one can define the solution in advance and even the path to an answer often won't be clear. That's why innovation so often requires a recursive process of trial and error with false starts, mistakes, and missteps along the way. Through a series of experiments, innovative groups act rather than plan their way forward, and solutions emerge that are usually different from anything anyone anticipated.

Consequently, innovation requires a large investment of time, energy, and other resources, and leaders need patience and the willingness to learn and change course along the way. Rather than following some linear planning process, the real path to innovation is far messier and more unpredictable. Some leaders we studied called it "a numbers game" in which the challenge was to produce multiple ideas and avenues of inquiry and then test those options as quickly as possible.

Still, even though innovation may require time and follow an unpredictable path, organizations require performance. The goal is always a solution, and no leader or group gets credit for effort alone. From the tension between the learning by doing that innovation requires and the results that organizations rightly demand springs the next two paradoxes. The leader's ability to navigate these paradoxes will determine her organization's ability to experiment, collect feedback, and modify.

Foster experimentation, learning, and performance

Without losing sight of the necessary outcomes, the leaders we studied were willing to let their organizations experiment, iterate, debrief, learn, and then start the process over again if necessary. At Pixar, people who worked on a film were encouraged constantly to try new approaches, but behind all those efforts stood one huge constant: the film's release date that had to be met. The director carried overall responsibility for the movie and its timely delivery and success, but at his or her side throughout the process was the film producer whose main job was to make sure the film was done on time and on budget.

The tale of Toy Story 2 is a good example of balancing a willingness to try new approaches with the need for performance. After the great success of the original Toy Story, Pixar focused throughout 1997 and 1998 on the next feature film, A Bug's Life. At the same time, it put together a small group to work on a Toy Story sequel. This sequel, however, would be something different, an experiment. Instead of a feature film shown in movie theaters, it would be released direct to DVD for playing at home. Consequently, it was expected to cost less and require less time, and those assumptions drove the decision to assemble only a small team, which was housed in a separate building away from the main Pixar studio.

For some time, as the studio focused on the current feature film in production, A Bug's Life, the Toy Story sequel remained almost an afterthought.

But at a certain point, key people took a good look at *Toy Story 2* and decided it was an experiment that wasn't working. First, the story was good but not great because it was too predictable. Second, as Catmull said afterward, it was "bad for our souls" to make, on purpose, a cheap, second-rate movie. In its current form, this was not a film Pixar wanted to put its name on.

The studio quickly decided to take a drastically different course: *Toy Story 2* would be a full-fledged feature film released to theaters. Production on the first version halted, and the story was reworked to make it into a movie that would meet the studio's highest creative and technical standards.

The problem was the original release date, which couldn't be moved because too much had already been planned around it. So Pixar sent its people home for the holidays at the end of 1998 with one piece of advice: rest up because we're about to make a Pixar-quality movie in nine months.

The studio met that goal, and *Toy Story 2* was a great success. But it was a success that came at great cost to everyone involved. The stress and pain, physical and emotional, were enormous. Many suffered repetitive stress injuries from working hundred-hour weeks. Many burned out. All said they never wanted to do that again.

When the movie was done, the studio went to great lengths to articulate and digest the lessons that would help it avoid such pain and suffering in the future. The combination of experiential learning constrained by the need for performance made these lessons painfully clear and helped the studio improve the way it made great movies.

The difficulty of the learning-versus-performance paradox is only heightened by the unavoidable fact that most ideas, options, and experiments fail—like the effort to produce a cut-rate Pixar movie—and it's not possible to foresee which will succeed. Time will appear to be wasted on pursuits that after the fact may seem to have been misguided. Economies of scale and efficiency are likely to suffer in the short or even medium run. All involved must be comfortable with the reality that missteps, mistakes, and failures will happen. The leaders we studied always treated them as sources of learning and not occasions for censure and punishment. They did insist that people work quickly and nimbly. Speed based on a real sense of urgency was a key way they matched the need for experimentation with the need for performance. Like Pixar with *Toy Story 2*, they learned from experience and experiments, while still meeting the demands for performance.

Accepting the need for experimentation and learning, with inevitable missteps along the way, doesn't mean leaders should throw up their hands and accept complete chaos.[3] Experiments must be relevant, designed properly, and run rigorously so that they produce real learning. There need to be boundary conditions—guardrails—so that failure isn't catastrophic. And trial efforts need to generate good data that can be analyzed objectively to make reality-based decisions. Pixar, for example, recorded and tracked far more hard data throughout the process of making a film than an outsider might imagine, including shots per week for every department, hours per frame, and run time of the film. And frequent review meetings, like the dailies at Pixar, kept people connected to what others were doing and such ultimate realities as deadlines and budgets.

Promote improvisation and structure

That innovation tends to emerge from trial and error makes it highly improvisational. A group or organization trying to innovate will improve its chances of success if it acts more like a jazz ensemble than a marching band. Yet the highly structured marching band is the approach many organizations prefer—a preplanned set of notes to play, rather than a theme to explore; clear, rigid, predetermined roles for each player; and everyone marching in tight formation to some preestablished destination.

In contrast, the leaders we studied created settings where people had great latitude and autonomy, though no leaders granted complete, unlimited freedom. There were always limits and conditions. Even a jazz band doesn't improvise from nothing. Nor do improv actors simply say whatever they want; they're bound by an initial idea of a situation or setting and the expansions of that idea already expressed by fellow actors. There will always be limits of some kind, and they're not necessarily bad.

People at Pixar believed that a firm release date and a budget play key roles in pushing people to greater creativity. In chapter 1, we showed a diagram of the messy, complex process for making a CG movie, with its seemingly endless iterations, feedback loops, and improvisations (figure 1-2). That apparent chaos was reality, but we also showed, before that, the process in its neater, more conceptual form (figure 1-1). The point of the two diagrams was not to say that the second was real and the first merely wishful thinking. Both were real. The second, messy diagram showed what the process *looked* and *felt* like, while the first showed the core structure that kept it from being complete chaos. The second, messy diagram showed what the work of making an animated film actually *looked* and *felt* like; the first provided only a simplification of the core activities associated with the process. Everyone understood the underlying structure in filmmaking, so as they worked together they were not overwhelmed. Similarly, Pixar's open communication practices, in which anyone could offer a comment about a movie in production, did not create a sense of ambiguity or confusion because decision-making rights were clear and understood by everyone.

Postmortems following every major project were another form of structure used by most companies we studied. Pixar was no exception. Almost from its beginning, the studio had conducted reviews after every film wrapped. Over the years, the way it did them had evolved, but the purpose was always to learn how the process might work better next time. After experimenting with various approaches, Pixar adopted the tactic of asking the people involved to identify five ways the process of making the just completed film had worked well and five ways it hadn't (and how to change them).[4]

However necessary and beneficial they can be, constraints, goals, boundaries, and conditions—all forms of structure—will always live in tension with the desire to explore as many ideas and variations as possible, for as long as possible. Not every possibility can be pursued. Nor are all possibilities equally worthwhile.

Constraints can take several forms. Detailed plans, tangible goals, even a broad overall purpose are certainly necessary as targets and boundaries, but at some point they can go beyond useful guidance and stifle the freedom to learn and innovate. People obviously need to know what they're responsible for, but task assignments and role descriptions can be so specific that they put boxes around people that constrain imagination and thinking. Preconceived models and expectations about the right outcome can be helpful, but they can also limit unnecessarily the search for a solution. And rigid processes, rules, and ways of working may make a group more efficient and rapid, but can also limit or predetermine the outcomes if taken too far.

Of course, hierarchy can also impede the free flow of information and generation of diverse ideas. We've already seen how Pixar was careful to distinguish its hierarchy for decision making from people's freedom to communicate. Structure is meant to simplify and focus effort, but it's always a means to an end. Too often we've seen it assume a life and rationale of its own, in the same way that plans and rules often persist even after the conditions that spawned them have disappeared.

Finally, expertise or experience itself can become a limiting structure. Most of us have seen someone join a group and suggest a better way of doing something, only to be told, "Oh, we already tried that, and it didn't work," whereupon the newcomer drops the idea. But a little digging might have uncovered the fact that what they had tried wasn't really what the person was currently suggesting. Or it was, but the world had changed and the idea may now be more likely to succeed.

Many leaders, of course, like structure because it provides the comfort of control. Left to their natural tendencies, organizations, even successful ones, ironically, will proliferate the number of control structures they use—specific goals, detailed plans, progress reports, hierarchy, processes, policies, and the like—even in the search for innovation. They neither understand nor feel comfortable with the improvisation and autonomy that innovation requires.

The effective leaders of innovation we studied understood all these dangers. They recognized they could not plan for innovation, but they could organize in ways that encouraged it. They limited team and group sizes to foster connection and mutual impact among members. They created forums where diverse groups could interact in both formal and spontaneous ways. They consciously created space for experimentation. They required just enough goal setting, planning, and performance metrics that the group could tell if it was making progress, but no more. They defined people's work broadly, often assigning roles that overlapped, but were specific enough to provide clarity about what people could expect from each other. Effective leaders involved people in each other's work, encouraged cross-specialty collaboration, and even gave people at-work time to pursue their particular passions and ideas. They constantly wove together reviewing, planning, and doing, with a heavy emphasis on learning from doing. They knew they could not eliminate hierarchy, but they worked hard to overcome the limits that hierarchy and expertise or experience could impose on open communication. They encouraged peer feedback. And they resisted unnecessary structures and systems.[5]

In short, innovation leaders viewed structure in all its forms as a tool for facilitating the process of collaboration and discovery-driven learning. They used it sparingly. How much did they use? Just enough.

The Paradoxes of Integrative Decision Making

Much of creating something novel and useful arises from combining existing ideas, including ideas that once seemed mutually exclusive. To do this requires moving from either-or thinking to both-and thinking. Finding solutions that exploit the diverse ideas of a community in this way calls for an integrative decision-making process.

As straightforward as it sounds, integrating diverse ideas requires the leader to grapple with two paradoxes.

Show patience and *urgency*

The leaders of innovation we studied understood that creativity followed its own schedule. It could not be rushed or commanded. To combine existing ideas in new ways, they and their people needed time to absorb and digest the ideas. Integration rarely happened overnight.

Integrative decision making needs patience. But in a competitive world, there's urgency, too. At Pixar, there was that unyielding film release date with hundreds of millions of dollars riding on it, and a budget that, though generous, was finite. The tension and pressure were enormous.

We can see the need to balance urgency and patience in the way systems people at Pixar solved the problem of fur in the feature *Monsters, Inc.*, where one of whose characters, Sully, was a furry beast. That was a problem because of the difficulty of portraying fur realistically in a CG film. In a way, fur was the holy grail of the CG industry. It had been done before but not on the scale of *Monsters, Inc.* It presented multiple challenges, from how to make the shadows on hair look right, to keeping strands of hair from seeming to move through each other, to designing software that freed animators from animating each hair (impossible, given the more than 2 million hairs in Sully's coat).

Many people—at one point, up to twenty from different parts of the studio—spent months of trial and error trying to figure out how to animate fur and hair realistically. The movie depended on it, and they, artists and systems people who were determined to find the ultimate solution, grew more and more desperate as time ran out. Finally, said one of the group's leaders, "We stopped looking for the perfect solution that would work in all cases and converged on a solution that worked in the specific instances we needed." It was a jerry-rigged simulation program that made the fur move and shade more or less realistically by, in effect, adding springs to individual strands randomly. It was improvised, makeshift, and even crude. It wouldn't work for long hair, but it worked for Sully in this movie.

Tight budgets and drop-dead release dates are hard enough, but other forces also take their toll. What integration requires is inherently discomforting, both emotionally and intellectually. Leaders often don't know what to do with opposing and seemingly incompatible possibilities. Only human, they crave the certainty of simplifying and choosing quickly, especially when the situation feels urgent. Suppose options A, B, and C appear mutually exclusive. Most leaders will make an early choice of one and eliminate the others. At the least, they will identify and eliminate the most unlikely options, just to simplify things. In some organizations, such rapid and decisive decision making is considered a hallmark of leadership.

The pressure on leaders for quick resolution can be acute. The longer opposing ideas remain in play, the more frustrated and uncertain people are likely to become. They won't know where to focus or what to do. Hating uncertainty, they're likely to think, "We need some leadership around here! Someone who knows what they're doing and is willing to make decisions!" In the face of such reactions, leaders need courage to persist in looking for the best possible solution, especially when they desperately want to see themselves as decisive. This is another way that leading for innovation can go against the grain of conventional notions about leadership.

Finally, in addition to making arbitrary, premature choices, many leaders accept or pursue other methods of early closure, such as compromising or taking a vote. Unfortunately, these methods rarely produce the best possible outcome and seldom please anyone. They're used when a group and its leader lack the patience and fortitude to press through to something better. In the end, they sacrifice all the value that might have been realized, with patience and deeper consideration, by finding clues to a superior model in the tension among ideas.

As we saw in a previous paradox, however, urgency is not necessarily a bad thing. Many of the leaders in our research considered necessity the mother of invention. They felt strongly that constraints could spur innovation. Part of the leader's job, they felt, was to confront the group with critical deadlines or budget realities, which could foster creative thinking by forcing the evaluation of key assumptions and the reframing of opportunities. As one leader said, "Our creative process will go on forever unless there's a hard stop. Constraints seem to sharpen thinking because they force the team to find ways to get around them."

To make integrative decisions possible, leaders must know when to allow debate and discovery and when to move on to decision making and execution. Leaders must provide the support and resources time, in particular, as well as shelter from external pressure—to develop and integrate ideas. They know ideas need to marinate and simmer, but they also know when it's time to move forward.

Encourage bottom-up initiative and intervene top down

Most innovation is the result of grassroots efforts. Thus, the final paradox reflects the need for a delicate balance between bottom-up initiatives and top-down interventions. The leaders in our study understood that unless they encouraged ideas to bubble up from the bottom levels of the organization, there would be fewer ideas and less innovation.

These leaders encouraged peer-driven processes of self-organizing and self-governing. Much as we see in Web 2.0 practices, online multiplayer games, and social networking sites, innovative organizations are places where natural hierarchies often replace more formal ones as groups advance in the innovation process. Influence and status are determined more by contribution than by title.

Yet to create the conditions necessary for those efforts, selective and timely direction from the leader is often required. Even in most highly innovative organizations, hierarchy is alive and well. But it's used as needed and very selectively.

We've noted more than once how open the moviemaking process at Pixar was—how virtually everyone involved could contribute their ideas through the way they did their piece of the work, through comments at the dailies, or through notes they sent to the producer and director. Yet, in the end, making a movie wasn't a democratic process; no votes were taken and there was no effort to reach consensus. A film's director was the ultimate arbiter of what the audience would see and hear on the screen. The best directors, however, were those open to a wide diversity of ideas, willing to let people try different approaches, and able to keep possibilities open in their minds. Remember the story in chapter 1 about the animator who added an ironic twist to a character's personality. At first, the director rejected that subtle but significant shift, but he later came back and incorporated it. While a movie director at Pixar was ultimately responsible for the film and so had final say, there were limits on his or her authority. Studio leadership at times did replace directors midway in a production when they failed to move the film forward on schedule. On those occasions, the problem was often the director's inability or unwillingness to enlist people's help in solving a story problem.

Consider this important distinction about how anyone leading innovation uses authority. The leaders we studied created a place that fostered bottom-up innovation, but they knew that place needed constraints and boundaries as well. They did not hesitate to exert strong direction, however, they did it not to set direction or impose a vision but *in support of creating a place where innovation could occur*. For example, they reminded people of deadlines, budgets, and other overall constraints. They made sure people had the information and other resources they needed. They kept the group focused on its fundamental purpose and the organization's overall needs. They pointed out when someone was violating the rules of engagement—the way people were expected to treat each other—especially when conflict was becoming personal rather than focused on ideas.

They provided valuable new data or insights. They created bridges with outside sources of support or important information. They constantly asked leading, probing questions—What about ... ?, What if ... ?, When ... ?, Why ... ?—that encouraged the group to test its ideas, reflect on what it was learning, be more rigorous in its analysis, or collect more data. And they never hesitated to press for better solutions or to refuse compromises or trade-offs.

In figure 2-1, we summarize the six paradoxes we've just described as they relate to the fundamental paradox—unleash *and* harness—behind them all.

The leader's challenge is to help an organization move appropriately between "unleash" and "harness" on each of the six scales in a process of continuous recalibration. The right position at any moment will depend on specific current circumstances. But the goal will always be to take whatever positions enable the collaboration, experimentation, and integration necessary for innovation. Leaders who live on the harness side will never unleash the full slices of genius in their people. And those who always stay on the unleash side will have constant chaos and never solve any problems for the collective good.

The leaders we studied understood how to adapt their behaviors according to the situation at hand. Conventional notions of leadership, discomfort with conflict or loss of control, or personal preferences could limit

Figure 2-1 Six Paradoxes

a leader's willingness to shift strategically across the scales. Many found it hard not to favor one extreme of the scales over the other. The versatility required to continually recalibrate the needs of their organizations and modify their behavior accordingly required superb judgment, courage, and persistence.

The Implications of the Paradoxes

Think about what the paradoxes are telling us about leading innovation.

First, they help explain why innovation is so difficult. It's difficult, of course, because finding solutions that are truly new and useful is not easy. But it's also difficult because the process of innovation is so messy and full of the tensions embodied in each of the paradoxes. Everyone involved must wrestle constantly with those tensions and the stress they induce. And the tensions never go away because the paradoxes are always there, requiring constant attention. That's why innovation is *inherently* difficult, and the difficulties can only be managed, never resolved for good. Knowing about them and why they exist can help, but it doesn't make them easy to navigate.

Thus, the paradoxes explain why organizational innovation requires both organizational *willingness* and *ability*. Clearly, any group that wishes to innovate must be able to collaborate, experiment, and integrate possible solutions. That is, it must possess the skill to undertake those activities productively. But, given all the barriers to innovation revealed in the paradoxes, leaders and their people must also be *willing* to do the hard work of innovation and endure the tensions and stress that work entails. This important idea is a critical aspect of leading for innovation that we will explore in coming chapters: first, *willingness*, of course, because without desire or inclination nothing else will happen, and then *ability*.

Finally, the paradoxes help explain why leading for innovation requires not only leadership but also a different approach to leadership, a different way of thinking about the role of the leader. As Andrew Stanton, the Academy Award–winning director of *Finding Nemo*, learned from his mentor, John Lasseter:

> *What I realized ... is, "Fine, I'm not an auteur. I need to write with other people, I need people to work against. It's not about self-exploration— it's not about me—it's about making the best movie possible." And as*

soon as I admitted that, it was amazing how the crew morale pivoted and suddenly everyone had my back. If you own the fact that you don't know what you're doing, then you're still taking charge, you're still being a director ... I learned that from John [Lasseter] on "Toy Story"—every time he got confessional and said, "Guys, I think I'm just spinning my wheels," we'd rise up and solve the problem for him.[6]

The paradoxes explain why many leaders may need to rethink what they must do if they want a more innovative organization. That is the subject we will explore in the next chapter.

I BELIEVE THAT IF THE CEO ALWAYS THINKS HE IS THE OWNER AND THE DOER, HE WILL NOT ACCOMPLISH THINGS. IT DOESN'T MATTER IF THE GOAL IS FLYING A ROCKET TO THE MOON, DIGGING OIL HOLES, OR GETTING THE BRITISH OUT OF INDIA. I GO BACK TO MY THREE HEROES [MAHATMA GANDHI, NELSON MANDELA, MARTIN LUTHER KING]. I DON'T THINK THEY DID ANYTHING. INSTEAD, THEY ENABLED PEOPLE TO DO WHAT THESE PEOPLE THOUGHT, IN THEIR HEARTS, WAS THE RIGHT THING TO DO. THAT IS THE FUTURE OF LEADERSHIP.

—**Vineet Nayar**, then CEO, HCL Technologies

RECASTING
THE ROLE OF
THE LEADER

eaders of innovation create organizations where people are willing and able to do the work of innovation, where everyone has the opportunity to contribute his or her slice of genius to the collective genius of the whole.

That may seem obvious, but most of those in positions of authority have been taught a concept of leadership that actually stifles innovation. They think their job is to come up with the big ideas and mobilize people to execute them. Somehow they see themselves as the ones who make innovation happen. But this approach makes no sense when the goal is the creation of something original. In that setting, no one can know in advance, by definition, what the outcome will be, not even the leader.[1]

Consequently, many leaders who truly seek to foster innovation must start by abandoning the "Follow me! I know the way!" approach that many consider the core role of leadership. They need to replace it with a different mindset about how leaders foster innovation from everyone in their organization.

In this chapter, we will look at Vineet Nayar. As president and then CEO of HCL Technologies (HCL)—with tens of thousands of employees, a much larger company than Pixar—he led the transformation of a faltering Indian computer company into a dynamic global provider of innovative IT services. In him we will see a leader who used his authority to take actions far different from those of a conventional CEO. He exemplified the kind of leadership needed to create an organization where people are willing and able to innovate.[2]

A New Leader for HCL

"We don't need a Band-Aid; what we need is a tourniquet!" Nayar was sitting at his desk in the Delhi headquarters of HCL. On a dusty street outside, hoards of cattle, motorbikes, chauffeured town cars, trucks, and pedestrians battled for right of way. The air was thick and wavy with heat and the nonstop honking and bleating of horns.

To Nayar, the bedlam outside mirrored the chaos inside his company. It was April 5, 2005, his first day as HCL's president. As far as first days go, this was a bad one. It was early afternoon when he learned that two customers wanted to cancel engagements. Unfortunately, this was not a surprise.

A pioneer of the Indian computer industry, HCL, part of the HCL Enterprise, had grown into a company with $764 million in revenues, a market cap of $2.3 billion, and twenty-four thousand employees. Once one of India's most innovative companies, it had slipped in recent years to number five in revenue among its Indian counterparts. Still growing at a cumulative rate of 35 percent, though more slowly than most competitors, it was living off its past reputation and customer base. More ominous, employee turnover was high, the company no longer attracted the best talent, and the market was growing even more competitive each year.

A classic start-up founded in 1976 in an Indian garage by Shiv Nadar, HCL Enterprise flourished in the 1980s—"a golden period" for the company, said an employee. But the seeds of change were also being planted in that decade. The personal computer appeared. Open source systems began to replace proprietary systems. Most important, focus in the industry was moving to software from hardware, which was increasingly a commodity.

This was the period when Indian software companies rose to prominence, including such firms as Wipro, Tata Consultancy Services (TCS), and Infosys.

In spite of these changes, HCL Enterprise entered the 1990s determined to retain its focus on hardware. But by the end of the century, founder Shiv Nadar realized the need to expand HCL Enterprise's strategic focus to include software. In 1998, he split HCL into two companies: HCL Infosystems, an Indian-facing firm focused on hardware and on software integration; and HCL Technologies, a global IT services company that provided software-led IT solutions, remote infrastructure management services, and business process outsourcing.

By 2004, the Indian IT industry had estimated annual revenues of $36 billion and was growing rapidly. HCL struggled to keep up. Services were "the new game," said an HCL employee, "and we entered late." Building a brand as a services company was not easy, given HCL Enterprise's legacy as the number-one producer of hardware in India. Customers wanted experienced outsourcers that could provide real business value, not just hardware and low-cost commodity work.

Nayar's upbringing helped prepare him for his demanding new role. Because his father died when he was young, "the traditional command-and-control structure did not exist in our household," he said. As a result, he grew up less imbued than most in his culture with a reverence for hierarchy and formal authority.

Nayar joined HCL Enterprise in 1985 as a twenty-three-year-old engineer with an MBA and soon established a strong reputation as a top talent. As he made his way up through various managerial positions, he clearly saw what was happening to the company, and his beliefs about leadership evolved. "I was often asked lots of questions by my employees," he said.

> At first, I loved it. I enjoyed being looked up to. It made me feel impor-
> tant and successful. But very slowly, I began to see this style of manage-
> ment had its limitations. I could never know enough about everything
> happening in our company. Sometimes I gave answers that proved to
> be wrong and caused people trouble. Sometimes I gave answers and
> the people who had asked the questions ignored what I said ... I had a

sense that there must be a better way to manage a company. I decided in order to find out what it was, that I would have to leave HCL and start my own enterprise and make it a very different kind of company. It would have little hierarchy, be highly creative, and fast moving.

When Shiv Nadar heard of Nayar's plans, he proposed an alternative: become an entrepreneur within HCL Enterprise. The Indian government at the time wanted to create a new stock exchange. Nayar realized that developing a more reliable and transparent electronic exchange using satellite-based technology was an attractive opportunity. He accepted the challenge, hired a few colleagues, and in 1993 founded Comnet, an IT infrastructure and networking business wholly owned by HCL Enterprise.

Nayar and his fellow Comnetians spent two years developing a proposal for using satellite technology to modernize the stock exchange, something never done before. "We were battling the best in the world," said an early Comnetian, "and the stakes were so high we had to be innovative." Comnet won the deal and navigated huge logistical challenges to open the National Stock Exchange in November 1994.

By the late 1990s, Nayar had earned a reputation as an exceptional leader who had made Comnet one of HCL Enterprise's most agile, innovative, and successful businesses. With close to a thousand employees, Comnet had won many high-profile deals. "At heart we were all entrepreneurs," said Anant Gupta, then Comnet's chief operating officer, "and we were constantly transforming our business to adapt to market dynamics."

Regular transformation was a core part of Comnet's culture. As Nayar said, "We believed that if we did not innovate every eighteen months or so, if we did not bring a new product or service to the market, we would not remain competitive and would lose our position as market leader." In 2002, the company successfully went global and opened offices in eleven countries.

Comnet's growth surged through the 1990s and early 2000s, while HCL continued to lose ground to competitors. Shiv Nadar began looking for new leadership for HCL and offered the presidency to the young leader of Comnet. Nayar hesitated. He knew the difference between building a successful start-up and turning around a large, declining firm. He finally accepted with one condition: "that I could do things my way. I wanted to make drastic changes that had never been made before. It was risky but Shiv said okay."

Nayar spent the following weeks visiting dozens of customers and HCL offices in India, the United States, China, and Europe. Immersing himself in the company revealed the true gravity of its problems. Customers continued to be unhappy and threatened to cancel; new business was coming in at a trickle; attrition had risen to more than 20 percent. "I had been running my own little shop inside HCL," he said, "and didn't realize how much the company had slipped in the past few years. Within a few weeks, I stopped being polite."

Nayar Understood the Market Had Shifted

When he took over the leadership at HCL, Nayar knew that the role of IT in most major companies was changing. Not only was it central to their operational success, it had become transformational, capable of changing their businesses in strategic ways. However, he saw greater opportunity than merely joining the throng offering software and services in response to this shift. He wanted HCL to become a full partner with clients in harnessing the transformative potential of IT.

Nayar thought about this in terms of where value for the customer was created. In the old HCL—in fact, in all traditional companies that sold actual products—it resided mostly in those who created products. The "value zone," as he called the place where value was created for the customer, had essentially been *inside* the company and that had been where innovation was most needed.

Becoming a services company, especially one that aspired to transform clients with innovative IT solutions, shifted the value zone. In the new HCL, it would reside at the outer edge of the company where HCL people worked with the customer to solve the customer's problems and ultimately to transform its business. In short, the new value zone would be the *relationship* between HCL people and the customer. That was where the new HCL would most need innovation, not inside but on the edge, at the interface with customers.

Nayar saw the possibilities that this new way of thinking offered. He saw that HCL's competitors were far ahead in offering basic IT services beyond hardware, but none was yet working with customers to apply the full potential of IT. He saw here an opportunity to leapfrog competitors by moving even further up the value chain and focusing on larger, more complex, and transformative engagements. That market space would still be uncontested, especially if HCL could combine its new approach with its traditional Indian focus on low cost and value.

The Real Problem

Seizing the opportunity would be difficult. To become a transformative partner for its customers, HCL would have to undergo its own transformation. Nayar needed an organization focused on this new value zone, and, he would have to create one not from scratch, as he had at Comnet, but from a traditional organization designed to support a traditional value zone inside the company. The new value zone would require creation of value in a long-term partnership with the customer. And that would require an organization in which innovation came not from management and a few product designers, but bottom up from people in the "zone," to use Nayar's term for it, who were willing and able to innovate continuously.

His challenge was that these employees and the organization supporting them had never been asked to do any of this before. During those intense early weeks when he traveled to company offices around the world, he discovered that too many employees were complacent and reactive. They didn't share their ideas, let alone debate them with one another, and they weren't taking responsibility for company performance. Above all, they weren't willing to innovate to meet customers' increasingly complex and strategic needs. They expected management to set direction and come up with new ideas.

However, Nayar knew he couldn't blame the employees for these attitudes and behaviors. At HCL, as in many companies, managers often focused on setting direction and making sure no one deviated from it, so traditionally people tended to look upward for instructions, which hampered self-driven innovative problem solving. The HCL organization, he realized, was "shackling people and keeping them from contributing all they could and in the ways they longed to."

The fundamental obstacle in the way of his hopes and plans for the new HCL was how people were being led. It was the employees themselves that HCL was offering to customers. "The value zone was between the employees and the customers, not me and the customers," said Nayar. "Without that employee value zone, and the value created there by innovative employees, HCL was nothing but a shell—layers and layers of management."

"It's laughable," he added. "Can you imagine a company with only senior managers? Management would not be able to deliver innovative solutions to customers. We had to find a way to put the value zone at the center of the company."

Early Steps

Nayar knew he had to act quickly, and so one of his first steps was to halt people's ability to keep doing things the old way. He realized that small engagements with limited scope and duration could not serve as vehicles for the kind of value he wanted HCL to create for customers. In early July, three months after joining HCL, he convened a three-day meeting—called the Blueprint meeting—of the company's top one hundred managers. There he announced a new operational strategy. HCL would stop going after the small, project-based work that constituted much of what it was currently doing, and, instead, it would pursue big deals. To do that, he told the group, they needed to differentiate HCL by offering "multiservice, unique propositions that transform customers' businesses." They were going to start competing against global majors like Accenture and IBM, "so it was critical that we get our house in order."

To make this new direction real, he set out a tangible challenge. By chance, a major European electronics retailer, DSGi, had just emerged as an opportunity. It was seeking a vendor to which it could outsource its internal IT support. Putting together a proposal would take months, Nayar said, but it, "could turn around everything for HCL. It could be a rallying point and I thought we should go after it."

To support this new direction, he took a number of other steps. He restructured the company around lines of business, rather than geographic areas. He pushed to automate consistent systems and processes across all lines of business and worldwide, so all employees would receive timely and consistent information. He fostered the development of an extensive talent development program that linked business goals to the individual learning needs of each employee.

He paid particular attention to reviving the Sales and Delivery groups because, when he arrived, he'd inherited a demoralized sales team that was accustomed to losing. The new head of Sales, a transplant from Comnet, reorganized the group around vertical markets and installed new sales tools, incentives, and programs to encourage and support megadeal wins.

He created a Business Finance group that worked with Sales and Delivery to make sure every deal was a financial win for both HCL and the customer. To make sure HCL could start delivering right away on big deals, he created the Multi-Service Delivery Unit and staffed it with two hundred technical people, all selected through a rigorous process that considered not only technical but business and social skills as well. This elite group focused exclusively on winning and then helping deliver large, exclusive deals like the one HCL wanted with DSGi.

Nayar pushed through these and other changes. Operating with a real sense of urgency, he put in place the organizational structures and tools that would foster the innovation HCL needed to win and deliver on big deals.

Though important and necessary, however, such steps by themselves would not create the kind of organization Nayar wanted. He could not take it by fiat where it needed to go. He could use the power of the CEO's office to reorganize and mandate new systems and processes, but he could not direct employees to innovate. Nor could he tell HCL managers simply to change the way they managed. That would require a different approach.

As Nayar pondered this challenge, a radical idea occurred to him. "What if," he said, "we turned everything upside down? What if management were accountable to the value zone and the people in it? What if we could put employees first?" As he thought of it, HCL would have only three components: the value zone where HCL people interacted with customers, enabling functions that supported the zone and those in it, and, last, management.

Changing How People Think

In July 2005, three months after he became president, Nayar set up a team of about thirty young employees to work on this idea. He called them "Young Sparks" and installed them in offices on the same floor as the executive suite at HCL headquarters in a Delhi suburb. He met with the group frequently as it planned the launch of an internal campaign aimed at fostering employee engagement around the value zone. "I wanted to change how employees experienced HCL," he said, "and I knew it needed a brand."

The Young Sparks' mandate was to develop a tagline and an intranet portal on the theme "Employees First." After much deliberation, and tests of various logos and phrases that tried to capture the spirit of the new HCL, "We came up with 'Employees First, Customers Second,'" said a member of the group, "because it had shock value and showed we were doing something radical."

The group also sought an icon that would symbolize the importance of the individual and the power of the collective. It settled on *Thambi*, which meant "brother" in Tamil, the major language in southern India. Symbolizing an extraordinary individual with pride, passion, and a focus on results, *Thambi* was meant to remind people that they were all members of the same community and that behind *Thambi* stood the entire organization, an idea captured in an HCL slogan: "The Force of One." Every employee could bring the full resources of the company to bear on a customer's problems.

Nayar loved what the Young Sparks had conceived. *Thambi* symbolized the HCL employee who could innovate in the value zone. By the end of July 2005, the group had launched a campaign that introduced "HCLites," as they decided to call HCL employees, to "Employees First, Customers Second" (EFCS).

Some Indian and non-Indian employees were skeptical at first. "Most of us took a wait-and-see approach," said one. Another noted, "At the Blueprint [meeting], it had been made clear to us how broken HCL was. Having something called 'Employees First, Customers Second' to fix us seemed inadequate."

Nayar kept stressing, though, that EFCS was in truth "hard not soft." Because the customer-employee interface was where value was created, he said, "I want value-focused employees who are willing and able to drive an innovative, sophisticated experience for our customers." EFCS was about "investing in employees' development, unleashing their potential to produce significant bottom-line results. The ultimate goal was to radically change the business model," said Nayar.

EFCS was how Nayar talked about making the organization serve those employees who, directly or indirectly, created value for customers through innovation in the value zone. Though it attracted much attention inside and outside the company, it was only one of several ways he sought to undertake what he called "inverting the organizational pyramid" (see figure 3-1).

Inverting the pyramid was about flipping the organization—customers at the top, management at the bottom—and putting in place structures for change so that the focus was clearly on serving the value zone and those in it.

For employees to take responsibility, Nayar believed, the company had to demonstrate its trust in them in a variety of ways. He called these efforts "Trust through transparency—creating the culture for change." He knew mutual trust was important because it would enable a level of candor and honest two-way dialogue that let people feel free to speak their minds without fear. Trust would enable people to accept his interventions without feeling unduly or unfairly controlled, while candor would let people push back if they felt the interventions were becoming intrusive.

One notable effort was something HCL called "trust pay," which applied to the 85 percent of employees, mostly junior engineers, who weren't senior managers or salespeople. "In the industry, it was typical for engineers to get 70 percent of their pay fixed, and then have 30 percent variable," said the head of HR. "But many companies set internal targets so high that only a small portion of that 30 percent was ever attained. So rather than telling

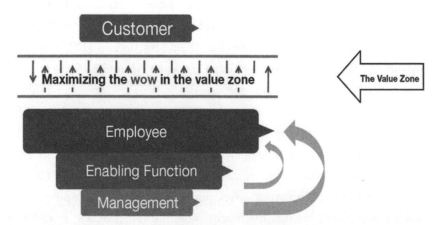

Figure 3-1 Inverting the Organizational Pyramid

our employees their fixed pay was Rs. 14,000 per month and variable could be up to Rs. 6,000 per month, we just gave them the full Rs. 20,000." It did increase the company's cost base, Nayar said, "but the idea was, we'd pay you fully, but we trusted that you would deliver. It reenergized the company, as suddenly people from the competition were joining us."

Above all, Nayar believed that the biggest driver of trust was transparency, and many of his actions were aimed at making the company and its management more open. HCL began using its intranet much more extensively as a lively, personalized place where employees could get almost all the information and processes they needed to do their jobs. The intranet made that information more timely, consistent, and transparent. It was a key way to communicate with people about EFCS. And, with weekly polls, it was a useful way to gather data from employees.

Transparency meant more candor about the condition of the company. Through an initiative he called "Mirror, Mirror," Nayar held up a metaphorical mirror when he interacted with employees that revealed HCL had been "pretty for twenty-five years" but hadn't been for the past five. He wanted people to abandon their "it's okay to lose" mind-set, set their sights higher, and then take responsibility for change. "There was no soft landing for anyone," he said. "I was holding up a mirror to the entire company. We had to transform from the inside out, and I was hoping that the employees really wanted to do the same—they just needed to know how!"

The Smart Service Desk (SSD) was an online system brought over from Comnet. Similar to a help desk, it allowed employees to log in and raise issues or questions about almost anything related to work—HR, finance, IT, training, and so on. The system issued a ticket, and the employee could then track the process of resolving the issue. What made SSD different was that only the employee could declare a ticket closed and the issue resolved. Its purpose was to give employees a sense of empowerment through their ability to raise a problem and follow it to resolution. An issue was an issue so long as the employee felt it was unresolved.

"U & I" was an online channel Nayar created where employees could ask him any question they wanted. He answered a hundred questions each week, and all questions and answers were posted and open to all employees. Employees asked so many questions that HCL had to dedicate a staff member to opening, uploading, and categorizing them. Nayar spent hours answering them himself. "I threw open the door and invited criticism," he said. "We were becoming honest, and that was the sign of a healthy company."

"Directions" meetings were annual events where Nayar and senior managers traveled to all HCL locations and held face-to-face town hall discussions. Nayar spent over half his time traveling to the company's global locations. "Directions created a common language across the company," he said, "so that everyone knew and could articulate what HCL stood for, what were its key strategies and how they fit into the big picture."

One employee commented that communications at HCL were once "handed down from on high," but Nayar replaced that with much more direct contact through video conferencing, online tools, and face-to-face talks. "In the UK," said this employee, "we frequently gathered in a room to watch Nayar speaking somewhere in the world. We had a sense of clarity about where we were headed."

Trust-building transparency also meant greater openness about performance. Nayar had the company install a balanced scorecard system using automated project portals to keep track of work on specific customer projects. Project performance and customer profitability on every project were completely visible to *all* project managers.

Another of Nayar's actions that provoked much attention was 360-degree reviews. In August, four months after he became president, he announced that by September all managers would receive 360-degree feedback. Nayar stressed that this process was for development, not evaluation. He explained that Comnet had used the approach successfully for the previous five years. He also announced that he would post his own feedback on the intranet for all HCL employees to see and even promised to resign if his 360-degree review dipped below a certain level. One of his early reviews said he was a "tough taskmaster." He said he wouldn't require his senior managers to post their reviews, but he asked for volunteers, and more followed his example than he had anticipated.

Nayar was pleased with the process: "When the thirty-seven thousand employees all over the world had the chance to view their top management transparently, I think the message really got across for the first time that we were truly a different company. The transformation process was becoming less dictatorial and more consultative." As an executive noted, "With the 360's, there was a tipping point. For a while there were few believers, and then suddenly there were few nonbelievers."

Clearly, as Nayar promised, EFCS and "inverting the pyramid" were not about free lunches. They placed heavy expectations on employees. It was actually a reworking of the psychological contract—the set of expectations, most unwritten, between leadership and employees—that shifted the power dynamic in the company and responsibility for change toward employees. The message was clear. Leaders at HCL were accountable to employees. Some managers, scared off by transparency and loss of control, left the company.

By September 2006, when Nayar and his top managers hosted Directions meetings for the second time, they were hearing different questions from people. "During the first year," he said, "the questions were more transactional. Employees from all levels were asking about the future, about strategy, and how to add value. You could tell this was an organization undergoing transformation."

Recasting the Role of the Leader

Yet, even after Nayar installed all these changes, HCL essentially remained a centralized organization. Nayar had been named CEO in 2007, a position, he realized, that was still the sun of the organizational solar system:

> Everywhere I went I got questions—all good and useful questions about important topics, but it bothered me that I was expected to have all the answers. It was just that they'd gotten into the habit so common in traditional Indian companies—and corporations around the world: ask the executive. What bothered me was that I knew I didn't have the answers to their questions—but they probably did.

He wanted employees to accept much more responsibility. To do that, he decided he had to reframe the role of the CEO in people's minds, so they would stop thinking of it as the key driver of change. "Only in that way," he said, "could we continue to focus on the value zone, put employees first as our company continued to gain size and scope, and make the change truly sustainable."

He modified the "U & I" online portal he had set up where any employee could ask him questions. The portal, he realized, did make senior management more transparent, but it also reinforced the notion of the all-knowing CEO—the one with the answers—which was exactly what he wanted to change.

Why shouldn't the question asking go both ways? He had many problems he was struggling to solve. Why not ask employees? He created within "U & I" a section called "My Problems." There he asked employees strategic questions he couldn't solve. "I got incredible answers," he said. "Everybody was willing to help their poor, benighted CEO!" He wanted to shift ownership of HCL away from him to the employees. In effect, he was telling employees, in his words, "I have no idea how to run this company. That's your job."

In July 2006, all employees went through a new, automated 360-degree review process. This time, fifteen hundred managers posted their reviews. While the experience was once again generally positive, some managers still declined to share their feedback. Later, Nayar began requiring that all managers post their reviews.

Employees First Councils were voluntary, online employee communities that formed around different areas of common interest. Subjects ranged from art and music to corporate social responsibility, but most were focused on ways to delight customers. They were "if only we could" projects that would truly differentiate HCL's offerings in the marketplace. The councils, each with an elected representative in each office, caught on like wildfire. Eventually, there were twenty-five hundred council leaders around the world.

Impressed with the councils' popularity, HCL added some that focused specifically on business-related passions, such as a particular technology or line of business. These new communities quickly began to generate a variety of ideas and helped HCL develop plans and proposals for new business. One initiative that grew out of these communities was business-aligned IT, or BAIT. The goal of BAIT was to align HCL's services much more closely and quickly with customers' specific business processes. After a pilot, the company rolled out the full program over the course of a few months.

"When some of these ideas began to produce new revenue," Nayar said, "we realized we had stumbled on another unanticipated benefit: creating new business ideas through unstructured innovation." These were "communities of passion," he said, "built around personal interests and business issues." They helped transfer responsibility for innovation from leadership to "communities of people collaborating and creating alternatives outside the boundaries of hierarchy."

In 2009, Nayar added an element of crowdsourcing to the way HCL did business planning. Until then, his top three hundred managers had presented their business plans to the senior team, but he began to wonder if he should be the one reviewing all those plans. What did he know about the businesses of these three hundred managers? He wasn't in the value zone; they were. It would be better, he thought, if the managers shared their plans and experiences with each other, perhaps triggering new ideas or solutions for their respective business areas. Nayar hoped to transform the planning process from one dominated by top-down judgments to one characterized by peer-to-peer review.

In spite of some resistance by his senior managers, Nayar created a portal called "My Blueprint," where HCL managers posted their plans for open review by eight thousand other managers above and below them in the company. The effect, he recalled, was astonishing. First, he was surprised to find that the managers' plans sounded very different from the face-to-face presentations he had been hearing. The depth of analysis and quality of strategic thinking improved because, he suspected, the managers knew their own teams and their peers would be reviewing them. The managers were also more honest in their assessment of current challenges and opportunities, and they talked less about what they hoped to accomplish and more about the actions they intended to take to achieve specific results.

The HCL intranet started buzzing about the plans on My Blueprint. Knowledge sharing increased well beyond Nayar's initial hopes. People helped each other refine their plans. Many managers found the postings far more relevant and actionable than the information they'd previously received in briefings from their superiors. Managers found they had far more buy-in from their teams. "In the end," Nayar said, "the leadership team and I participated in the process, giving comments and feedback, but our voices were just a few among eight thousand."

Nayar launched "iGen," a limited-time online platform that followed the annual face-to-face Directions meetings. Employees could propose solutions there to problems HCL faced. Far more than another electronic suggestion box, iGen required a well-thought-out idea with supporting information and suggestions for execution, along with predictions for cost savings or impact on the company. The iGen application guided an employee through the process with ten questions. "The exact ideas employees proposed," Nayar said, "were not as important, usually, as the fact that they were thinking creatively. iGen was about the culture of creating ideas."

HCLites Become Innovative Problem Solvers

Because of all those changes, something fundamental began to happen at HCL, something on which the big, long-term deals would depend for ultimate success. HCL employees were beginning to innovate bottom up in the value zone. The following example is one of hundreds and, ultimately, thousands.

An HCL employee working with a global pharma customer noticed while reading some of its business reports that the pharmaceutical company had developed a vaccine for cervical cancer. On his own, the employee decided to start organizing communications events for women at HCL where they could learn about the disease and the vaccine and, if they chose, be vaccinated. It was not necessarily easy to set up. The HR department, among others, had many reasonable questions. Why should we do this? Is it safe? Has it been tested? He pushed through the barriers, created with his work team of programmers an outreach system for organizing and holding an event, and eventually was able to run an event where HCL subsidized vaccinations for fifteen hundred women employees.

Around this time, the CIO of the pharma customer was in India and by chance saw a poster in an HCL cafeteria publicizing the event. He brought up the program with the business side of HCL, which realized this outreach program, already designed, could readily be taken to market as a service. The program turned into one of the early components of HCL's emerging Business Process Outsourcing (BPO) business. The outreach program expanded to serve not only women concerned about cervical cancer but also patients with diabetes. It also became both a way for the pharma customer to expand sales and a BPO service that HCL could offer pharma companies for use in emerging markets.

As one HCL manager, who worked extensively with this pharma customer, said, "This was one little innovation, but when you imagine tens of thousands of people doing this every day, it can add up."

Progress

Six months after Nayar first announced the big deals strategy at the first Blueprint meeting, HCL won the $330 million DSGi deal that he had set as a goal. It surpassed the previous record for India's largest outsourcing deal, set by Tata Consultancy Services (TCS) with a $250 million contract in 2005.[3] Many employees had been skeptical that HCL could win something so big against the global majors, especially while it was undergoing its own transformation. Said Nayar, "We really chased this deal. In the past we'd let big deals get away, but we said, 'Not this one.'"

DSGi was only one of several big deals that started coming in. The first, a $50 million, multiyear contract with Autodesk, a California-based software and services company, came in before DSGi. Next came a strategic $100 million partnership with EXA Corporation, a Japanese system integrator that was a joint venture between IBM Japan and JFE Steel, Japan's second-largest steel manufacturer. These were "the type of work we wanted," said Nayar, "complex, long-term, and multimillion." More followed, with Teradyne, a leading supplier of automatic test equipment based in Boston; with Cisco, the networking equipment maker, that involved royalty-based revenue sharing; with Boeing for work on its breakthrough 787 Dreamliner; and with Celestica, the innovative Toronto-based world leader in electronics manufacturing services, a $100 million joint venture that launched HCL's "concept-to-manufacturing" service.

Many of these deals were won in stiff competition with global majors like IBM and Accenture and key Indian IT firms like Wipro and TCS. They were deals that, even a year earlier, HCL would probably not have pursued or won. Some, such as those with Cisco and Celestica, represented the next phase of HCL's transformation, which was about forming strategic partnerships that jointly created new and uncontested markets. "We were starting to win," said a senior HCL manager, "because Vineet had pulled all of the ingredients to success—which we already had—together. 'Employees First' was a wonderful glue."

With these wins and other signs of change and progress, HCL began to attract the interest of investors, the business press, and prospective employees. *India Today* ranked HCL one of the top ten "most wanted Indian stocks." IDC, a technology information firm, called HCL a "disruptive force" and said it "may very well be one of the contenders to lead the IT services world of the very near future."[4] *The Economist* cited HCL as a company to watch, especially for its unique strategy. It said IBM and the other global majors were "becoming increasingly nervous" about HCL. "Largely unnoticed," it said, "HCL has won several contracts worth $300m-700m for infrastructure management and business transformation."[5]

HCL's performance metrics showed the results of Nayar's leadership. In the global recession of 2008–2009, all its Indian competitors watched their revenues drop while HCL posted an increase of over 23 percent. In the five years before he arrived, HCL's compound annual growth rate had been the lowest among Indian IT firms by eleven to fourteen percentage points; for 2008–2012, it was the highest by six to nine percentage points.

One driver of this growth was HCL's 2008 acquisition of AXON, a leading enterprise systems integrator, for over $800 million. Instead of integrating the acquired firm into HCL, the standard approach in a merger, Nayar created a separate business unit, HCL-AXON, and reverse-integrated HCL's own enterprise applications practice and staff into the AXON operation. This approach, he said, "had the intended effect of accelerating HCL's growth even as the recession deepened." It was the next step in his long-term plan to provide clients with innovative, integrated services that would have an impact on and even redefine their core businesses.

For all HCL's success, Nayar was quick to point out that the transformation of the company was always an ongoing story. Not everything worked as intended. The acquisition and reverse-integration of AXON, for example, was tumultuous at times. Not every customer engagement went well. We talked to many customers who saw great innovation in HCL's work, but some were disappointed. As HCL began to see some success, Nayar said, it was difficult to keep people dissatisfied and eager to change. Neither he nor any of the leaders we studied believed that their organizations' past and current successes guaranteed anything about the future.

After three years as CEO, Nayar subsequently become its vice chairman in 2010. Then, in 2013, he relinquished his CEO position to focus on the activities of a foundation he had begun years earlier that was devoted to social and educational change in India.

During the time he led HCL, from 2005 to 2013, its operations expanded to thirty-two countries while revenues increased sixfold, from $764 million to $4.7 billion. Profits and market cap increased by the same factor. Under him, the company achieved, with eighty-five thousand employees, the highest revenue-per-employee of all India-based firms. This radical transformation led *Fortune* to recognize HCL as "the world's most modern management," while *Businessweek* named HCL "one of the world's most influential companies." In 2012, HCL was named one of the top-three global outsourcing leaders by the International Association of Outsourcing Providers. That same year, *Forbes* included it among its "Fab 50 Companies" in Asia. The company also received many prestigious citations, such as the "Most Democratic Workplace in the World," "Workforce Management Optimas Award for HR Innovation" in the United States, "Britain's Top Employers," "Best Employer in Asia," and many more. Nayar himself was chosen by *Fortune* for its first-ever global "Executive Dream Team" 2012, which was described as an "all-star leadership" that "could coalesce and dominate in any industry," in addition to his inclusion in the elite "Thinkers50 List" in 2011–2012, a definitive listing of the world's top fifty business thinkers.

Even in Nayar's absence, the leadership ideas he implanted continued to grow and develop. Employees First began paradoxically as a top-down effort to spur bottom-up initiative. Now, as we write this, employees themselves, excited by the Employees First philosophy, are pushing that initiative to its next stage. They're asking for, and in some cases demanding, corporate platforms to stimulate, celebrate, capture, and reward grassroots innovation. Some programs emerging from that effort include MAD Jam (Make a Difference Jamboree), an annual celebration of employee innovation, including a contest in which employees vote on innovations generated by different teams in the course of their regular work; Value Portal, a clearinghouse for employee innovations developed for one client with the potential to benefit many; and MAD LTD (Make a Difference, Lead the Difference), a kind of hackathon for college engineering and business students, designed to bring students' ideas for societal and other kinds of change to the surface.

Lessons from a Different Kind of Leader

It's impossible to read the story of Vineet Nayar and HCL without concluding that the leadership he provided was not leadership as commonly seen or conceived. Yes, he was a visionary, but he understood that was not his primary role. He could be and was at times quite directive, especially when he needed to remove obstacles to innovation or put structures in place that fostered it. But we believe he succeeded not because of those aspects of his leadership but precisely because he had the courage to take the unconventional steps he did. Despite terrific pressure to perform, he embraced and practiced what to most leaders would have seemed a revolutionary mind-set and approach.[6]

Given what he discovered at HCL during his first weeks as president, Nayar felt he had little choice. He was taking over a once-great hardware company that was declining as it faced faster competitors in a changing market. Customer companies wanted more than the isolated software solutions HCL primarily offered, and they had grown beyond the basics of using IT to automate old ways of doing business. They wanted an IT services vendor whose people could innovate in using technology to transform their companies.

Nayar understood what this required of HCL's leaders, starting with him. *Above all, he thought differently about his role as leader.* As we said, he never saw himself as the great visionary of HCL who would lead it to a glorious future. Instead, he saw himself, in his own phrase, as a "social architect" creating an organizational setting that encouraged and enabled the innovation that would be the company's value-add in the future. He actively, publicly refused to play the role of the one with all the answers, and he encouraged his managers to reject that role as well. He understood that he didn't know enough and wasn't smart enough—no leader is—to know everything. We saw this in the many systems and forums he created at HCL where employees could raise and answer questions themselves. He taught people not to look passively to leaders—to the "Hand of God," as he put it—for all direction. "I believe," he said,

> *Leaders must avoid the urge to answer every question or provide a solution to every problem. Instead you must start asking questions, seeing others as the source of [innovation], and transferring ownership of the organization's growth ...The greatest impact is that it unleashes the power of the many and loosens the stranglehold of the few, thus increasing the speed and quality of innovation and decision making ... every day.*

Nayar pressed people to take personal responsibility for organizational change. He worked hard to change what they expected from their leaders. Instead of answering the question, "Where are we going?" he focused on "Who are we?" and "Why do we exist?" He wanted people to see themselves as partners with HCL's customers in finding innovative uses of technology to transform their businesses.

This was why *Thambi*, the character developed by his Young Sparks team, was so important. *Thambi*, "brother," was the extraordinary individual, the idealized, proactive HCL employee who was able and expected to accomplish great things. *Thambi* was backed by the "Force of One," which was HCL as a whole—its collective genius, if you will. The Force of One referred to the ability of one person to bring to bear the collective genius of HCL on a client's problems and opportunities.

Nayar recognized people's individual slices of genius. He didn't believe innovation was the province of a few talented individuals. He believed instead that most individuals brought to work their own unique talents and had a genuine contribution to make. If he created the right setting, systems, and opportunities, people would combine their talents, their slices of genius, to create collective genius. This is something too few leaders realize or act upon. Even if they appreciate intellectually that everyone has a creative spark, they don't see it as their job to take advantage of that spark.

Nayar took a wide variety of actions—actually experiments—to bring about change and was constantly reviewing and learning from the outcomes. This large organization was spread around the world. Nayar not only had to take a different approach to leadership himself, but he also had to foster a similar change among the firm's eight thousand managers, far from an easy task in a culture that tended to give great deference to authority. As one HCL manager said of posting his own 360-degree review: "In India, people tended to value hierarchy, and transparency was not built into the culture. It was uncomfortable to be exposed like that, especially as someone with seniority."

Over the decades of its history, HCL leadership had set direction and then made sure everyone followed. People had been trained to look upward for guidance about everything important. Nayar knew that some of the managers were still struggling with their new role. He had to watch out for regression, given the challenging economic times and the unrelenting pressure to deliver. Indeed, some managers were scared off by the shifting power dynamics—the loss of control and amount of transparency expected. Some employees were frightened off as well; they were unprepared to accept the duties and obligations that came with their new freedom and responsibilities. Nayar was unfazed by the turnover, which he viewed in some sense as quality control.

When innovation was the goal, he knew a conventional approach to leadership made little sense. He knew that if everyone constantly relied on direction, it would most likely produce only frustration and failure.

The lesson for those hoping to lead innovation is clear. If you want your organization to produce something truly new and useful, you cannot know—by definition—exactly where to go. That's why leading innovation is not—cannot be—about being a visionary. The last thing you want is a team that defers to you to set a course, to be chief innovator and then simply implement your vision. That was the kind of organization Nayar inherited and had to change in order to save it.

If your goal is innovation, then your role must instead be to create an environment—a setting, a context, an organization—where people are willing and able to do the hard work of innovation themselves: to collaborate, learn through trial and error, and make integrated decisions.

Nayar's story and those of the other leaders we studied have convinced us that until leaders reframe their understanding of innovation and leadership, innovation will remain an exception in their organizations.

We cannot say that leadership is the only difference between the many organizations that rarely innovate and the few Pixars and HCLs where innovation is part of their DNA. But we're convinced it's frequently a key difference. Without the kind of leadership we saw in those we studied and describe here, we believe an organization will struggle to achieve its full capacity for innovation.

PART I:
LEADERS CREATE THE WILLINGNESS TO INNOVATE

I n the first three chapters, we presented the main findings from our decade of studying leadership in innovative organizations. We said that effective leadership is a key difference between firms that could innovate again and again and firms that rarely innovated at all. We said that innovation is so difficult because it embodies basic paradoxes that produce ongoing tension. Balancing and managing those tensions is at the heart of the challenge of leading innovation. And we pointed out how leading innovation requires leaders to rethink their roles and responsibilities.

The chief difference we've observed is that the best leaders of innovation don't see their role as that of conjuring up a vision and inspiring others to follow. That's not to say they're incapable of vision or inspiration; often they are. But they've come to understand that their most important role is to create a context in which others can collectively do the work of innovation. As Vineet Nayar at HCL said, leaders are "social architects."

Now we move on to the question—social architects of *what?* That is the subject of the next five chapters in which we explore what these leaders actually do—where they focus their time and attention.

In leading innovation, they face two basic challenges. First, they must create an organization in which people are *willing* to face the hard work of innovation with its inherent tensions and stresses. Second, they must build an organization in which people are *able* to do the work that innovation requires. Neither willingness nor ability can be assumed.

Willing to Innovate

The wise leader knows that innovation is voluntary. No one can be compelled to make a contribution or to care about a problem. Unless people freely open their minds and hearts, they're unlikely to offer their best ideas or endure the sense of vulnerability and anxiety that innovating creates. Why should they? This is the first challenge the leader must address. Without it, the ability to innovate will produce very little.

In the first of the next two chapters, chapter 4, we'll see how Luca de Meo took over a fragmented marketing group at Volkswagen and faced an immediate problem. His group and how it worked had evolved in ways that discouraged innovation. He found there a culture in which innovation was considered something engineers in product development did, not people in marketing. And he found that work processes and organization in marketing fragmented the work into discrete linear steps, which made marketing innovation difficult. Yet, without continual innovation, marketing couldn't support the company in meeting its stated ambition to become the world's leading automaker, both economically and ecologically. De Meo's first challenge then was to develop in his people a stronger willingness to take risks and try new things.

His response, as we saw in so many other innovative organizations, was to build a community of marketers united around and motivated by a compelling, mutual sense of purpose. Until he arrived, the marketing people, spread across 154 countries and 24 different time zones, had worked in silos, with narrowly defined roles, and had operated like a loose federation, seldom working closely with each other, let alone with others outside marketing. De Meo needed his marketing professionals to feel instead like citizens of a cohesive community willing to collaborate as a unit to produce what VW needed—innovative solutions to create a single powerful brand that spoke with one voice globally.

But, fundamental as it is to creating a sense of community, purpose must be built on a set of shared values and rules of engagement. In chapter 5, we will look at Pentagram, a partnership of world-class designers that has survived and thrived since its founding in 1972. Though each partner could have worked successfully on his or her own—to become a Pentagram partner, a designer must *already* have established a national or international reputation—they all chose to work together. They succeeded as a community not only because they pursued a common purpose but because they also shared fundamental values and followed certain rules of engagement that the founding leaders established and subsequent leaders continuously reinforced. These values and rules guided how they worked together and clarified the duties and obligations, rights and privileges that came with membership. In the story of Pentagram, we can see clearly all the elements—purpose, shared values, and rules of engagement—that create and sustain a community capable of innovating.

MARKETING IS NOT JUST A CORPORATE FUNCTION, BUT PRIMARILY AN ATTITUDE. WE HAVE WORKED HARD TO CREATE A GLOBAL COMMUNITY WITHIN MARKETING THAT HAS THE RIGHT ATTITUDE, WORKS COLLABORATIVELY, AND DELIVERS INNOVATIVE MARKETING SOLUTIONS THAT DELIGHT AND SURPRISE PEOPLE.

—**Luca de Meo**, then CMO, Volkswagen AG

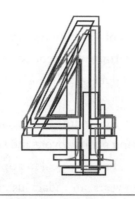

CREATING A COMMUNITY

While waiting for his flight to Munich in late summer 2012, Luca de Meo played the new Think Blue game on his iPad, which promoted environmental sustainability for drivers. It was a pleasant reminder of how far his marketing team at Volkswagen AG (VW) had come in three years.[1]

He had joined VW as head of marketing communications in 2009 to help create the marketing function the firm needed to achieve its ambitious corporate goals. After less than a year, de Meo had added product marketing to his portfolio. Later in 2010, he had also taken on a newly created position as chief marketing officer (CMO) of VW Group, which comprised nine brands.

When de Meo joined Volkswagen, it was already bucking industry trends. Even in the middle of a global recession, it sold nearly 6.3 million units, a new company delivery record, and produced sales revenues of €113.8 billion, an annual increase of 4.5 percent. It was expanding successfully in Brazil, India, and Russia, and in 2008, China had become its largest market, with sales of 1.2 million units or 20 percent of the company's total. It was also determined to rebuild share in the United States, a huge market where it had done well historically before losing ground in recent years.

VW leadership aspired to more. Not satisfied with the company's number-three ranking behind giants Toyota and General Motors, VW chief executive Martin Winterkorn had set a goal in 2008 that VW would become the leading carmaker in ten years, an audacious target in such an intensely competitive business.

It was a goal de Meo embraced and used to unite his fragmented group into an innovative team. Early on in his time at VW, he explained at a meeting of his staff that the corporate goal meant they had "to become the best marketing team in the automotive world." His thinking was simple and compelling. It was what you might call his "$1 + 1 + 1 = 1$" theory. To be a market leader, all the components of a company had to be the best. For VW to become number one, he and his people had to become the number-one most innovative auto marketing team.

During his three years at VW, he had worked diligently to create a marketing team that was up to this challenge, and the company had made significant progress toward its goal. Now in 2012, he was going to Munich to assume his new duties as head of sales and marketing—and to serve on the board of management, the top executive team—at Audi AG, one of the world's leading premium carmakers and the most profitable part of the VW family of vehicles.

With de Meo's three years leading marketing at VW, we take our story of leading innovation one step further to reveal how de Meo addressed the basic challenge we identified in chapter 2: *given the inherent paradoxes and tensions, how does a leader foster people's* willingness *to innovate?*

This is the first task for anyone who seeks to lead innovation. Unless people are willing, nothing else the leader does matters.

What de Meo Found at VW Marketing

De Meo was already a veteran of the European auto industry when he joined the giant German automaker. After earning a business degree in Italy in the early 1990s, he had spent six years at Renault before going to Toyota Europe where he became general manager for product management. In 2002, he moved to Fiat and, while there, revived the Lancia brand, was named CEO of Fiat Automobiles S.p.A at age thirty-seven, and then became CEO of Alfa Romeo, too. His team at Fiat launched the revamped version of the iconic Fiat Cinquecento (Fiat 500), which was selected European Car of the Year by a panel of fifty-eight car journalists from twenty-two countries. He was named "CMO of the Year" by Booz & Company in 2008.

Already fluent in five languages, de Meo learned German while joining VW and, from the beginning, he immersed himself in the history, culture, and organization of the company. Shortly after arriving, he set up thirty-minute meetings with everyone on his staff and listened as nearly a hundred people described their work. In addition, he met with colleagues in other functions at VW headquarters and traveled the globe for face-to-face meetings with management teams in numerous markets, including many of his marketing professionals who were spread across 154 countries and twenty-four time zones.

He was happy to find in his travels and discussions that there were many talented marketing people at company headquarters in Wolfsburg and in the field who admired the company. He also confirmed that this was a product- and engineering-driven company with deep core values of excellence and quality—values he shared. Since his first ride in a race car at age seven, he had become a car afficionado, and though not an engineer by training, he was knowledgeable enough to converse with auto engineers on their own level.

He also found reasons for concern. Marketing decisions at VW were historically decentralized. The marketing division at headquarters in Wolfsburg set parameters, but each market developed and implemented its own marketing strategy.

Smaller markets, which were handled by independent importers that brought in multiple brands from different companies, understandably relied more on VW corporate marketing than the larger markets like China, the United States, and Brazil. In those markets, VW owned national sales companies. But their marketing budgets were set by sales, not marketing, and the heads of marketing reported not to Wolfsburg but to the local CEO or general manager. Consequently, the marketing relationship between headquarters and country markets was often more administrative, as a marketer in the field described it—"sometimes too much about checking the boxes."

The relationship between corporate marketing and the markets was complicated and could be tense at times. For example, it was especially strained in 2007 when VW corporate launched a new global campaign around the tagline *Das Auto*, German for "The Car." Every piece of advertising from the company was supposed to feature it. Many markets resisted because they felt the phrase had little meaning in their cultures or languages. In some languages, it even carried unwanted connotations. In India, *das* was a common name for a person and *auto* was associated with service stations, not cars. In Brazil, Volkswagen had been established for so long that many locals considered it almost a Brazilian car. Marketers worried that *Das Auto* would remind Brazilians that VW was a foreign brand. De Meo heard many complaints about *Das Auto* during his travels to markets around the world.

De Meo also found problems in his own marketing communications department in Wolfsburg. Though VW was a global business, few marketers there had any experience working outside Germany and most knew very little about markets other than their own. In fact, few in his group had any experience outside their own unit.

Much as he loved cars, he also worried that the engineering- and product-driven culture of the company worked against his group in some ways. As often happened in many product-focused organizations, marketing could be perceived as a necessary and unavoidable expense—someone had to throw media parties, run ads, and print brochures. But it wasn't a strategic function crucial to the achievement of corporate goals. He feared that too many of his staff accepted this situation.

When he probed the way his group worked, he found it focused above all on execution via what he called highly linear processes. People had evolved ways of working in silos, with narrowly and specifically defined roles. They seldom met or interacted with each other or their colleagues outside marketing. For example, the marketing strategy for launching a new car was planned and carried out via step-by-step processes. Years before introduction, product marketing met with engineers and designers to define the model and its positioning. Then product marketing handed off to marketing communications, which, twelve to fifteen months before the car actually appeared, developed a strategy for communicating with customers. By that time, everything about the product had been decided.

Given all these features and ways of working, de Meo was not surprised to find that marketing across all the countries was not nearly strategic, global, or innovative enough. As a consequence, VW's brand identity varied significantly from market to market worldwide. It was strongest or most positive, of course, in Germany, followed by the rest of Europe. It was much less strong in such non-European markets as India and the United States, which were needed for continued growth.

The situation was "frustrating at times," according to a manager in de Meo's unit. Though everyone was well intended, he said, marketing often failed to speak with "one voice" in campaigns. "For example, in classical advertising, like TV or print, we went in a more lifestyle direction, but on the Internet we communicated something different."

De Meo's Challenge

De Meo's challenge was clear. Because of the linear and siloed way it worked, the marketing organization he took over wasn't ready to perform the innovative work the company needed from it. It was not, in short, an organization willing and able to collaborate, learn through discovery, and make integrative decisions. Indeed, such activities cut against the grain of the culture and traditional practices de Meo found when he arrived.

Above all, many in his group accepted the belief that marketing—the work they did every day—was a necessary but not strategic function. The company needed them, but its ultimate success didn't depend on them. Consequently, in this engineering- and product-driven organization, they too considered innovation the province of those who designed and developed products, not those in marketing. When he pressed his group to be more innovative, it was, according to a member of his staff, a "relatively new" idea.

De Meo's primary problem, then, was fostering people's *willingness* to do the work of innovation. "I was not sure," he said, "that people felt they had to change the way they played the game" in order to support the company's aspiration to become the leading automaker.

A Foundation to Build On

Fortunately, there was a foundation on which de Meo could build. As he took pains to learn the company's culture and history and get to know his people, he uncovered an underlying pride in the company and what it did, its global accomplishments, and its important place in modern German society. Even marketers spread around the world considered themselves a part of Volkswagen. People knew VW had been founded by auto engineering legend Ferdinand Porsche in the late 1930s to be an affordable "people's car" (the literal meaning of *Volkswagen*). Its purpose was to give common people the freedom of mobility, no small thing at a time when few people had cars. Since then, VW had played a key role in the economic revival of the country after World War II and had become one of the most important firms in the German economy.

People also recognized the prominent role the auto industry played and continued to play in society. "The car is bigger than the car. It still has a strong impact on society," was the way de Meo expressed this belief. Though it was easy to think of cars as an "old economy" business, he said, it remained a major source of jobs in the global economy and a continuing driver of innovation. The car industry revolutionized manufacturing with the invention of mass production. It was the first business to develop a vast collaborative network of suppliers; 70 percent of the value in a car, he pointed out, was created not by the automaker itself but by this supplier network, which provided millions of jobs worldwide. Even in the new economy, the auto industry was continuing to drive leading-edge research in more efficient combustion engines, electric engines, battery technology, alternative fuels, and ultra-light materials.

People in the company understood what was ultimately driving VW's corporate goals: behind the slogans and campaigns, company leaders talked about the impact VW would have on society, on people, and on progress. "They have this obsession for technical progress," de Meo said, "because they know technical progress creates added value for the country and society."

In that broader context of driving social, economic, and technological progress, VW leaders had chosen to build the VW brand around three core values: *innovative*, *responsible*, and *valuable*. They believed that if people everywhere considered Volkswagen the most valuable, innovative, and responsible carmaker, it would become, and deserve to be, the leading car company in the world.

When Winterkorn set out VW's ten-year goal, he meant, by "leading," far more than just the number of cars sold or revenues and profits. He also meant ecological leadership and having the most satisfied customers and employees. "Only an automaker who can achieve all these goals can really call itself number one with justification," he told *Forbes*.[2]

Brand was the key

Building the Volkswagen brand was the key to addressing the challenge de Meo found in VW marketing. First, building one strong brand worldwide was crucial to the company. VW needed greater growth outside Europe where the potential was much higher but the brand was weaker and fragmented.

"Product is and should continue to be the heart of Volkswagen," de Meo told his people, "but we have to go one step beyond product and work on the brand itself, which is what people associate with the product." Unless they built a brand that spoke globally, with one voice, about the three brand values of "innovative, responsible, and valuable," the company could not achieve its aspiration to become the world's leading carmaker—leading in every sense of the word.

De Meo challenged his team to create not only the leading auto brand but one of the top ten global brands across all products and industries. At the time, VW was fifty-fifth in the Interbrand ranking of all global brands, automotive and otherwise. Four other car brands—Ford, Mercedes, BMW, and Toyota—ranked higher.

Second, if brand was critical, then marketing had a strategic role to play. It was essential to the company's success, not merely a necessary expense. That made building the brand a powerful purpose that could align his team members' ambitions and values with those of the company, unite them as an innovative community, and foster their willingness to change how they did the work of innovation.

Early in his time at VW, de Meo told a meeting of his team:

Why are we all here? It's the same reason I joined Volkswagen. This organization has the ambition to become the best car company in the world. To do that, we must become the number-one automotive brand, the most innovative volume car brand, one of the top-ten brands across all industries. For that, we have to become the best marketing team in the automotive world.

They had to "unfold VW's full power *as a team*," and the brand values—innovative, valuable, responsible—had to become the DNA of marketing.

Prior to his arrival, marketing had been task- and process-driven, with each person focused on a specific task. Now it would be a purpose-driven community. As de Meo said: "People are more likely to cooperate when management pays attention not only to KPIs (key performance indicators) and processes, but also to ideas and beliefs—to the meaning of the work."

"Who's Going to Get Us There, If Not Us?"

Like Vineet Nayar at HCL, de Meo understood his task was not to be the source of innovation, the one who made it happen, but to be the "social architect," as Nayar said, of an organization that encouraged and enabled it. His job was to create a context where people's individual slices of genius could emerge and coalesce into collective genius.

Building the brand was the key, but de Meo would have to do more than talk about it to overcome long-ingrained patterns of thought and behavior. The problem, he concluded, was that the corporate and field marketing teams simply did not have enough incentive and opportunity to "work together as a team" and "share their know-how and ideas." In his experience, the mutual trust and respect needed to create a community came only from "interaction and dialogue," he said, and there was too little of either in the way people had routinely done their work.

Pushing people together

Soon after he arrived at VW, de Meo selected three junior members of his group to work with an outside firm headed by an Italian colleague, Maurizio Travaglini, to create a two-day design lab where people could come together and collaborate on a set of important marketing problems. He knew he must do more than tell people to act in new and different ways. Like the other leaders we studied, he put them in situations that forced them out of old behavior and catalyzed a new, more innovative way of working and thinking together. He'd done this at Fiat and seen, in his words, "people emerge, reinvent themselves, come together, and apply their talent and skills to a common end."

They called the VW lab "Marketing Worx!" and designed it to bring together staff members from headquarters and markets to collaborate on building a global brand. Instead of PowerPoint presentations or lectures, the lab would be a place for actual prototyping, testing, and arguing until the best solutions came to life.

The planning team identified several high-stakes projects for participants to work on, in a format that also allowed new ideas to emerge. But the goal went beyond specific projects. It was for people to experience and grow familiar with the innovation process of collaborating, experimenting, and integrating ideas. De Meo recalled:

> We decided to hold this three-day gathering inside one of the most inspiring buildings in the heart of Berlin, designed by Frank Gehry. We worked with an Italian firm to plan the session following their unique and unorthodox approach. We transformed the building into a true twenty-first-century laboratory: artwork everywhere, loud rock music signaling transitions between activities, snapshots showing the history of the automotive industry mixed in with conversations about the future of mobility. We felt that in order to unleash people's thinking and attitudes, some sort of "positive shock" had to be provoked. Unlike in the normal daily life of the organization, everyone was being invited (or even pushed) to be a codesigner of solutions, not just an implementer of others' ideas.

Participants—seventy-two marketing communicators, many of whom had rarely actually worked together—gathered in Berlin on a chilly day in December 2009. Rumors had spread about the design of the event, and some attendees were enthusiastic, while others were skeptical.

"Brand is not fluff," de Meo told them. "There is very concrete evidence of what great brands do. It's real business, not just magic." Strong brands—he cited Coca-Cola and Apple in particular—were known to drive customer preference and share, as well as loyalty and retention. In blind taste tests, he pointed out, Coke and Pepsi were about equally rated. But when people taking the test knew the brand names in advance, they preferred Coke 65 percent to 35 percent. For cars, brand was known to justify price premiums of 10 percent or more.

"Strong brands," he said, "have a clear identity, are unique, and consistent." They "play both sides of the brain—rational and emotional—and normally only make one promise to consumers." Communications from companies with strong brands "all have the same look and feel." But for global brands, he added, "consistent does not mean 'one size fits all;' we do need to tell the same story everywhere, but with the language and expression suited to the local market." He ended by saying, "Our challenge is to become one global brand." For that, they had to come together as one team.

Participants then broke into subgroups, but before diving into their separate projects, all worked on a common assignment: to define "the brand's current meaning and future potential." Based on marketing communication materials they were given to review, they could see that customers in different markets varied widely—in age, gender, income, and price paid—and that the VW brand was perceived quite differently around the world. De Meo recalled, "It is fair to say that people were in real shock at the beginning as they were convened inside a true laboratory, where everything was surprising: the place, the process, the roles. Marketing Worx! became a transformative experience for the marketing people in the HQ."

By the end of the lab, de Meo felt the participants had made progress, both in their assigned projects and in the way they worked together. Although many details still had to be worked out, they had, for instance, the broad outline for a "KPI-cockpit," as well as a plan for moving forward with a sustainability project. He could tell by the way people interacted—their energy, eye contact, gestures, and body language—that they had begun to make connections and gain new insights and perspectives on issues critical to the brand.

One participant described the meaning of Marketing Worx! for him:

I had never had the chance to meet with the other countries ... My perception was that it was Volkswagen for Germany, and then Europe, and then all the other markets. Now it's totally different. Now it's like we want to move this company and we're all a part of the brand. Luca [de Meo] is not dictating rules; he's gathering and trying to get common commitment.

Marketing Worx! showed what people can do, de Meo said, "when they work together collaboratively, without silos and process, and with the ability and mandate to innovate." It was a living demonstration of what it looked like to perform as a team at a higher, more innovative level in marketing.

A different way to handle launches

Focusing people on the brand required more than onetime events like Marketing Worx! De Meo also changed the way his group did its ongoing work, like developing and executing the launch strategy for new VW cars. Though launches required coordination with virtually every other department, and with countless field operations, they had always been done like any other marketing activity—in a siloed, linear, process-heavy fashion. Yet, because they required so many separate groups to work together, de Meo considered them golden opportunities for marketing to practice and improve cross-group collaboration and create a more powerful, consistent VW brand worldwide.

So, less than a year after arriving at VW, he created a cross-functional team to manage the launch of the next car in the up! series. A relatively new concept for Volkswagen, the up! was a city car for everyday use that competed with Daimler's Smart car and the Fiat 500.

During his time at Fiat, de Meo had often relied upon the energy and fresh perspectives of young people to come up with innovative high-impact marketing, including what were some of the earliest online efforts in the industry to codesign cars with customers. For the up! launch team, de Meo selected a core group of young marketers and added others from other functions, for a total of eleven members. He gave this group responsibility for all 360 degrees of the launch, which meant it had to develop an integrated marketing strategy for the car's entire life cycle, not just its introduction.

The team reported directly to him, and he located it in an area next to his own office where he expected members to work full-time for the duration of the project. "We need to recreate the spirit of a small company within a large organization," he said. Then he shocked the group by saying, "I'm not going to tell you how to do it. You'll have to do it. See you in a month." This was not how their bosses usually acted. "They had never experienced anything like this before," he said. "The rule was that the boss came in and told them exactly what to do—this, this, and this."

One team member remembered the kickoff meeting: "We said, 'Okay, when do you want us to start?' He said, 'Right now!' A few hours later, de Meo looked in the room and said, 'Where are you guys?' because no one was there. We had to finish our work before we left our departments."

Without providing specific direction, de Meo set high expectations, which he communicated by spontaneously dropping in for coffee and looking over the team's work "in an unstructured way," as he described his approach. He might "nudge them in this or that direction" but generally encouraged them to play out their own ideas. He urged them to take risks and reassured them that mistakes were part of the process. He "preferred that they try."

Afterward, de Meo recalled that the team floundered at times and had endless discussions about the important and difficult issues. He felt their thinking was good, much of it out of the box, and he was satisfied that many of them were discovering the benefits of working in a diverse group.

Unfortunately, the group was unable to reach final conclusions on its own. With a presentation to the company's board of management only two months away, de Meo finally granted the team's request for a formal leader. But, instead of naming a senior manager or leading it himself, he picked someone from outside the group who was also young but had experience with other launches and with presenting to the board. This leader, whom de Meo told to think of himself as "the first among peers," found that the group had already developed good data and "worked absolutely in the right direction. We only had to proof it," he said, "reduce the complexity, bring it to the point, and 'sell' it in the company."

The board was impressed by the up! team's 130-page launch plan— "probably one of the most integrated launch strategies done recently at

Volkswagen," de Meo said. Though the up! team had struggled a bit, he continued to believe that launches were a perfect opportunity to test continually "that the different pieces are able to work together ... a kind of acid test ... real life stuff ... not theory." He took the same approach with the launch of the new twenty-first-century Beetle.

Pushing people together II

Eight months after joining VW, de Meo took over product marketing, as well as marketing communications, and thus became responsible for all Volkswagen AG marketing. (He would be named chief marketing officer a few months later in 2010.) He felt he'd made progress in creating a more collaborative marketing community that thought about not just process but innovation and creating the premier auto brand. More and more, he heard people refer to the "marketing team" and the "marketing community." People understood that they were expected to collaborate, learn, discover, and decide together.

Now, with both marketing departments under his leadership, he decided to hold a second design lab called Marketing Worx! II. This time, the objective was to engage both marketing departments in collaborative planning for the coming year. As he addressed the attendees from around the world and across all of marketing, he once again emphasized the need to build the brand by collaborating in ways that embraced the experience and expertise of everyone.

Working in diverse groups as before, the participants focused on new high-relevance projects that reflected four key drivers: innovation, sustainability (a key component of responsibility), and brand value, along with customer satisfaction. This time the goals of the lab went beyond encouraging participants to discover the value of collaboration and joint learning. This lab aimed at actually advancing participants' thinking about projects in those key areas.

Project leaders updated the group about work done in the previous six months and sought advice concerning next steps. De Meo made sure minority opinions were heard, even unpopular views or those that "slowed down progress," in his words. He wanted people to challenge traditional thinking and processes, as well as try new ideas and take more risks. At the same time, he pushed people to be more agile, 50 percent faster, and more integrated in how they work.

When it was over, he felt the two Marketing Worx! labs had given people a chance to feel what it was like to collaborate as a community. Because people in the different marketing groups had come to know each other better, many commented later that they were starting to call on each other more often for ideas, advice, and feedback.

It took a multitude of efforts

Like Vineet Nayar at HCL, de Meo found that fostering change required him to rework many structures and systems in ways that supported greater collaboration and innovation.

Marketing roundtable

Before de Meo arrived, the marketing teams from around Europe had met with corporate marketers once a quarter in Wolfsburg for a day of discussing ideas and plans. "It used to be," he said, "that you [the market] came here and told me what you were doing and I told you if it was good or not. There was no exchange between one country and another because everyone was doing their own thing."

De Meo replaced those meetings with a quarterly marketing roundtable, which involved all major markets and lasted two days. Participants discussed priorities and developed specific plans for key initiatives that would be implemented by cross-functional, cross-country teams.

With this different approach, his groups made real progress in clarifying and distinguishing the roles of corporate and country marketing teams in building the brand. The team in Wolfsburg would support the local teams and help co-develop potential solutions with them as a sparring partner. The local team would take the lead in identifying challenges and adapting actions to local demands in order to build the brand and reach mutually agreed-on targets. As his people began involving the markets more in the development of strategy and key initiatives, de Meo noticed there was far less complaining from the field about "those guys in Wolfsburg."

Centers of Excellence

To acknowledge that "ideas have no boundaries," de Meo began to designate markets that had demonstrated expertise in specific areas as Centers of Excellence. If a market had become particularly good at, say, some aspect of sustainability, it would be given supplemental funds to develop its ideas and share them with other markets. When he discovered that the US marketing team was adept at digital business strategy, his people in Wolfsburg began working collaboratively with the US team to develop and deliver in phases a superior digital experience for VW customers everywhere.

Dedicated launch team

Pleased with the work of the up! and new Beetle launch teams, de Meo created a permanent team that would develop and implement the launch plan for all cars. Reporting directly to him, this team was to create a road map for each launch that integrated the efforts of sales, communications, and after-sales. Its first project was to manage the launch of a special model of the Golf GTI, a sporty hatchback, on its thirty-fifth anniversary. Lucas Casanovas, the team leader, was pleased with the outcome. After the GTI launch, he said, "other successful launch projects followed, and ... the results are becoming better and better. Internally you can feel in the atmosphere that something has changed and is working very well."

International management

To address the dearth of international experience among marketers in Wolfsburg, de Meo and the head of group management development sales and marketing, Ariane Reinhart, set a goal: by the end of 2012, they wanted 50 percent of marketing managers to have international experience. They would achieve this target through a combination of hiring those with work experience abroad (for example, by bringing talented people from the country markets to headquarters) and sending managers from Wolfsburg to work in the markets.

Think Blue—the Power of Common Purpose

One marketing program under de Meo deserves special attention. Think Blue was a prime example of what his marketing people were able to accomplish—throughout the company—by working together in building the brand.

De Meo had urged the original Marketing Worx! planning group to include an environmental project. Sustainability was a key part of VW's "responsible" brand value, an area that a small marketing group had already been pursuing for some time and that he and many of his colleagues were passionate about. He thought it could be a way to unite his marketers around the local and global meaning of the brand.

Concern for the environment was hardly a new idea at Volkswagen. The company had first set up a Department for Environmental Protection in 1970 and had taken a number of proactive measures in the decades following. More recently, Martin Winterkorn, chairman of the company's board of management, had written of VW's ambition to "become the world's leading automaker, *both economically and ecologically* [emphasis added]."

So de Meo was especially pleased that the environmental sustainability team had made real progress during the two-day lab. The heart of what they'd done was their decision to make sustainability a big marketing concept called "Think Blue" that united all the unconnected sustainability activities currently scattered around the company.

The Marketing Worx! team preferred the color blue, instead of the more traditional green for the environment, because, as de Meo said, "green was about limits, about being against, about refusing technology and looking backwards. Instead, blue is about looking for opportunities, for possibilities, about embracing the future and about progress." The color of the sky and the ocean, blue is also, he pointed out, "the background of the Volkswagen logo," and the same color featured in the original "Think Small" Beetle campaign decades earlier.

During Worx!, the team created a Think Blue manifesto that outlined the principles behind the initiative. When Christian Klingler, de Meo's boss and the VW Group board of management member responsible for sales and marketing, arrived on the last day, he too signed the manifesto, signaling his personal commitment to the cause.

De Meo had made clear he expected plans that were ambitious, doable, and measurable, so the Think Blue team—ten full-time marketing employees, assisted by interns and external partners—developed a strategic plan for implementing and monitoring a credible and consistent international rollout of the program. It set out four basic objectives: (1) support Volkswagen in becoming the most ecologically sustainable brand; (2) push an ecological sustainability perspective throughout the company; (3) provide a unique and distinctive brand appearance with Think Blue; and (4) push and ensure international communication of Think Blue, that is, create higher awareness in the markets.

Team members developed a cutting-edge companywide communications program that combined the way products were made and the way they worked, as well as the steps drivers could take to support sustainability. They also developed a Think Blue KPI quarterly report to track progress and developed a number of tools to help colleagues think and act blue every day, as one team member expressed it. For example, they produced a monthly newsletter showing projects and important topics; standard presentation modules, such as a collection of charts on aspects of Think Blue; a style guide for Think Blue design; an exhibit service that assisted in the development of concepts and exhibits for fairs and events; campaign material, such as television commercials, print ads, and billboards; event concepts such as a fuel-saving championship; and online modules for the Think Blue website and Facebook that could be adapted for different markets.

The team officially launched Think Blue as a key component of the VW brand at the Geneva Auto Show, alongside the new Polo BlueMotion model, the company's most fuel-efficient car. "We immediately involved consumers," de Meo said, "explained the project internally, and opened the possibility to other functions to make their interpretation of Think Blue in their field. We introduced the project in more than thirty countries within the first twelve months." In 2011, more than 25 projects were carried out internationally, and in 2012 that number grew to 320 Blue Projects. Two years after its formal introduction as a corporate program there were more than six hundred Think Blue projects in marketing alone, across more than forty countries.

De Meo and the Think Blue team were, perhaps, most proud of Think Blue Factory, a broadly focused cross-departmental initiative for all Volkswagen plants worldwide. Its aim was to make more efficient use of energy, materials, and water, and to reduce emissions of CO_2 and pollutants. The team set a target, to be tracked by a new KPI system, of reducing environmental impacts by 25 percent at every VW plant by 2018.

"Normally, marketing and production are not next together in the company," said Doerte Hartmann-Kerl, the head of the Think Blue team. "What we achieved with this approach was to bring marketing and production as close as possible. It was attractive for them and also for marketing. To find this bridge was a great step for the company."

As measured by a new KPI system, the team's activities were having a positive effect on the brand. In the top twenty-seven VW markets, Think Blue significantly supported the perception of Volkswagen as an environmentally friendly brand.

The VW management board agreed to integrate Think Blue into the company's brand strategy. And management declared Volkswagen's intention to be not only the most successful and innovative carmaker in the world but the most sustainable as well. It pledged to invest over €50 billion over the next four years to reduce the environmental impact of VW's cars and factories.

Think Blue tapped into a reservoir of broad interest. With de Meo's support and blessing, it became a project of the highest priority for both marketing and the entire company, a core piece of VW's "responsible" brand value. Sustainability is "*the* new battlefield of innovation and therefore the key to staying ahead of the game," said de Meo in a speech at the time. "The challenge is to get people not only thinking blue, but also 'acting blue' every day."

Think Blue was one example of the catalytic role marketing was coming to play in the company. What started as a marketing program grew into a guiding principle for the whole organization, a cause every part of the company could pursue together.

"Blue marketing is at the heart of the organization," said de Meo. "[It's] a mind-set that is seeded in all aspects of [the] business and across the complete life cycle of the products. Blue is collaborative, engaging all actors into participation. Blue marketing is marketing with meaning."

It emerged not because de Meo invented and decreed it but because he created the setting and context that allowed it to happen. "Luca [de Meo] was the patron of Think Blue," said team leader Hartmann-Kerl. "The working structures and network Luca developed were really essential ... With the structures and communication we had five years ago, it wouldn't have been possible."

Company Results

During de Meo's time in Wolfsburg, Volkswagen's overall success continued and, if anything, accelerated. As *The Economist* commented in 2012: "Last year the VW group's profits more than doubled, to a record 18.9 billion Euros ($23.8 billion). As other European volume carmakers seek to close factories and cut jobs, VW is seizing market share in Europe, booming in China and staging a comeback in America. It plans to spend 76 billion Euros on new models and new factories by 2016. Its global workforce is more than half a million, and growing."[3] By that news magazine's qualified reckoning, VW became the world's biggest carmaker by volume in 2011, seven years ahead of schedule.[4]

A year later, in an article titled "The Best Laid Plan," *Forbes* noted that the company's plans to lead the auto industry by 2018 were already "looking conservative." Sales were up 49 percent from 2008 when it set out its ten-year target; revenues were up 63.5 percent. In 2012, it earned 13.2 percent on sales of $250 billion, far ahead of the 8 percent margin it targeted for 2018. And worldwide share was up 0.5 percent to 12.8 percent.[5]

VW's journey to becoming a top-ten brand was well underway. By the time de Meo left VW for Audi, the VW brand had risen in the ranking of all brands worldwide from fifty-fifth to thirty-ninth.

In addition, de Meo encouraged his people to seek outside recognition for marketing excellence. It was a way to stimulate collaboration around the brand. During his time at VW, the company received a number of awards. Interbrand selected it (based on consumer surveys) as the top global green brand in 2012, primarily for the Think Blue program. The prestigious CLIO Award recognized VW as the "2012 Global Advertiser of the Year" for its creative leadership and commitment to innovation in advertising. And the company also walked away with an unprecedented twenty-three Lions (prizes) at the Cannes International Festival of Creativity.

Community Drives Willingness

Given the obstacles, how did de Meo—how does anyone leading innovation—foster people's willingness to do what innovation requires?

The answer is simple in concept, though not easy in practice. People are willing to face the personal challenges of innovation when they feel part of a community engaged in something more important than any of them as individuals and larger than any could accomplish alone.

A sense of community is powerful because it's about belonging and, above all, identity.[6] Members consider their inclusion in the community a key part of who they are. Its collective "we" helps define the "I" of each member. Thus, members feel a strong bond with each other and are eager to do their part in supporting the vitality and advancing the cause of the group. They feel responsible both *to* it and *for* it. They believe its survival and success depend on each of them. No one wants to let his or her colleagues down. That shift in perspective—when "we" becomes as or more important in key ways than "I"—is what enables every member to do work that feels unfamiliar or risky but is needed for the good of the community.

No leader can declare a community. One will not form on command. Instead, the leaders we studied built innovative, collaborative communities around a compelling mutual purpose that people already considered important and would strive collectively to fulfill. These leaders couldn't manufacture a purpose to serve their own ends. It had to be something that already resonated with people, the way de Meo built on the foundation of people's feelings about VW.

Purpose is often misunderstood. It is not *what* a group does but *why* it does what it does. It's not a goal but a reason—the reason it exists, the need it fulfills, and the assistance it bestows. It is the answer to the question every group should ask itself: if we disappeared today, how would the world be different tomorrow?[7]

Purpose can be anything that benefits people and society in some way, from producing family films that move people to laughter and tears, to revolutionizing companies' business models through IT, to giving people the gift of mobility in the most innovative, responsible, and valuable ways possible. Whatever form it takes, purpose is the glue that integrates the work of one into the work of many. It lifts people's efforts above the level of everyday, self-centered activity.

Purpose—not the leader, authority, or power—is what creates and animates a community. It is what makes people willing to do the hard tasks of innovation together and work through the inevitable conflict and tension.

Like all the leaders we studied, de Meo was careful not to define exactly how to pursue his group's purpose. He knew he couldn't force people to collaborate, but he did use his authority to install practices, forums, and structures where people could discover for themselves the benefits of collaboration, learning through discovery, and integrative decision making.

He shoved people together in new platforms where they could try out different ways of interacting and communicating.[8] People still had jobs and responsibilities, but in these new contexts they had to do them while actively engaging with others. Work would no longer be done like passing buckets of water from hand to hand in a fire brigade. As de Meo said, he wanted his people to know and trust each other so well that they worked "with the agility and passion of a pit-stop crew."

His efforts were built on a foundation of corporate history, people's pride in their company, the sense of duty and discipline that imbued VW's culture, and a newfound belief that marketing had a crucial role to play. From his efforts emerged a marketing community in which purpose motivated people to collaborate, experiment, and integrate ideas day after day. It was a place where individuals were willing to contribute the best their talent could offer to create collective genius in service to something bigger than themselves.

IN OUR BUSINESS, WE
CONSTANTLY HAVE TO CREATE
NEW THINGS. YOU NEED
CONFIDENCE. YOU NEED TO
KNOW THAT YOUR PARTNERS
BELIEVE IN YOU AND IF YOU
ARE STUCK, THEY'LL HELP YOU
WORK OUT A NEW OR BETTER
SOLUTION. WE'RE A GROUP
OF PEOPLE WHO ALWAYS BARE
A PIECE OF OUR SOULS IN
OUR WORK, AND WE KNOW
HOW IMPORTANT IT IS TO
CONTINUALLY NOURISH EACH
OTHER.

—**Kit Hinrichs**, Pentagram partner

BEYOND PURPOSE: VALUES AND RULES OF ENGAGEMENT

Kit Hinrichs was making last-minute changes to the presentation he would make the next day. It was evening in Jackson Hole, the Wyoming ski resort where he and fellow partners of Pentagram, the international design firm, were holding their semiannual partners' meeting.

Hinrichs, a graphic designer, was going to present his work for the California Academy of Sciences in San Francisco, an iconic institution that had been a centerpiece of the city's and state's cultural life for more than 150 years. He and his team had been selected to help the Academy reinvent itself from the ground up after its buildings had suffered near-catastrophic damage in the 1989 Loma Prieta earthquake.

Hinrichs was proud of his and his team's widely acclaimed work. The project was a crown jewel in his own portfolio, the kind of high-impact project every world-class designer dreamed of doing. Renzo Piano, a Pritzker Prize winner, was the architect of the new $500 million revolutionary, environmentally sustainable facility. Creating what he called the "new identity of this next generation museum," had required Hinrichs and his team to play at the very top of their game. Hinrichs had relied upon some of his partners in the room to help him work through the myriad of "deliciously wicked problems" that had come up along the way.

But he was anxious about the presentation: "It's unbelievable that, at this point in my life, I still get nervous about presenting to my partners, but I do, and every partner will tell you the same thing. They all have international reputations at a very high level, and so it's not like presenting to a group of students."

Partners' meetings were a Pentagram ritual. Attendance was mandatory—that was understood when you became a partner—and every partner was expected to present his or her work at roughly every other meeting, that is, once a year. Comments and discussion were candid, even blunt—but not personal or cruel. After all, these were professionals operating at the top of their disciplines.

"We want our partners to say, 'Wow, that was a knockout!'" Hinrichs said. "Sometimes you get that, sometimes you don't. We all know when we've done a better piece or not. If ... you only get some polite applause, you say, 'Not a good day.' You know."

Imagine a firm that included the likes of Steve Jobs, Bill Gates, Jeff Bezos, Konosuke Matshushita, Larry Page, Sergey Brin, Li Ka-Shing, Kazou Inamouri, Ratan Tata, and Ingvard Kamprar in a partnership that held regular meetings where each presented his or her ideas and work for the others to critique. If that seems unlikely, and it is, then you can begin to appreciate how unusual Pentagram was because each of its partners was a rock star in the field of design. In fact, before being invited into the partnership, a designer must have already earned national and even international prominence.

The way Pentagram was organized and run made it distinctive among design firms. Though it was a collection of high-level design talents—the kind of passionate creative individuals not often known for cooperation—it has operated successfully for nearly four decades (and is still going strong as we write this). On one hand, each partner was responsible for working directly with clients and for hiring and maintaining a fairly autonomous team of designers; on the other, each partner was expected to function effectively as a productive member of the partners' community.[1]

But why would such stars choose to join a community where they had to share responsibility with others when they could have been fully independent and most likely made more money on their own? This question was exactly why we chose Pentagram, as we continued to pursue the broader question of what makes people *willing* to innovate. In chapter 4, we said the first part of the answer was that people are willing because they belong to a community whose members are bound by a common purpose. That purpose imbues their collaborative work with higher meaning and leads them to endure the stresses and turmoil that inevitably come with innovation.

From the unusual but successful community of supremely talented individuals at Pentagram, we can learn what more is required, beyond mutual purpose, for innovative communities to operate effectively over long periods of time. Even better, we can see how all the elements that produce willingness fit and work together. From that insight, we can understand better what leaders must do to ensure people's willingness to innovate again and again.

Pentagram

Pentagram was founded in the 1970s by five internationally known designers—three graphic designers, an industrial designer, and an architect—as a partnership in London. Within only a few years, it had joined the ranks of the most esteemed firms in its field, and its clients included such prominent companies of that time as IBM, United Airlines, Olivetti, British Petroleum, Pirelli, Thorn EMI, Kodak, Penguin Books, Reuters, Roche, Xerox, Polaroid, Neiman Marcus, and British Rail. Known for work that was witty, clear, and intelligent, it was on the short list for many high-profile projects, and one journalist dubbed it "the designers' designers' designers."[2]

By the turn of the century, the partnership had 160 employees in five offices—London, New York, San Francisco, Berlin, and Austin, Texas. William Drenttel, a former president of the American Institute of Graphic Arts (AIGA), said it was "at the top of the heap, if you're talking about power and clout and prestige."[3]

For its first twenty years, the firm was chaired by Colin Forbes, one of the founding partners. Though his position did not carry much formal authority, he was the acknowledged unofficial leader and chairman of the twice-yearly partners' meeting. He tended the organization, more or less set direction when it floundered, and played an outsized role in establishing the purpose and culture that distinguished Pentagram.

Key to that culture were a few principles that have remained in place through the life of the firm to date. Its explicit founding principles were equality and generosity. There were no junior or senior partners, just partners; all were equal shareholders. Formal leadership, the ability to influence corporate matters, fell evenly on all partners, regardless of tenure.

Generosity meant that each partner in an office earned the same salary and bonus, regardless of each partner's individual profitability (differences across offices were based on cost-of-living differences). Each office sent 7 percent of gross billings to the corporation to pay for joint activities like partner meetings, seminars, and communications. The resources to run an office came from that office—except to cover shortfalls in a down year, an office could draw funds from the corporate account.

All decisions were made by consensus. If one partner was against a particular policy or prospective partner, it did not happen. As Forbes once said, "Votes are anathema to us. We would rather drift together than set course with a minority voice." At the same time, there was no "tyranny of the minority." As Hinrichs said, "If something gets too heated, we'll revisit it later."

Partners were almost always, by design, outsiders who were invited to join. Besides needing to have already earned a national or international reputation, they had to be able to generate business, manage projects, and contribute to leadership of the firm. And they were expected to be "proactive members of the group and care about Pentagram and the other partners," according to Forbes. This meant that, among other things, they had to attend the partners' meetings, participate in the business conducted there, and, far from least, present their work. The presentations, in fact, were considered one of the firm's most important rituals.

All these features and requirements—restrictions, actually—not only highlighted how different Pentagram was but also raised again the question of why, in an age of celebrity and worship of individual achievement, superstars would be willing to give up their autonomy. Certainly, there were reasons a good designer might want to join such a firm. Because its daily work was organized around more or less independent teams, it offered the artistic freedom and limited bureaucracy of a smaller firm. Because of the close ties among its world-class partners, it also offered the intellectual stimulation, ability to undertake large-impact projects, and financial security of a larger enterprise. In simple terms, it offered the advantages of size while comprising, in effect, a number of small firms that shared a name, office space, and some business functions, and whose heads operated as a collaborative community.

But these weren't merely good designers. They were among the elite. Had they remained independent, they could have done better financially, enjoyed more autonomy, and not had to share their reputations. There was a cost, financial and otherwise, to being a Pentagram partner. A key element of the nonfinancial cost was embodied in the policy, set out from the very beginning, that none of the partners' names would appear on the firm's shingle. This was contrary to the practice of most design organizations whose eponymous names tried to build on the fame of their founders.

Hinrichs was one of those who gave up his own design firm when he became a Pentagram partner. He recalled the time when he first became a partner: "I was giving up my own name that had been associated with my work for twenty years. There was that thirty seconds when the fellow comes in and scrapes your name off the door before he puts 'Pentagram' there and there's a little pile of dust on the floor. It made me think."

Yet he and his fellow partners did join. Equally noteworthy, most stayed for long periods of time. Over those first four decades, partners came and went, but the average stay was many years. Why? The answer says something important about innovative communities and what's required for them to operate successfully over time.

Purpose at Pentagram

To understand, we must begin, as at VW, with purpose, the foundation of any community. For Pentagram partners, the goal was always clear—to come up with innovative solutions to a client's problem, on time and on budget. But their purpose grew from their deep shared belief in the social importance of design. For partners, as one commentator said, "Design was not just a service supplied to clients ... it was a calling, a style of being, a whole way of life."[4] They believed in the power of design to improve the quality of people's visual and intellectual lives. Hinrichs described it this way:

... design is in everything. Advertising. Products. Communications systems. Signage. Branding. Architecture. All kinds of things. For me, the role of design is to make the complex simple; the opaque, transparent; the unstructured, concrete; the obtuse, accessible; and the ordinary, beautiful. It is the responsibility of those in the design profession not to treat this lightly.

Based on their belief in the importance of good design, Pentagram partners shared something else—a desire for impact. This was the glue that brought and held them together. They sought to spread good design far and wide throughout society. As individuals, they could have only limited influence. They needed size to attract the largest clients. Working for a small local company couldn't compare with the opportunities for impact offered by the regional presence and international reputation of a California Academy of Sciences or by the global reach of an IBM, GE, ABB, or Citi.

"Pentagram's founders conceived of design's role in the grandest terms," said an observer of the firm, "but they knew that however well intentioned designers might be, on their own they are weak. They lack influence with clients, especially larger, more powerful clients, and they lack power and influence in society and politics."[5] For this reason, Pentagram generally eschewed small design projects that would touch only small groups of people; there was too little impact for the work involved.

"At Pentagram," wrote one partner, Paula Scher, "I have attained the power, status, and credibility to more easily persuade clients to a given design."[6] And, as Hinrichs said, "the idea in the long term was that we would be able to influence larger organizations because they influence the world." And he added:

All the partners ... saw that ... by joining together, we would actually be able to have more clout, more impact in the business world as a larger organization, that because of the reputation of the combined talents, we might be able to change how business uses design. I think we all felt that if we can do this collectively, with the talents that we all individually

possess, we could actually have great impact on our culture. A simple
statement and very high-minded. And, whether we were successful or
not, I think it was something we all strived for.

Thus, we see at Pentagram the same dynamic we saw at Volkswagen—
the power of a compelling purpose to create a collaborative community. Certainly there were personal and career advantages to joining the firm, but
they all supported the greater purpose—to exert the maximum impact on
society through good design.

Have those advantages been enough, however, to hold the enterprise
together over time? Such collections of diverse, independent talent typically don't last several years, not to mention decades. The forces of disintegration—the need for individual recognition, frustration over equalized
incomes, differences of opinion about direction, and a dozen other desta-
bilizing factors—sooner or later (usually sooner) overwhelm the forces of
integration. Then some crisis, difference of opinion, or even an opportunity causes the community to blow apart or slowly come unraveled. That
can happen even though the individual members still share the common
purpose that first brought them together. So, even a compelling purpose by
itself cannot serve as the glue that binds over time.

The retirement of Colin Forbes in the late 1990s tested Pentagram
itself. Many outsiders predicted the firm would fall apart. In fact, Forbes's
departure hit the firm hard—a New York partner said he left "big, empty
shoes"—but the remaining partners adapted. They collectively decided that
the chairman's role would change hands every two years, in keeping with
the principles of equality and generosity. The title would bestow no additional power, and the person in the role would be chosen by tenure and then
by age. His or her primary responsibility would be to plan and run the partners' meetings and, when problems arose, to be a mediator and "the advo-
cate of common sense," as one partner said it. Though it changed hands
biannually, the title of chair was more than honorific. This person had to
guide the firm through difficult times, such as when three London partners
were asked to leave because of poor financial performance.

In the partners' reliance on the firm's first principles, we begin to
see the second ingredient, beyond purpose, of the glue that binds together

members of a community and enables them to do the collaboration, learning through discovery, and integrative decision making that produce innovation.[7]

The Importance of Shared Values

Members of a true community share values. They agree about what's truly important. Sometimes these values are stated. Remember the brand values—innovative, responsible, and valuable at Volkswagen—but often they remain implicit. If its shared purpose defines "who we are" for a community, its values define "what matters most to us." By shaping priorities and choices, they influence individual and collective thought and action.

Communities and organizations obviously differ in their purposes and the values that support those purposes, but in our studies of multiple innovative organizations we found four basic values that all of them held in common. The organizations didn't always use the names we do, but, as we'll see at Pentagram, they were there, and leaders actively fostered, supported, and rewarded them. The four basic values are: *bold ambition, collaboration, learning,* and *responsibility.*

Shared value: bold ambition

Clearly, Pentagram aspired to something big and audacious. Its partners wanted not only to solve their clients' most difficult problems but also to use those problems for an even bigger purpose—to improve society through good design.

That's why its partners looked for large, complex challenges as vehicles for realizing this purpose. They believed that as designers they had an especially important role to play. As one chronicler of Pentagram aptly observed, "Pentagram became the grown-up ideal ... Grown up because they admit and court the realpolitik of commerce; ideal because they truly believe in design's potency to modulate the alienating aspects of commerce."

In the same way, members of all the innovative communities we studied wanted to tackle big audacious problems. They wanted to take on uniquely complex challenges that conventional ideas or processes couldn't overcome or resolve. They sought to be stretched, to do work that would require them to find new and useful solutions. They strove to do the best individual and collective work possible. But it was more than delivering excellence. They wanted the world to be different and better because of what they were doing. Through his design work for the California Academy of Sciences, for example, Hinrichs played a key role in building public support and raising the funds necessary for the Academy to reconceive and revive itself.

Shared value: collaboration

Innovative companies value collaboration and take conscious, proactive steps to build it into the way they work. They understand that the best, most innovative work happens when diverse people interact closely and integrate their ideas. They know individuals working by themselves can only take an idea or project so far.

Pentagram's founders and partners knew that they could only achieve the bold ambition of their purpose through collaboration. They could deliver the kind of innovative projects they wanted—work that would have the impact they wanted—only when they worked together and combined their abilities and ideas. As Hinrichs pointed out: "Like producing a play, design is not a solitary act, but a collaboration that requires inspiring the talent and spirit of writers, illustrators, photographers, strategists, and technicians. We can do something collectively as a group that we can't do individually, which is why we're together."

From its earliest days, Pentagram founders devoted time and attention to nurturing the human connections among partners. They did this by ensuring that there were many opportunities to engage in meaningful interactions—the key opportunity being the twice-yearly gathering of partners.

Pentagram's most basic operating principles of equality and generosity—and all that flowed from them: equal pay, no senior or junior partners, decisions by consensus, and so on—were specifically aimed at fostering and maintaining a community. In almost every way, Pentagram was built on the idea of collaborative practice, an all-for-one and one-for-all approach the firm has been able to maintain for more than four decades. As partner Paula Scher said of her expectations when she first joined the firm, "I assumed they were going to do this and they were going to do that. I thought ... 'this is going to happen to me from them.' Then you find out—there is no them. When you join Pentagram, there is only 'us.'"[8]

Though partners ran fairly autonomous teams within each office, the firm did expect them to follow certain work practices it considered conducive to open, collaborative work. For example, a Pentagram architect designed the firm's London offices without private offices so partners could sit and work with their design teams. When the firm opened its second office, in New York, one of the London partners flew across the Atlantic as a carrier of culture. One of the first things he did was initiate the tradition of the London office where partners and their teams ate lunch together every day unless they had an outside commitment.

Pentagram's work with clients was collaborative, too. One of Hinrichs's major projects was with Muzak, the music distribution company. Pentagram was the only design firm willing to take on the assignment, given the challenge and the client's limited budget. Hinrichs was hired to help the struggling company execute a turnaround. His task, as he described it, was to rebrand Muzak "from the inside out as the organization that created experiences through audio architecture." He and his team, along with their associate Brian Jacobs, did a complete overhaul of the company's marketing and sales collateral and were actively involved in the change management process of getting the franchisees on board. When the company needed an architect to design its new headquarters, Hinrichs suggested his partner, James Biber, from the New York office. Hinrichs described his thinking:

> I had never worked with Jim on a project before, but I knew his aesthetic from partner meeting presentations and thought it would be a good fit. Also, I knew that if we collaborated, we wouldn't get caught over who should have the "most say." He would know that Muzak was my client, but when it came to architectural issues, he'd have precedence, and when it came to the internal signage, I'd make the calls. We were on the same side; no need to protect your turf.

Based on a deep understanding of the logic behind Hinrichs' work for Muzak, Biber said, he was able to design a building that both embodied the essence of the company's new identity and provided an important piece of the company infrastructure—the space where people worked—needed to fulfill that identity. Biber explained:

The question was, "How do you make a community out of a big warehouse-like room?" From previous work, I knew that space defined social interactions. I thought the place could have an urban energy, like an Italian city, with big common spaces and a network of more private ways.

In the end, Pentagram's multidisciplinary, collaborative approach played a critical role, according to the client, in transforming Muzak from a stagnant brand with disillusioned employees into a fast-growing, reenergized organization. The CEO of Muzak noted that, before the transformation, the equity firm that owned Muzak offered to sell it to a competitor for $100 million. The offer was rejected. Two years later, the equity firm sold Muzak for $250 million. Both Hinrichs and Biber won awards for their designs, and Biber's success with the Muzak building helped him land one of the most sought-after commissions in the United States at the time, designing the Harley-Davidson Museum.

Unlike many service firms where partners competed for business, all Pentagram partners viewed each other as allies in helping clients solve problems. Every Pentagram partner could present other partners' work to a potential client as examples of Pentagram work. No partner took personal credit for another's work, but the message was clear: because the firm was a collaborative community, you got Pentagram and *all* its capabilities when you hired a Pentagram partner. Each partner's team usually focused on its own work. But if a team lacked, say, social media skills, it could call on another partner and team that did possess such skills. Partners with one design expertise, say, graphic designers, knew they could call on other partners with different design skills—in product design or architecture, for example—without worrying about losing control of the project or losing the client to a competitor. In offices with multiple teams and partners, there was much informal day-to-day collaboration. It was almost unavoidable, given the open architecture of the office space, such practices as communal lunches, and the close informal ties forged among partners, largely through the partners' meetings.

Shared value: learning

A desire to learn is at the core of the innovation process, especially collaboration and discovery. It makes people willing to go through the multiple iterations required to tackle a tough problem and fulfill a bold ambition. And it leads people to benefit from the missteps and mistakes inherent in innovation.

Biber called Pentagram his "postgraduate education." He said, "We all craved to be around others who were a little faster, a little sharper than ourselves. When a group of stars gets along and strives to always be better, it creates wonderful things."

The partners' meetings and especially the partner presentations were, and were intended to be, intense learning experiences. Each presentation was followed by questions and discussions from which both the presenting partners and their colleagues could learn. Hinrichs called these sessions "Pentagram at its best."

Another partner concurred. "I always learned something from my partners," he said. "Being around smart people made me smarter, made me perform better." One writer who knew Pentagram well wrote, "The culture of Pentagram encourages openness to diverse views and sees intellectual curiosity as necessary for creative innovation. The creative opposition is both painful and enjoyable."[9]

Shared value: responsibility

The partners all felt a deep sense of obligation to the Pentagram community as a whole and to one another. The actions and work of each reflected on all the others, and so they felt bound to live up to the high standards set by each other's work. Maintaining these standards was another key function of the presentations at partners' meetings. There was a Pentagram "we" that transcended all the individual "I's," and every partner was responsible for maintaining that collective identity.

Partners' responsibilities also extended beyond the quality of the work. They were expected to generate new projects, to remain personally and deeply engaged in the actual work itself and not delegate all or most of it to their teams, to be proficient at leading and managing their own teams, and to engage actively and effectively with clients throughout the course of a project.

Partners enjoyed wide latitude in how they managed their engagements and teams. But they could not act in ways that departed dramatically from good work practices throughout the firm or reflected badly on the firm and other partners. For example, a partner who chose a daily schedule of arriving at the office in the late afternoon and working all night was finally told by his colleagues that such behavior was unacceptable. It disrupted the work of both his team and the office as a whole; and his constant absence when clients called reflected badly on all Pentagram partners.

Most such matters were handled at the office level, but if they could not be resolved there, then the partners addressed them at their semiannual gatherings. "It's very subtle, the weight of the partnership that each partner carries," said Hinrichs, "because we all want to be part of this organization and ... we know we have obligations. It's not all Camelot."

That was certainly apparent when it came to financial performance. Every partner and his or her team were expected to carry their own weight financially. Every month, the firm prepared monthly financial statements that detailed individual partner or team profitability, balance-sheet net asset value, retentions, capital use, and individual partners' worth within the operation. At partners' meetings, these financials and a list ranking all partners by profitability were routinely presented and discussed.

Since everyone knew how everyone else was doing, as one partner noted, "You didn't want to be at the bottom of the list. But, if you were, you knew your partners were helping to support you." As another partner explained, a major benefit of income sharing was that when one partner struggled for whatever reason, the other partners were motivated to join in and help.

However, no partner wanted to be—and none would be allowed to be—at the bottom of the list for long. That occurred in the London office, where in the early years of the new century a confluence of factors brought hard times. Because of Pentagram's prominence, the office's problems attracted coverage in several industry publications, and so they reflected on the firm as a whole. London's continuing losses were the subject of discussion at successive partners' meetings. Finally, in 2005, to cope with the strain, the London partners all agreed to cut their salaries. Unfortunately, the losses continued, and three London partners with persistent losses were ultimately asked to leave, following a severance procedure established years earlier.

Purpose and Shared Values Aren't Sufficient

Critical as they are to the formation and survival of an innovative community, however, more than shared purpose and values is needed if a community is to do the work of innovation—to collaborate, learn by trial and error, and make integrative decisions—and to cope with the tension inherent in that work.

Remember the paradoxes we outlined in chapter 2 that must constantly be kept in balance if an innovative group is to function effectively over time. They all apply to Pentagram. We've focused already on the continuous tension between the individual partner and the collective. The fact that, even to be invited into the partnership, a designer must have already established a national or international reputation only heightened the potential for conflict in this domain. Imagine the constant tug on partners exerted by the realization that they could almost certainly earn more and enjoy more prominence as individuals on their own.

Other paradoxes also came into play at Pentagram. In the financial standards just described, we could see the tension both between performance and learning and between patience and urgency. In Pentagram's practice of letting each partner's team operate autonomously, within limits, we can see the tension between bottom up and top down, as well as the constant struggle between improvisation and structure. These paradoxes, in all their different guises, were often the subjects of business discussions that, besides partner presentations, constituted much of the partners' meetings.

To deal with these tensions that constantly threaten to tear every community apart, a creative community needs what we call "rules of engagement." Innovation and rules may seem like an odd couple. How can creativity and improvisation require rules? Aren't innovators rule breakers, people willing—eager, even—to challenge the status quo? For the most part, they are. Yet even innovative communities must set rules or norms for how people interact with each other and approach their collective work—rules, for example, for expressing and responding to disagreement. Rules help to preserve the ability to collaborate, learn through trial and error, and make integrative decisions. If purpose and shared values are the glue that binds members into a coherent community, rules of engagement are the grease that keeps member interactions running smoothly.

Pentagram is a good example of this need. "There are rules and regulations that go along with being part of Pentagram," according to Hinrichs. "It's very easy-going ... but we understand that we have responsibilities to each other." Pentagram worked as an innovative community because it had guidelines for the basic activities that touched all partners—how to join, leave, work together, share the economic rewards of their work, and review each other's professional, aesthetic, and financial performance.

Rules of Engagement in Creative Communities

While rules of engagement vary from organization to organization because the work of every organization is different, we uncovered a pattern of underlying rules at work in all the innovative groups we studied. Think of them as the informal behavioral rules or guidelines that support a community as it does the work of innovation.

The rules or norms we found fall into two categories:

1. How people in the group interact
2. How people in the group think

Rules are an important way of implementing and focusing on purpose and values. They are also key ways of fostering and enabling the three characteristics of the innovation process: collaboration, learning through discovery, and integrative decision making.

How People Interact

If collaboration is central to innovation, then the way people interact is the essence of collaboration. Even a brief glance at the paradoxes we noted in chapter 2 makes this apparent. Only a clear set of expectations or rules that group members can count on will allow a group to undertake the work of innovation. Such rules, for example, create the psychologically safe environment where creative clashes can happen because individuals are willing to share their craziest thoughts. Who will volunteer ideas—the foundation of collaboration—if they know that others are likely to belittle or attack them personally, or take credit for their ideas? Nor can any group enjoy the benefits of diversity, also a core element of collaboration, if differences of opinion are discouraged. And, without rules, people will hesitate to experiment to avoid failure.

Mutual trust

Mutual trust starts with the belief that everyone in the community is driven by intentions based on the group's purpose and shared values.[10] It is the belief that everyone essentially wants the same thing for the same basic reasons and that no one has goals or agendas that supersede the community's.

Trust is critical because it encourages members to take calculated risks as they explore new ideas and approaches, and to live with and learn from the inevitable missteps. Trust is also what makes members willing to endure the risks and vulnerability of sharing their ideas, the raw material of creative clashes. People will only volunteer their thoughts and suggestions when they feel their talents are recognized and utilized by the group as it pursues its purpose.

Trust is hard to build if people lack firsthand experience working with each other. It's why Pentagram's process for admitting new partners was so lengthy and painstaking. Pentagram considered it essential to build trust in prospective partners *before* they were finally admitted to membership. It's also why the semiannual partners' meetings were so important to the firm. That was where partners saw and reviewed each other's work, learned from each other, discussed and made firmwide decisions, and, far from least, built the personal bonds that underlay everything they did together.

An invitation to a partner candidate was only the first step. (Remember, this was someone who had already built a strong professional reputation.) If the candidate was interested, he or she would then spend up to a year traveling to every Pentagram office and meeting every partner face-to-face. Then the current partners voted on the candidate, and the vote had to be unanimous. Any partner could cast an unquestioned veto. Even when the vote was unanimous in favor, the candidate became a partner-elect—and enjoyed the appearance and all the privileges of partnership—except he or she was on probation for two years. After that period, the candidate could leave if he or she chose, or the other partners could declare a bad fit and ask the new partner to leave. This lengthy process was aimed at building trust. It explains why the firm in its first thirty years invited and accepted only forty partners and why most partners once in place stayed so long.

Mutual respect

Mutual respect means that community members all consider each other competent, even though each brings different abilities and strengths. It is the belief that every member has something of value to offer. That belief is critical because it fosters the listening, openness, and transparency that are necessary for innovative collaboration and risk taking.

Again, Pentagram's lengthy partner-selection process ensured that no one joined the community who did not command everyone's respect. "All partners have different talents and this means that people have different contributions," said Forbes. "Some of us are better at bringing in business, others at keeping clients happy, and others at winning awards while collaborating on an engagement they didn't initiate. While we're all paid equally, differences in profitability are often as much as three times. But we know that everyone's playing an important part."

One partner, Lorenzo Apicella, said of his colleagues, "At the partner meetings, there was always an element of grandstanding to put your view across. But you had to listen, too. We had very strong—and very different— characters in the partnership, and no one was a wallflower. But it worked because we all deeply respected each other."

Mutual influence

Mutual influence refers to the expectation and reality that everyone in the community has the potential to influence outcomes and even make decisions. If members feel that they can make a difference in what the group does, then they will feel accountable for the outcomes of community efforts because they had a hand in creating them.

Effective leaders of innovation consistently told us that one of their most important responsibilities was to make sure the minority voice was heard; that they felt responsible for ensuring that the fresh perspectives of the inexperienced weren't drowned out by the fixed ideas of experts. Without this kind of leadership, an organization cannot benefit from its members' diversity of knowledge, insight, experience, and attitudes.

As we said earlier, all significant firmwide decisions at Pentagram were made by consensus among partners. Consensus was different from majority rule. No formal votes were taken. Nor did individuals have formal veto rights (except in the selection of new partners). If the group could not reach a decision acceptable to everyone, it would put the issue aside and revisit it later until consensus eventually emerged.

Mutual influence produces three important effects on the innovation process. First, it ensures that problem solving will be an inclusive process that seeks and incorporates the widest possible range of ideas and suggestions. Second, it helps to counter the destructive idea that disagreement and conflict are about winning and being right, rather than learning and finding the best way forward. And, third, it helps ensure that decision making will float to the best and most appropriate parties, rather than always going to those with the most clout. Pentagram partners and their teams were given great latitude in how they worked, and other partners involved themselves only when someone's actions affected or reflected on all of them.

With all its design stars and their often high self-regard, Pentagram could function well as an innovative community because the partners observed these rules of interaction. This was apparent in multiple ways, not least in the partner presentations, which were occasions of real personal vulnerability. As Hinrichs observed:

> No one said, "Gee, that work sucks." We had to live with each other and
> [a presentation] was as close to a personal statement as you could make.
> You put yourself out there. We all know it's a very personal thing. We
> were very good about complimenting the best work. And we were all very
> civil to each other all the time during those situations.

How People Think

To be effective at innovation, every group must also agree on basic ground rules for how it will go about solving problems. Otherwise, members will argue not only about possible solutions but also about *how* to proceed, that is, how to identify and evaluate alternatives and then select a solution.

Question everything

At its heart, innovation requires that a group create a portfolio of ideas, test and refine them, and finally choose a solution, all of which involves questioning the status quo. Declaring certain practices, policies, ideas, or assumptions off-limits can only stifle every step of this process. Innovative groups consciously practice an approach of questioning everything. Anyone who observes such a group at work will be struck by its lively spirit of inquiry and even friendly skepticism.

Leaders of innovation consistently told us that based on their experience, permission to question everything seemed to attract the most talented people, people who approached challenges like eager explorers venturing into unknown territory. We saw this at Pentagram, especially in the partners' meetings and presentations. In a book about Pentagram based on interviews with partners, coauthor Delphine Hirasuna described their presentations this way: "As cacophonous as these peer reviews can be, the feedback, sharing of personal experiences, and different perspectives stimulate fresh thinking and challenge everyone to consider solutions outside their comfort zone."[11]

Be data driven

The second key characteristic of the innovation process—discovery-driven learning—refers to the practice of testing a portfolio of possible solutions as you search for a solution. As we've said, the conventional view of innovation attaches far too much importance to the initial idea, the flash of insight, as though answers appear fully formed and perfect. In truth, solutions rarely appear that way. Innovation requires a process of trial and error, which can truly occur only in an environment of respect for results and data.

If "be data driven" sounds obvious, recall how often groups make choices *in spite of* hard evidence because members didn't like what the evidence was telling them. When this happens, a group typically finds some reason to ignore the data—"it doesn't apply to us; we're different," or "the data is flawed; it wasn't collected properly," or "We're the best at this; we know what to do." Sometimes, hard evidence is simply ignored because it delivers an unwanted message or its implications are too difficult to face. Yet innovators, we've found, consistently pay attention to data. They not only pay attention to it, but actively and voraciously collect and analyze it.

For all the creativity required in its work, Pentagram as a firm was driven by hard metrics, just as we saw at VW, and full recognition that, above all, its work wouldn't succeed if it didn't solve a client's problems. Pentagram believed that design success and the ability to find and perform impactful design work would ultimately lead to business success. If it couldn't make money, the firm couldn't carry out its purpose. Thus, an important portion of each partner meeting was the discussion of the financial performance of each office and partner.

We saw earlier how economic losses led to the departure of three London partners. As difficult as that was, it was an outcome driven by the data, not by personal considerations. The great advantage of being data driven is that it avoids disagreements and conflicts that are based on personal preferences or individuals' differing beliefs and that consequently are almost impossible to resolve objectively and fairly.

See the whole

Innovation requires all members of a group to keep in mind the whole problem, the way all of its parts are interdependent, rather than focusing on or trying to optimize one part. The best solution is often one that combines disparate approaches and can only be uncovered by framing a problem holistically. Otherwise, possible solutions that at first seem mutually exclusive are unlikely to be identified, much less combined in fresh ways. It's too easy and only human for individuals to emphasize almost exclusively their pieces of the puzzle when they need to see a problem from multiple stakeholders' points of view. In the end, the solution or innovation should work for all involved.

Think about all the practices and principles we described at Pentagram, such as the exhaustive process of vetting prospective new partners, detailed financial reports, required attendance at partners' meetings, the presentations in which partners showed their work to all their peers, and standards for financial performance. These were all ways of applying and reinforcing the purpose, values, and rules that created a community and bound its members.

We hope now that the idea of values and rules that guide an innovative organization as it pursues its purpose seems less strange. All three elements work together to keep members focused on what's most important, discourage unproductive behaviors, and encourage activities that foster collaboration, discovery-driven learning, and integrative decision making. Every innovative organization has them, even if they're tacit or rarely discussed. Exactly what they are and how they are articulated and played out is specific to the particular organization and its unique work. But behind the specific rules can be discerned a more general set of norms that shape how group members work with each other and how they go about solving problems.

This completes our description of what we've found that leaders do to encourage a group's *willingness* to innovate. Ironically, the social nature of the innovative process—people working with people—not only makes the process challenging but can also sustain people as they work through it. In looking at Luca de Meo and Volkswagen in chapter 4, we described the crucial necessity of creating a community by rallying people around a common compelling purpose. In this chapter on Pentagram, we added to purpose the equally important ingredients of shared values and rules of engagement. All three, intertwined, are what make a group *willing* to undertake the difficult and arduous work of innovation. Indeed, early in his time at VW, de Meo created a number of spaces where his emerging global community could break routine and work together in new ways consistent with the rules of engagement we saw so carefully nurtured at Pentagram. Because Pentagram was able to get these components right and worked persistently to keep them vital, it was able to keep working and innovating productively for decades, even as the founders left and other partners slowly came and went.

Part II:
Leaders Create
the *Ability*
to Innovate

A decade of observing innovative organizations has convinced us that the best leaders of innovation don't see themselves as people with all the answers who set a direction for others to follow. That's not to say they're incapable of those things. Often they are even visionaries in their own right. But they've come to understand that the primary role of the leader is to create an environment where diversity and creative conflict flourish, experimentation is encouraged, intelligent missteps tolerated, and integrative decision making embraced. In short, what they do is shape a context in which others are willing and able to innovate.

With part I, chapters 4 and 5, we completed the *willing* half of the puzzle. Now, in part II, chapters 6, 7, and 8, we turn to three companies that were pioneers in their fields—Pixar, eBay, and Google—and focus on what leaders there did to foster the organization's *ability* to innovate. Both halves are essential, of course, for neither willingness nor ability by itself will suffice.

The organizational ability to innovate matters because innovation actually requires certain organizational skills that a leader can encourage and help develop. There are three such capabilities, and they correspond to the three key aspects of the innovation process—collaboration, discovery-based learning, and integrative decision making—that we said were the areas where effective leaders focused their attention.

Innovative Capability 1: Creative Abrasion

Creative abrasion is the ability to create a marketplace of ideas, to generate, refine, and evolve a multitude of options through discourse, debate, and even conflict. Potential solutions emerge from this process; they almost never spring complete from a solitary mind in a mysterious flash of insight.

In chapter 6, we look at how an innovative solution emerged from conflict around a critical technological challenge at Pixar. Unforeseeable events created a situation in which two important productions required the full resources of the company's data center at exactly the same time. Meeting the demands of both simultaneously was physically impossible and the unique requirements of computer animation meant the work couldn't be done outside. Yet the company had to have both films completed on schedule, and there was no money to throw at the problem.

Innovative Capability 2: Creative Agility

Creative agility is the organizational ability to test and refine ideas through quick experiments, reflection, and adjustment. Creative agility drives the second aspect of the innovation process—discovery-driven learning—that we outlined in chapter 1. The best solution for a problem rarely appears quickly. More often it emerges from vigorous and proactive trial and error and the learning it produces, often from efforts that don't initially succeed.

In chapter 7 we will examine this critical capability through the story of eBay Germany, widely considered one of the most innovative and successful countries within eBay's pioneering global platform that fundamentally changed the way the world shopped. Originally a German start-up that enjoyed rapid growth, Alando.de was acquired by eBay, became eBay Germany, and struggled within the constraints of the larger organization—until it discovered a way in that setting to continue the constant experimentation that had brought it early success.

Innovative Capability 3: Creative Resolution

Creative resolution is the organizational ability to make integrative decisions. In many companies we've seen, differences are resolved by one dominant individual or group, or they're settled by compromise, some form of splitting the difference that usually ends the conflict but pleases no one.

Innovative organizations, on the other hand, are able to make choices that integrate disparate and even opposing ideas into a single superior solution. Many innovations are the result of such choices, new combinations of existing ideas that seemed at first incompatible or mutually exclusive.

Creative resolution is what moves a group past the limits of binary decision making—pick either "A" or "B"—and lets it produce a synthesis of the two (or more) options that is far better than either option by itself. Instead of settling for "A" or "B," innovative teams frequently create a third way that combines and improves on both.

Such integration is far from simple to do, and in chapter 8 we will see the process of resolution at work as two teams under Bill Coughran, a senior leader at Google, explored alternate ways of storing the immense and rapidly growing amounts of data the company had to handle.

Ironically, conventional leaders often stifle development of all three capabilities. Those who seek to preserve harmony by muffling creative disagreement will limit the number of good options considered. Those who exercise discipline and control by marching their groups directly to a predetermined solution will discourage the trial and error efforts that lead to the best answer. And groups led by someone who believes it's the leader's job to make choices early and often are less likely to develop the most creative and thoughtful solutions.

JOHN LASSETER HAS A SAYING: "ART CHALLENGES TECHNOLOGY. TECHNOLOGY INSPIRES ART." PART OF THE MAGIC OF PIXAR IS THAT THESE TWO DISCIPLINES BUMP UP AGAINST EACH OTHER AND CREATE SOMETHING BETTER THAN EITHER COULD CREATE BY ITSELF.

—**Greg Brandeau**, then head of systems, Pixar Animation Studios

CREATIVE ABRASION

reative abrasion is the first of the three core capabilities that enable a group to innovate.[1] It is the ability to develop a marketplace where rich diverse ideas compete through discourse and debate. Possible solutions emerge from a series of sparks, not from a single flash of insight, as group members play off one another, each member's contribution inspiring the next.

Abrasion refers to the process of two or more substances rubbing together. That is the key dynamic of a collaborative marketplace where ideas jostle against and contend with each other. As that happens, the ideas change, improve, and perhaps even spawn other, better ideas.

Creative abrasion always involves some level of conflict—disagreement, contention, argument. That's why it works best when practiced by a diverse community whose members are bound by a common purpose, shared values, and rules of engagement that contain the conflict and keep it productive rather than personal and destructive.

Collision in the RenderFarm

We will watch the process of creative abrasion in practice as we return to Pixar and look at a problem that suddenly confronted Greg Brandeau, senior vice president of systems technology, and the systems department he headed.

The difficulty first became apparent late in the summer of 2008 at a regular meeting of Brandeau and three of his key people: John Kirkman, director of systems technology; Anne Pia, manager of the Render Pipeline Group (RPG); and Chris Walker, tech lead of RPG.

"We have a problem," Pia announced. "*Up* and *Cars Toons* need to be rendered at the same time." She and Walker shared responsibility for managing the RenderFarm, the data center where rendering was done. Experience had taught Brandeau that two heads with complementary skills were often better than one when a group needed leadership with high levels of both technical and managerial skills.

Pia's group planned and scheduled jobs through the RenderFarm and was responsible for troubleshooting any problems there. She and her people tracked all current productions and mapped out the compute power they would need when they entered the final rendering stage for each production.

Up was a feature film with a projected value stream of $1 billion. *Cars Toons* referred to the first four shorts in a planned series based on the characters from *Cars*, a previously released feature film that would air soon on cable television.

Rendering was the final step in the complex process of making a computer-generated (CG) film (see the diagram and explanation of this process in chapter 1). Using RenderMan, Pixar's Oscar-winning software, computers take all the artists' instructions—how characters look and move, for example, or the placement of lights and objects—that were created in previous steps and perform the calculations that create each frame of the final film that audiences will see in the theater.

Rendering a feature film requires an enormous amount of compute power. Depending on the complexity of what is in it, a single frame might require anywhere from less than an hour to several hours of CPU time to render. At 24 frames per second, a typical feature film comprises more than

120,000 frames, each of which must be separately calculated. No wonder the Pixar data center was one of the top ten, privately owned, large-scale computer systems in the world at that time.

The looming problem was that final production of *Cars Toons* had fallen behind schedule, and so Pia and her people had been working with *Cars Toons* people to understand and schedule their rendering needs. What she had just learned was that *Cars Toons* would be ready for rendering at the same time *Up* was scheduled to start rendering.

Brandeau trusted Pia's judgment. She had joined Pixar a decade earlier as his assistant and worked her way into her current position. Though she lacked previous technical experience, she'd quickly learned the ropes and demonstrated a high level of both managerial skill and the ability to work well under pressure. If she thought there was a problem, there probably was.

Nonetheless, he was mystified. He knew the RenderFarm, for all its compute power, was a finite resource, and he knew that with feature films, shorts, and marketing collateral, the scheduling of the RenderFarm was growing more and more difficult. But still.

"How is that possible?" he asked. "*Cars Toons* is a short. How can a short cause a problem?"

Brandeau understood the rendering needs of *Up*. It was technically ambitious; an aging widower makes an intercontinental trip with a young boy in a house carried aloft by thousands of balloons. Many *Up* characters were human, which were much more complex to portray than toys (*Toy Story*), fish (*Nemo*), bugs (*A Bug's Life*), or rats (*Ratatouille*). And it was the first feature film Pixar would release in 3D.

As for *Cars Toons*, Pixar had always done shorts, as well as feature films. They represented a different kind of artistic and technological challenge that people enjoyed. Without the pressure of a feature film, they offered freedom and flexibility to experiment with new software and hardware to create new special effects. They also served as good training grounds for new directors and producers.

What was difficult to understand was why *Cars Toons* needed the entire RenderFarm for two whole weeks. Everyone knew that the compute power shorts needed was hardly more than a few notes in the vast symphony of computing at Pixar. Feature films with more frames and more people submitting frames required massive computing power, while shorts could be fitted into the nooks and crannies of the RenderFarm schedule.

But *Cars Toons*, it turned out, was no ordinary short. It was technically challenging in the extreme. Its frames would require as much compute time—many hours—as the frames for *Cars*, by far the most technically difficult feature film that Pixar had made to date. The reason was a complex CG technique called ray tracing that Pixar had developed.

In *Cars*, the director had wanted the dazzling desert landscapes where parts of the film were set to look fully authentic—intense sunlight playing off a car's specular body, the look and feel of peeling paint on a sun-blasted building, the ruby glow of a desert mesa in dusty twilight, the palpable shadows of a car coasting in the harsh midday sun. Ray tracing allowed CG filmmakers to mimic the many forms and guises of real light, such as reflection and refraction.

Its stunning visual effects came at a high cost, however, because frames using it took so long—many hours—to render. The first Pixar film to use extensive ray tracing, *Cars* was a technological tour de force that required compute power on the order of three hundred times the power needed for *Toy Story*.

Still, *Cars Toons* had only a fraction of the frames of a feature film. Even with ray tracing, it should have been easy to fit all four shorts into the RenderFarm schedule. But it was a problem because of three additional factors.

First, the shorts were technically even more challenging than could be explained by ray tracing. Parts of *Cars Toons* were set in Tokyo, which meant the designers had to create a CG set of that vast city. With limited people and time, they took an approach that minimized their own design time but increased the render times. They were making the frames visually stunning by taking technical shortcuts that didn't reduce ultimate quality but did make the frames more complex to render, which required more render time.

Second, on most productions, final rendering was done shot by shot as shots were completed and approved, which meant rendering got done in smaller chunks over a longer period of time. However, because *Cars Toons* had a small crew that was extremely busy, they decided to leave final rendering until the very end when all shots would be done at once.

Third, *Cars Toons* had been scheduled to begin rendering during the summer when the RenderFarm was only 50 percent utilized. But when the filmmakers began to show their work in progress to key people at Pixar, they were given notes for improving the stories and they wanted to make those changes, which delayed production and pushed rendering into September.

These factors, combined with the fact that the deadline for final completion of *Cars Toons* didn't change, meant final rendering would require the entire RenderFarm for one intense two-week period in September.

Systems people had known that *Cars Toons* would involve ray tracing, but no one told them about the Tokyo set or the production delays. That was no one's fault, given the way shorts had always been made at Pixar. The demands they made on corporate resources were typically little more than noise, and so few groups outside those directly involved worried much about them. Nor did the people making them worry much, or need to worry, about coordinating with other groups. Shorts were typically made with small staffs that included only a few dedicated planners or coordinators because those functions had never been a problem. That's why the *Cars Toons* people never spoke up about the changes. They simply assumed what had always been true in the past—that a short would get the resources it needed, when it needed them, because its needs were only background noise.

Consequently, the systems department was looking at a collision in the RenderFarm in early September, only a few weeks away and fast approaching. *Cars Toons* would need 100 percent of the Farm for two weeks just as *Up* began final rendering and would need the Farm's full capacity for six to seven months.

That was the problem, but no one in systems was deeply concerned. It was something they could and would work out because the implicit rules of the road at the studio were clear. Pixar was in the business of producing blockbuster feature films, and so everyone knew that the feature film currently in production *always* got top priority. If it needed the RenderFarm tomorrow, it would get the RenderFarm tomorrow, and everything else would wait.

The immediate issue was that for the moment, only Brandeau and his group knew about the conflict. The *Up* people naturally assumed they would get what their film needed, exactly when it was needed. And the *Cars Toons* people were obviously assuming their shorts would be fitted in as soon as they were ready.

All this was occurring in a broader context of growth and change at Pixar. The pioneer of CG feature films, the studio had thus far produced only one at a time. But now it was beginning to think about rising to the next level. "We felt we now knew how to make CG films," Brandeau said, "and we were hitting our stride. So we were in the process of scaling up to release two films, maybe three, a year, instead of one."

In addition, Disney had recently bought Pixar for $7.4 billion with the expectation of not only more feature films but also more shorts like *Cars Toons* to help build movie franchises. More of everything would seriously test the capacity of the studio in every way, not least the ability of the systems department to handle sudden spikes in demand for computer resources.

Brandeau and his people in systems were already anticipating the demands and pressures of more and more production. They had always prided themselves on their ability to anticipate and plan for even the worst contingencies. Pia and her group were constantly building and improving tools for projecting how much compute power would be needed over a sliding six-month window. These tools measured exactly how long frames were taking to render for every shot in every film in production. Using this information and the show schedule of when shots were expected to be in production, systems people could combine all productions in a graph and look at where demand peaked. With a six-month rolling window, they could react in time if there were a sudden spike, either from a single show or from productions overlapping each other. As demand for computer resources increased, they were working to make these planning tools even more sophisticated.

What was most troubling about the conflict between *Up* and *Cars Toons* wasn't just the two-week overlap but that the systems group had been blindsided for all the reasons we noted. It hadn't foreseen this sudden surge in demand. "We thought we knew," Brandeau said, "how our universe worked and could use that understanding to handle whatever came up. Now we began to wonder if maybe we didn't understand it as well as we thought."

Brandeau liked to work at the edge of what was possible—it was his "bold ambition"—but he never anticipated he'd be doing it in show business. At Pixar, he was applying massive computing power to make the kind of animated films never made before. With two electrical engineering degrees from MIT and an MBA from Duke, he had been director of operations at NeXT, the computer company Steve Jobs founded in the mid-1980s after he left Apple. A few weeks after Pixar's first movie *Toy Story* hit theaters, Jobs called Brandeau to his office and asked if he would consider a move to Pixar. Jobs had bought the studio from George Lucas in the 1980s and had pumped tens of millions into it before it was finally about to be profitable. Pixar needed someone to lead its mission-critical technology systems, and Jobs wanted Brandeau to be that person. Curious, Brandeau decided to interview, and after a few meetings at the studio, he took the job.

Make a Decision, Please

To resolve the looming collision between *Up* and *Cars Toons*, Brandeau and his people first had to let everyone involved know what was about to happen. Any problem is hard to deal with when no one considers it a real problem. The response was always the same whenever someone in systems mentioned the possibility of a conflict, "What? No, it doesn't work that way. This is a short and shorts don't need many resources."

There was nothing to do but meet with the people from *Up* and then those from *Cars Toons* and make clear they had to find a resolution. Everyone in systems knew that if *Up*, in the end, couldn't find room in its rendering schedule, *Cars Toons* would have to wait. In any case, it wasn't the job or place of the systems people to make those decisions.

"How exactly is it that a short needs the entire RenderFarm anyway?" Steve May, the supervising technical director (or suptech) for *Up*, wanted to know. Because they understood both the systems and the artistic production sides of the business, suptechs could serve as a bridge between the two groups.

After the systems people explained, May said he might be able to shift a few things around, such as production of especially complex scenes, to make some room for *Cars Toons*. But he could only find a few days, not the two weeks *Cars Toons* needed.

He made it clear that without the necessary compute power, his film would not finish on time. *Up* was going to be released in nine months, and once that date had been set, his hands were tied. Hundreds of people at Pixar and Disney, distributor of the film and now owner of Pixar, were preparing for the big day. Suppliers around the world were already making toys, clothing, books, and all the other ancillary products that would make *Up* a billion-dollar property. Slipping the date would create havoc that would put everything at risk.

"You're kidding! Nine months!? We can't render *Cars Toons* for six or seven months?!" Kori Rae, the producer of *Cars Toons*, and her suptech were sitting in a meeting room with Brandeau and his team. Rae had just learned that her show was going to collide with *Up*, which meant *Cars Toons* might have to wait nine months.

"We can't wait several months!" said Rae. "We promised to deliver *Cars Toons* this fall!" *Cars Toons* was going to air on the Disney Channel and ABC Family, which Disney also owned. The Disney marketing powerhouse was counting on *Cars Toons* being delivered on time. "And John loves *Cars Toons* and wants to see them," Rae added. John was John Lasseter, the Pixar cofounder and director who had made *Toy Story* and *Cars* and now was taking an interest in *Cars Toons*. It was his notes that had strengthened *Cars Toons'* story lines—and delayed production.

It wasn't just a matter of filling the time slots on those channels. There were three consumer product lines at Disney that then produced significant revenue; one was the toys and other items tied to characters in the original *Cars* movie. *Cars 2* was still years from release. Not wanting the *Cars* characters to fade from viewers' memories, people at Disney believed a series of *Cars* shorts—*Cars Toons*—released on cable television and online would keep the characters alive and maintain the sales of *Cars* consumer products.

Everyone knew how deeply Lasseter cared about the characters in his films. More than mere animations, they were part of his world, and he wanted kids to make them part of their worlds too. For him, the toys and other products were ways for children to play with the characters and make up their own stories around them.

The meetings with *Up* and *Cars Toons* ended at an impasse. For the *Cars Toons* people, their "short" was no ordinary short. It deserved as much priority as anything else. For the *Up* people, there was no question that the feature film currently in production would get whatever it needed, as always. Anything short of that would be crazy.

After the meetings, Brandeau and his people reviewed next steps. Clearly, they were facing two sets of nonnegotiable demands that were physically impossible to meet. They were frustrated because this was a perfect storm that they couldn't have planned their way around. (See the sidebar, "Brandeau Recalls Another Perfect Storm.") Not discussed but on their minds was the clear subtext of expectations that production people had communicated in the meetings. "This is your problem, systems. Solve it." So much for hoping the production people would work it out.

This was not a position Brandeau was used to nor particularly enjoyed because, much as he wanted to, he "couldn't magically conjure up" the compute power needed. "When you have these constraints," he added, "everyone is forced into a weird box. You're all friends, each of you is handcuffed to the others, and you all have knives. Everyone is trying to support their own point of view about what should be done, but it's a difficult situation. People are competing with each other to achieve their goals and simultaneously trying to accomplish the company's goals."

Buy More Computers or Delay Something

"Options?" said Brandeau later in a meeting with his team. "Ed will want to make sure we've considered everything."

Ed was Ed Catmull, Pixar CEO, founder, and a legendary computer graphics pioneer. If the production people couldn't resolve the conflict, Brandeau would ultimately have to get a decision from him.

The discussion of options had gone quickly, because it was a list Brandeau and his people constantly reviewed, kept up to date, and expanded.

Brandeau Recalls Another Perfect Storm

In the midst of the sprint to make *Toy Story 2,* a system command accidentally deleted the entire film. When he learned of the problem, Brandeau was concerned, but he knew they had a safety net. As Brandeau explained:

> *We knew that a Pixar film was worth a billion dollars and my backup team, the team responsible for protecting Pixar's data, had four very robust, independent systems for data protection and someone on-site manning backups 24/7. However, in an almost impossible chain of events, each backup system had failed and we could not recover the movie. We had no movie.* It was gone. *I wrote my resignation letter.*

Fortunately, they got the movie back. Thanks to the sense of community at Pixar, the lead technical supervisor, who was on maternity leave, had been trusted with a copy of the whole film on her home computer. But that's not why Brandeau didn't get fired, though Ed Catmull, John Lasseter, Steve Jobs, and Brandeau's then-boss Lawrence Levy did discuss the option. They told him, "We know you're smart and trying your best. So when you messed up, our first thought wasn't that you're incompetent; it was that you're up against really tough problems. It's ok that you made this mistake once. Don't let it happen ever again." It didn't.

How leaders handle missteps can have lasting impact on a team's sense of mutual trust and responsibility—a critical foundation for the kind of candor and agility Greg's team needed now in order to engage in innovative problem solving in a tough situation. He observed:

> *When you are working on the cutting-edge, you are not always going to get it right, and, for sure, you don't want to depend on luck. Think about the colossal mistake my team and I made— and we weren't fired! What message did that send to everyone about being safe to try new things? That's why people were always looking ahead to figure out how to get the work done, instead of looking over their shoulders to see if they're about to be fired.*

They were always looking for cheaper, better, faster ways of providing the compute power the Pixar filmmakers needed.

One option was to render frames overnight on the hundreds of powerful desktop computers—thousands of CPUs, actually, because each computer had four—that sat on Pixar employees' desks. In fact, Pixar had used employees' computers this way in the early 1990s to complete *Toy Story* on time. But this was years later, and CG technology had grown so much more complicated that there weren't enough hours each night to render many of the frames. Artists would either have to wait the next morning while their desktops finished rendering or cancel the rendering and lose all the work done overnight. Anyway, most desktop computers weren't configured properly for rendering.

Renting or leasing made sense in principle. People in finance often suggested that the systems department own a base of computers for ongoing work and rent more during demand peaks. But every time systems people looked at that option, the cost of renting was only about 10 percent less than an outright purchase, and you didn't get to keep the equipment when you were done with it. Computers became obsolete so quickly that the owner/leaser had to recoup its money quickly. Unless something had changed, which was unlikely, buying was a far better option. Even if Pixar needed the extra compute power for only a short period at the moment, its growing needs would certainly absorb the excess capacity in the future.

More optimization—preparing frames beforehand so they required less time to render—was another possibility. Feature films could afford the staff to optimize frames. But *Cars Toons* didn't have such people or the time it required. Even if optimization were possible, it wasn't clear that it would save enough render time.

A new option someone raised was the possibility of doing the rendering at Disney Animation in Burbank, a one-hour flight away, assuming its RenderFarm was available. Brandeau knew the people and operation there well, and he gave Pia the name of the person to call. Disney had bought Pixar both because it was a thriving business *and* because Disney wanted to inject some Pixar magic into its own flagging animation business. It would be ironic then, Brandeau thought, if Pixar ended up relying on Disney Animation to solve this problem.

Another, more recent possibility they'd been tracking was to use a capability just coming on the scene—cloud computing. Brandeau and others in systems had met with Google and Amazon, but nothing had yet come of it for mainly technical reasons. Cloud computers weren't ideal for rendering, and available broadband connections couldn't handle the volumes of data. But it was a fast-emerging capability. There was no reason to think the limitations had been overcome, but it was worth checking.

As Brandeau and his people discussed the possibility of using the cloud, someone noted that probably the only way such banks of computers could work was if they were physically moved to Pixar. In the spirit of considering all possibilities, they discussed for a moment the option of physically borrowing the 250 computers they needed, but the discussion ended when someone called the idea "insane," an opinion they all more or less shared—for good reason. How do you quickly and safely pack, ship, unpack, install, modify, debug, use, repack, and return hundreds of computers worth millions of dollars in a few days? Even more problematic, how can you be sure the computers will run Pixar's software properly? No new computer had ever done that without modification. Besides, firms like Google and Amazon weren't going to let you actually take their computers.

Those were the options, but no one felt very confident. Every alternative presented huge unknowns and risks, and most likely wouldn't be able to solve the problem. Reluctantly, Brandeau and his systems people concluded that the only way to finish both *Up* and *Cars Toons* on time was to spend $2 million on new computers. It seemed ironic. If *Cars Toons* had to put a line item in its budget for rendering, the extra $2 million would probably have killed the project before it even started.

Now the only real option was to delay one of the two productions. "I don't see how we're going to get out of this mess," he said. "Ed will have to make a decision."

Seeing Catmull was no longer as easy as it once was. Since Disney had bought Pixar, he had been spending significant time in Burbank. When Brandeau was finally able to set up a meeting, he summarized the situation—first, the reasons for the conflict and, second, the options, none of which looked especially promising. He said the only real option for doing both *Up* and *Cars Toons* together was to buy more computers.

Catmull's style in these situations was to listen laconically, maybe ask questions for clarity, and then share his perspective. "We don't have $2 million for new computers," he said. Brandeau understood. It was hard to justify that amount of money to use computers for two weeks.

"Then, do we delay *Up* or *Cars Toons*?" Brandeau asked, fully expecting the answer to be "Delay *Cars Toons*."

"Neither," said Catmull. "We need both done on schedule. See if you can figure something out."

––––––––––––––

"So what are we supposed to do?"

"I don't know," Brandeau said as he sat with his people. "Ed didn't say."

"But we still have to finish both on time?"

"That's right."

"This isn't our fault, but we're going to get blamed," someone said.

Throughout its brief history, Brandeau often pointed out, Pixar had lived on the edge of what was technically possible. "Making every movie was like jumping out of an airplane and putting together the pieces of a parachute on the way down. Inevitably, some piece would be missing and we'd have to invent a solution as we were dropping. The release date, like the ground, wouldn't budge."

But, thus far, the systems department had always been able to improvise solutions at the last minute. In those situations, systems people would say flippantly to each other, "Lack of planning on their part doesn't constitute an emergency on our part," and then they'd find a solution anyway. But this time, they were looking into the black abyss of failure. The future they'd seen on the horizon had just arrived.

September was now less than two weeks away when, if the systems people couldn't find a solution, they would have to tell the *Cars Toons* people the bad news. They knew the response would be heard all the way from Emeryville to Burbank.

The problem had started as a conflict no one saw coming. As it morphed into a real crisis, it turned into one of the most unnerving times Brandeau and his systems group ever experienced at Pixar. People usually willing to collaborate began pointing fingers at each other, desperate to finish their projects on time. "You're crazy!" said one group. "You're violating the fundamental principles of how we run this place. The feature film at bat gets what it needs." "If we don't finish *Cars Toons*," said the other, "Disney is going to be unhappy. Plus, JL [Lasseter] loves *Cars Toons*."

Ultimately, everyone began pointing fingers at the systems department. "The people in *Up* and *Cars Toons* clearly felt it was our fault that we hadn't planned for their needs," said Brandeau. "People were seriously stressed and behaving in ways you'd never see otherwise."

"Let 'em go over the cliff," said someone in a systems meeting.

"Right. Maybe they'll finally learn where the edge is."

Later, Brandeau would say of that dark moment:

We were so depressed about being caught in a situation we didn't make that we talked about letting Cars Toons *crash and burn because, at the end of the day, it was the short. But that was frustration talking and definitely not in our nature. We actually cared about not letting the rest of the studio down. These were colleagues who were counting on us. So we pressed on.*

People in systems knew they had no choice but to keep trying. As John Kirkman, director of systems technology, said: "If we had gone to *Cars Toons* or *Up,* and said, 'We can't do your show. Tough. Next time, plan better,' that would have been a disaster for the department. We couldn't win that argument."

But, in fact, Brandeau and his people never tried to make that argument. In spite of their frustration, no one in systems wanted to disappoint their colleagues in production. This was a key reason Brandeau had joined Pixar. It was clearly a three-legged stool—art, technology, and production. People in every part considered each other peers, all essential to the company's one goal—making great computer-generated films. He drummed into everyone who joined systems an important truth: "CG movie-making is a team sport. It requires all of us. No one does it by themselves."

On Thursday of the next week, Brandeau and his people were reviewing their options—for the umpteenth time. On Monday, only four days away, both *Up* and *Cars Toons* needed to start rendering if they were to stay on schedule.

Using desktop computers wouldn't work. Render times were too long. A quick check had confirmed that renting or leasing rates were no better than before. Optimization was unlikely to save enough time; anyway, there weren't enough people to do it. Another quick check had confirmed that the cloud remained an unlikely option. Amazon and Google computers were configured for running web services, not rendering. Above all, Internet connections were too slow. Pixar had evolved its software to take advantage of its own ultrafast on-site networks, which were roughly one hundred times faster than the fastest link it could find to the Internet.

"Disney isn't using their RenderFarm right now," Pia said. She had just heard back from her contact there. But rendering at Disney Animation was also unworkable, they quickly decided (again), because Disney had tuned its network, file servers, operating systems, and software to support the way it worked, which was radically different from the way Pixar systems worked. Whatever the solution was, someone said, it had to involve somehow physically adding more computers to Pixar's RenderFarm.

With the whole group depressed and stressed about the impossible situation, someone said, "Can we borrow Disney's computers and use them here? We've ruled out borrowing because it's so tricky. But we've bought whole new RenderFarms in the past and installed them. How is borrowing computers and installing them any different?"

No one objected that borrowing was an option they'd only recently reviewed and labeled "insane." No one reminded the group that they'd never done it before and didn't know of anyone who had. The questioner was saying, in effect, "We need to think about this some more." So, because as a group they were always open to a new or old idea, that's what they did.

For borrowing to work, Disney's computers would have to be trucked from Burbank to Emeryville, almost a full day's drive. Pia called Disney back. People there, it turned out, were willing to pack up and ship 250 of their RenderFarm computers to Pixar immediately. Then her team figured out how physically to fit the extra computers into Pixar's RenderFarm and how to automate installing them once they were put in place.

"Desperation made this seem possible," said Brandeau later. "We all knew there were big potential problems. None of us could recall ever buying any equipment that worked right out of the box. Everything needed modifying and configuring, which we knew we could do, but the question was time. Would we have enough time?"

The trucks from Disney Animation arrived Friday, and people worked through Saturday unloading, installing, cabling, and powering a thousand processors. It was no small task. Each server containing multiple CPUs weighed upward of forty pounds, a total of four or five tons of equipment, which meant a very long day for the small systems crew doing the work.

While the computers were being physically installed, other systems people pulled one or two machines aside for testing. This was the hard part, not because they couldn't figure it out but because they didn't know how long it would take. They had to determine how to reconfigure the borrowed equipment to make it work in the Pixar world. The ultimate test was to render the same frame on both a Pixar machine and a Disney machine and get the same result.

Once they'd achieved that goal of matching frames, they built an environment in which the machines—once installed, powered, and cabled—could install the software themselves.

That occurred on Sunday. In groups of around twenty servers at a time, the borrowed machines lit up, looked on the Pixar network, and said, in effect, "Here I am." At that point, the network recognized them and said, "Okay, here's your operating system. Load the software and reboot." By Monday morning—the whole process had taken four days, Thursday through Sunday—the expanded RenderFarm was ready.

Although it wasn't easy, *Cars Toons* finished production as planned. Lasseter and Disney were thrilled. *Up* remained on schedule and hit its release date. It went on to be nominated for best animated picture, which it won, *and* for best picture overall. Though it didn't win the Oscar for best picture, it was the first time a computer-generated movie had even been a nominee.

Crisis averted, everyone outside systems just remembered it as systems doing its job, and they forgot the tension and high feelings. Even when people in systems thought back to those events, no one could clearly recall who first raised the possibility of borrowing equipment from Disney Animation.

"In hindsight," said Brandeau, "the answer we came up with may seem obvious. But, believe me, when my peers in other companies heard this story, they were amazed. Borrowing a compute farm, shipping it around, and getting it to work quickly in a totally new environment hadn't been done."

———————————————

This story is actually the story of both a tactical innovation and a strategic innovation. The tactical solution resolved an immediate problem, while the strategic solution gave systems a better way to operate in a more complex world.

First, of course, the story was about the short-term innovation—borrowing computers to expand the RenderFarm temporarily—that resolved the immediate conflict between two productions that needed rendering at the same time. As Brandeau and his people struggled to resolve this problem, they learned several things: they could find computers to borrow; transporting and installing hundreds of computers quickly was a fairly straightforward logistics challenge; and they could fairly quickly adapt the software to run on systems that at first were incompatible.

The strategic innovation grew from the first. It was that the systems people found a better way of thinking and operating in a new world where the old rules no longer applied—where the feature film currently in production no longer automatically got highest priority and where short productions couldn't always be fitted into the schedule somehow. The innovation was a new way to think about and handle the increasing complexity and uncertainty of Pixar's computing needs.

The key was something Steve May, the suptech for *Up*, said to Brandeau after the crisis was past. Brandeau told May what the systems group had done and mentioned the problems and uncertainties that surrounded borrowing servers on short notice, especially the difficulty of anticipating the time and effort required to make them work in Pixar's unique Render-Farm environment. May reacted with a suggestion: systems should identify pools of outside servers that might be available and test them in advance to learn how to make them work if and when they ever needed to be used.

That remark percolated in the back of Brandeau's mind and finally led him and his people to change completely how they thought about preparing for the future. In the past, their response to increased complexity and demand had always been better planning—learning how to make better predictions about what was coming over the horizon. Their goal had been to have a six-month window for preparation. But the conflict between *Up* and *Cars Toons* provided painful evidence that perhaps not every need could be anticipated. Systems did have to plan, but it also had to develop ways of responding quickly when planning fell short, as it always would on occasion.

"We learned," said Brandeau, "that with more and more balls in the air, no matter how good our planning, a crisis would arise. With shorts and other work coming from Disney, project time frames were getting shorter and many of the projects, like *Cars Toons*, couldn't fit into the cracks. If planning wasn't sufficient to avoid all crises, we had to be able to react quickly."

For this more flexible approach, the systems group built a new set of tools designed for the efficient modification of RenderMan to fit a variety of different CPUs. And borrowing became an accepted if not frequent practice that let Pixar deal with demand spikes that couldn't be foreseen. At one point, Pixar even borrowed a pool of servers from Morgan Stanley, the financial firm, to finish another short on time.

Creative Abrasion

Creative abrasion is a process in which potential solutions are created, explored, and modified through debate and discourse. It can and often does involve heartfelt disagreement or heated argument, but not always. Abrasion in essence means simply that ideas and options compete in order for the best idea to emerge.

It's a process with multiple steps because, as we've pointed out, innovative solutions rarely appear fully formed in a flash of insight. Instead, the evidence is clear that most innovations arise from the collision of different ideas, perspectives, and ways of processing information. For this to happen, groups must first generate lots of ideas and keep massaging them, as we saw at Pixar, in order to find one breakthrough idea. As Thomas A. Edison reportedly said, "to have a great idea, have a lot of them."[2]

Don't confuse creative abrasion with brainstorming. Both seek to develop as many ideas as possible. The difference is that creative abrasion, as its name implies, includes the ongoing discussion, evaluation, and critical comparison of ideas, while brainstorming forbids critical comments in favor of generating as many ideas as possible, no matter how farfetched. Think of the difference in terms of the support-versus-confrontation paradox we mentioned in chapter 2. Brainstorming is all about support and only support. Creative abrasion, on the other hand, is about support *and* confrontation. That's why it only works with a community built on purpose, values, and rules. In that setting, members can feel safe to offer ideas *and* to hear criticism of their ideas because they know the goal is finding the best way to achieve the community's common purpose.

The Pixar story illustrates nicely how creative abrasion works. Its essential ingredients are *diversity* and *conflict*. We understand that both those words come with associations, and so here's what we mean by them:

- By diversity, we mean people who *think differently*.
- By conflict, we mean *cognitive conflict* not interpersonal conflict, that is, conflict over ideas and approaches, as opposed to personalities; conflict aimed at learning and improving, not winning, losing, or dominating.[3]

Diversity

When people think of diversity today, they typically focus on demographic diversity—differences in nationality, culture, ethnicity or race, and gender. But just because people look different doesn't mean they'll have divergent points of view.[4] Different life experiences and personal identities may lead to different outlooks, but not necessarily.

Creative abrasion requires a different kind of diversity: *intellectual* diversity. For innovative problem solving, you want to bring together people who think differently, people who have different skills, knowledge, working and thinking styles, and different preferences for how they gather, process, and assimilate data.[5]

John Seely Brown, the former head of Xerox PARC, contends that innovation flows from the friction of multiple views coming together. "Breakthroughs often appear," he says, "in the white space between crafts ... These crafts start to collide, and in that collision radically new things start to happen."[6]

Not only does diversity lead to innovation, it also attracts talented individuals. According to growing evidence, such people gravitate to communities that "provide the stimulation, diversity, and richness of experiences that are wellsprings of creativity." The reasons are clear. "Diversity means 'excitement' and 'energy.' Creative-minded people enjoy a mix of influences ... a place seething with the interplay of cultures and ideas ... They also happen to be qualities conducive to innovation, risk-taking, and the formation of new businesses."[7]

Pixar clearly was such a community. It successfully bridged three different worlds—technical, creative, and business. Other studios were usually driven by one or the other, but not Pixar. It treated people across these worlds as peers and colleagues valued for their different but equally valuable perspectives. This sense of mutual respect, trust, and influence created a fertile context for the kind of idea sparring necessary for creative abrasion. "It was clear to me," said Brandeau, "that Pixar hired artists and technologists in as peers. Everyone could talk to anyone else at the studio. Many of these people were the best in the world at what they did—and they were all focused on pooling their talents to achieve a shared goal: make terrific films."

Even within the key groups inside Pixar, leaders actively sought diversity. In systems, for example, Brandeau wanted more than technology whizzes. He wanted people with a mosaic of different talents, sensibilities, personalities, subject-matter expertise, backgrounds, age, and so on. Many of those people did not come to Pixar with traditional technology backgrounds. They included a cultural anthropologist who had worked with Jane Goodall, someone who had managed concessions at a major state fair, an erstwhile music producer and video jockey, and even a professional cheerleader. Regardless of their backgrounds, they all thought of themselves as filmmakers.

The two systems people we met in the story, Anne Pia and Chris Walker, were good examples. They shared the same job running the RenderFarm but brought to it different backgrounds and skills. Both were smart, of course, but Pia brought a liberal arts background and a high level of managerial skill, while Walker brought a deep technical background and great skill as a technical leader.

Conflict

When passionate, diverse people collaborate on solving a problem, differences, disagreements, and conflict are inevitable. That's good because when alternatives compete in a marketplace of ideas, they get better and the competition often sparks new and better approaches. Thus, collaboration of diverse individuals produces healthy conflict, and that produces more and better ideas. So important is this kind of conflict that its absence constitutes a flaw that limits innovation. "If you have no conflict," said Jim Morris, the general manager of Pixar who came to the company from Lucasfilm, "you're going to have something that's pretty average."

Conflict presents the leader with significant challenges. Not all conflict, of course, is desirable or productive. When advocates oppose each other instead of each others' ideas, conflict can turn personal and destructive. Leaders of innovation, while they want creative conflict about alternatives, point out and discourage interpersonal conflict wherever they find it. The Pixar manager just quoted also went on to say, "People here are blunt with each other but in a collegial way with the intent of making things better."

Keeping intellectual conflict separate from interpersonal conflict is difficult.[8] Even debates about ideas can get heated. It's human for people to become attached to their ideas and feel personally attacked when someone disagrees. In defense, they sometimes strike back at a personal level, which generates a like response, and the debate spirals downward. In response, leaders who don't fully appreciate the necessity of positive conflict seek to minimize all conflict. In the process, they limit the ability of their group to find new and useful solutions.

Even if debate never turns personal, it can still feel threatening and unpleasant. Most people find it stressful and exhausting when they have to explain and defend constantly everything they say. So why then even suggest an idea if someone is just going to attack it and force them to uphold it vigorously? In short, conflict, even positive conflict, can lead some people to remain silent, and that obviously stifles innovation.

Most people also find it challenging to work with others who approach problems differently. Unless they simply withdraw—not a response that

---

The Paradoxes of Creative Abrasion

Recall the two paradoxes that leaders must manage as members of a group develop and debate options for solving a problem.

Individual versus Group Identity

In every community, each member's need for individual recognition and identity is pitted against the needs of the collective. This paradox arises from a fundamental tension within human nature itself: each of us wants to belong *and* we want our uniqueness recognized, not lost in the crowd. In the Pixar story, this clash took a slightly different but still common form—the necessity of balancing the needs of subgroups in the studio (systems, *Up* production team, *Cars Toons* production team) with the needs of the Pixar community overall.

Support versus Confrontation

How can a leader productively encourage team members to support one another while simultaneously encouraging them to provoke and challenge each other through robust debate? Creating the context where this can occur is tricky, to say the least. The answer is to build a community in which there is a strong sense of "we" and a belief that "we all succeed or fail together" and that no individual can succeed if the team fails. Managing this paradox is possible only if people seek to fulfill some higher collective purpose.

---

produces innovative ideas—they must constantly inquire about others' ways of thinking, and sometimes that thinking will shake the foundation of their own firmly held beliefs. (See the box, "The Paradoxes of Creative Abrasion.")

The Critical Role of Community

Even in the best circumstances, such as we saw in the systems group at Pixar, the challenges of diversity and conflict underscore the critical need for community. For people to offer ideas that allow creative abrasion to occur, they need to feel both motivated and psychologically safe. Those conditions can only exist when the group is a community where members feel bound by a mutual purpose and collective goal, shared values, and real rules of engagement. When people feel allied with others in pursuit of something larger and more important than any of them individually, they're more likely to contribute and feel valued, even when colleagues disagree with them.

In the Pixar story, although we saw some debate, we saw little actual conflict within the systems department as it sought ways to render two productions at once. People there had already coalesced into a genuine team or community. Though the pressure and tension reached a high pitch because of competing interests within the company, and people in systems vented their exasperation with talk of "crash and burn," the bonds of community and sense of equality among groups were strong enough to hold everyone together. That produced the extra work that led to an ultimate solution. The existence of a community certainly doesn't preclude heated disagreement. It does mean the community won't blow apart because of it.

Because of the sense of community, people also felt free and safe to offer ideas [9] The solution to their problem came when someone felt able to raise an idea again—borrowing computers and bringing them to Pixar—that the group had earlier declared "insane." In many groups, members would feel unable to return to something already rejected so decisively. Yet this person was able to ask the innocent question: "Are the problems of borrowing computers that different from buying a new RenderFarm and installing it?" Well, actually, they're not, the group realized, and from there it moved to a solution.

The community provides the context of psychological safety in which people feel able to offer ideas and options. Even if their ideas are attacked, they know the disagreement is aimed not at them but at the search for a solution that serves the higher purpose they're all pursuing. For the same reason, group members are motivated to speak up in service of that purpose.

The Leader's Role in Creative Abrasion

What we saw at Pixar mirrored what we saw across the organizations we studied. The pressures of the moment and situation could lead any group to forget why it existed and what it considered most important. When this happened—for example, when people confronted differences in dysfunctional ways—it was the leaders' role to bring the group back on course by reminding it of its purpose, values, and rules of engagement. It was Brandeau who reminded his group, when it understandably fell into a pit of despair and frustration, that it had a bigger purpose. If discussions in his group had grown personal and dysfunctional—they didn't, but if they had—it would have been his crucial role to remind people of their values and the rules of engagement.

For creative abrasion, it was also the leaders' role to espouse, encourage, expect, and practice communal norms that valued and even amplified diversity. For example, they hired people who were not only collaborative but who could also bring to problems a range of training, experience, outlook, and approaches.

The leaders also pushed people together and created situations in which diverse thinkers were put in close proximity to each other. They knew that, unless people with different perspectives came together to share ideas and debate competing solutions, the value of diversity would go unrealized. As obvious as this may seem, many leaders keep diverse thinkers isolated, physically and symbolically, precisely to avoid contention. But this only stifles innovation because the very act of pushing diverse people together brings out the differences that spark new ideas.

Leaders also create organizational bridges. For example, many roles at Pixar, such as the supervising technical directors on a production who worked with systems, were explicitly designed to serve as links between the two groups. Many practices, such as the "dailies" meetings where work in progress was critiqued, purposely brought together a variety of viewpoints. Even the physical layout of Pixar's building, which clustered such common areas as cafeteria, restrooms, and meeting space, was carefully designed by Steve Jobs to throw together spontaneously people from throughout the company.[10]

Instead of acting as arbiter or imposing solutions, effective leaders fostered diversity through the questions they asked. If they believed an alternative hadn't received full consideration, they would ask "What about … ?" questions. If they believed someone wasn't being heard or wasn't saying everything on her mind, they would return to that person and ask for more.

And if they believed the group wasn't considering all possible conditions, they'd ask "What if ... ?" questions. Without imposing ideas or approaches, such questions expanded the group's thinking and forced it to consider a full range of possibilities.

In short, the leaders of innovation we observed knew that creative abrasion was an organizational skill that could be encouraged, learned, practiced, and improved. Their role was to make sure all the ingredients for a healthy community were in place and remained vital—purpose, shared values, collective goal, rules of engagement. Without a community, real creative abrasion could not occur. Without a collective identity, a sense of "we" or community, no group can survive the passionate discussion, confrontation, and intellectual conflict that creative abrasion and innovation require.

As Brandeau reflected after both *Up* and *Cars Toons* had been successfully rendered:

> *Our sense of community enabled us to keep going and ultimately find a solution. At Pixar, everyone's shared purpose was to get the director's vision up on the screen and make great family movies. But here we found ourselves cornered and we felt we were unfairly being blamed for causing the crisis. We were on the verge of giving up in frustration, which was something we had never done. However, our deep-rooted sense of responsibility for something bigger than ourselves kept our team from flying apart under this tremendous pressure and allowed us to poke at a seemingly crazy solution that we had already decided would never work and make it work.*

We used to launch products in an "all or nothing" mode to all of our users. Now we had the capability to test multiple different live versions of new products on 1 percent samples of our users. This yielded huge data sets and brought with it a change in mind-set for approaching innovation. We began to avoid projects that only allowed for "zero or one" decisions, instead choosing projects that could be rolled out and evaluated in small slices.

—**Philipp Justus,** then head of eBay Germany

CREATIVE
AGILITY

Members of groups that develop an innovative solution often recall afterward that it appeared unexpectedly—out of the blue. But in studies that carefully monitor such groups' activities, it's clear that the solution almost always emerges step-by-step, even when that's not what people remember.

This is the experience of most groups when they innovate. They develop and test different options, learn from the outcomes, and try again—and, in many cases, again and again. In this way, they learn what actually works and are able to evolve even better options. The organizational ability to do this we call *creative agility*.

To explore this important capability, we turn to eBay Germany and a little-known chapter in the history of eBay, the e-commerce pioneer that changed the way the world shops.* Though not well known outside its

---

* The events described in our story of eBay Germany occurred primarily in the period 2002 to 2005.

home country, eBay Germany became one of the most successful auction sites within eBay's global empire, more successful by some key measures than even the US market. Its achievements demonstrated the power of agility and the discovery-driven learning that let it keep meeting the needs of its user community.

eBay Germany's Growth Challenge

Our story begins when eBay was almost ten years old and then CEO Meg Whitman, accompanied by Philipp Justus, visited eBay Germany's offices near Berlin. Justus was the former German country manager who had just become the new eBay senior vice president in charge of all Europe. In that meeting, he and Whitman challenged the leaders of eBay Germany to find ways of spurring growth in their core auction business.[1]

Not long after that visit, Stefan Groß-Selbeck, the German country manager who had succeeded Justus, called him to report that the German team was actively experimenting with new ways of driving traffic to its site at little or no cost. According to Groß-Selbeck, the results of these efforts— he called them "micro-projects"—looked promising and perhaps even scalable to other countries. But, he admitted, they were "not risk-free." The comment made Justus smile—"Far from it," he thought—based on his close knowledge of the German group and its audacity. Groß-Selbeck promised to explain more the next time Justus visited the offices in Berlin.

eBay Inc. and eBay Germany

Everyone familiar with the history of the Internet knows the story of eBay. Founded in 1995 by Pierre Omidyar in California, it quickly became the leading online auction site, a person-to-person trading platform where buyers and sellers of used goods and collectibles like Beanie Babies, antiques, and rare coins could find each other and transact business. From nothing in 1995, eBay shot up by the end of the century to 10 million users and gross merchandise sales, the total value of goods sold on the site, of $2.8 billion.

Almost from the beginning, Omidyar and Whitman, whom he hired as CEO, moved rapidly to expand beyond the United States through start-ups, joint ventures, and acquisitions of some of the local auction sites that were springing up around the world. One of those sites was alando.de (Alando), a site founded in Berlin by six German friends in 1999 that Omidyar began tracking almost from its inception.

He was attracted by how similar it seemed to eBay. It too had passionate employees focused on responding to and growing their community of traders through quirky, innovative campaigns. For example, Germans tended to be bargain hunters, and so Germany had many Internet sites listing competitions and giveaways. Alando ran mini-competitions that got it listed on those bargain sites. It also ran fun promotions, such as giving a voucher for a free Big Mac to any user who signed up a friend. And it ran audacious guerrilla marketing stunts, such as selling tickets it didn't yet have to the premiere showings of a *Star Wars* prequel (it obtained tickets eventually). As a result, Alando had virtually no user acquisition costs and had quickly become widely and fondly known.

eBay bought Alando for $47 million after a brief courtship in June 1999, its first acquisition of a non-US auction site, and renamed it eBay Germany. Months later, when most of the founders decided to leave and start a new venture, eBay selected Philipp Justus, an outsider, to head the site. After university in Germany, Justus had earned an MBA in the United States, returned to Germany, and was working for the Boston Consulting Group in Munich. At thirty, he was already seasoned in comparison with the rest of the eBay Germany staff, which comprised mostly twenty-somethings, many of them interns still in college.

On Justus's first visit to eBay headquarters in San Jose, Whitman, Omidyar, and other senior leaders charged him with several key tasks: build strong working ties between his staff and eBay; manage triple-digit growth while professionalizing his organization with better processes and systems; and, far from least, sustain the agility, passion, eagerness to try almost anything, and strong sense of community that already existed among his people. This last feature—a strong sense of community—was especially important to Whitman and Omidyar who believed, first, that eBay's success depended on building a community of passionate buyers and sellers around the world and, second, that eBay internally reflect the same sense of community built on trust.

If Justus had a concern, it arose from the one obvious difference between eBay's and eBay Germany's cultures. Because it was slightly older, eBay was ahead of the Germans in maturing from an entrepreneurial start-up to a larger organization with more formal structure and processes. Merging with a larger organization had advantages: joining a global trading community, for example, and access to greater corporate resources and expertise. But there were costs, too.

The Trials of Merging Alando and eBay

As the new country manager, Justus began almost immediately installing eBay marketing and management practices. Impressed by eBay's success with customer segmentation—focusing on the 20 percent of users, "Powersellers," who were trading full-time and generating 80 percent of eBay's volume—Justus led his colleagues at eBay Germany to identify their top 350 Powersellers and interact with them in a much more high-touch way.

Listing fees were a second major change, a practice they adopted from their new parent. From its beginning, the German site had offered free listings to encourage volume. Its only revenue came from a final value fee, a small percentage of the final sale price. However, eBay corporate had been profitable from inception and considered listing fees vital to its success. "If you don't have a listing fee," said an eBay executive, then "people put junk up, your site is not profitable, your users get bored because the stuff is junk, and top sellers are upset because of the low conversion rate."

When eBay Germany implemented listing fees, its community erupted in outrage, as many employees had feared and predicted. Users fulminated about the Internet being free, created sites protesting the fees, bid items up to outrageous amounts, and mail-bombed the company's mailboxes. Listings plummeted from 1 million to 250,000 items, and staffers' morale sank with them. It was a time people remembered as *Das Tal der Tränen*—the Valley of Tears.

After a short period, however, listings bottomed out and began rising as users discovered that a higher percentage of auctions actually closed because cheap, low-quality items no longer cluttered the site. The change ultimately turned out to be good for the community and hence for business, as eBay had predicted. It improved the quality of items listed, which improved the experience for buyers, and that began a period of steady growth in transactions.

The next major change came when eBay moved the eBay Germany site from local servers in Berlin to the company's global platform, then being built in San Jose. eBay Germany employees understood the logic of the migration. For eBay to become a global trading platform where a seller in Boise could trade easily with a buyer in Kyoto, all its local sites had to use the same technology platform. Still, they feared that the global platform would change something fundamental about the way they had always operated. A key to their rapid growth and success had been the ability to make the quick site changes that let them rapidly test a variety of promotions and other ideas. Would those changes be as quick and easy to make when their site was hosted not on local servers but on corporate servers thousands of miles away?

After a great deal of planning, the migration finally occurred in 2001 and quickly turned into a second Valley of Tears. Initial technical problems required a few days to resolve. More problematic were enraged users who hated the many changes required by the migration. They flooded eBay Germany with questions and complaints in tens of thousands of e-mails and thousands of phone calls. Within a week, listing volume was down by half.

When the initial switchover problems were resolved, however, more fundamental, ongoing problems emerged. Users found the new site too complex and bemoaned various lost functions. Expecting these complaints to diminish with time, the German team grew concerned when certain complaints did not diminish and, especially, when growth in listings, once it resumed, did not return to the premigration rate. Clearly, key aspects of the new site were feeding persistent community dissatisfaction and needed to change.

Alarm bells went off when German leaders pressed for further site changes right away and were told by corporate that, since the new site was technically stable, all change requests had to be scheduled through eBay's normal procedures, which meant a delay of weeks or even months. "We were getting put in a process," said a German manager, "but we felt that we were in an emergency."

At a meeting six weeks following migration, Justus and his key people identified the site changes they considered essential and discussed how they could get eBay in San Jose to make them immediately. Realizing that e-mails and conference calls wouldn't work, Justus decided on the spot that he and a colleague had to fly to California for face-to-face meetings. Three hours later, they were on a plane.

Going to San Jose and meeting with eBay leaders led to rapid resolution of the more urgent problems. Justus's quick action was key. "If Philipp hadn't stepped up and said, 'We're flying to the US,'" said one of his German colleagues, "the management team could have been seriously hurt, if not broken." Those changes, along with an aggressive marketing campaign, eventually enabled eBay Germany to rebuild its user community. Ultimately, the site resumed its premigration rate of growth and won back the support of the German public.

Life after migration—not the same

Over time, Justus and his German team grew adept at collaborating with eBay corporate and came to appreciate the value of eBay's global platform. Conversely, eBay came to consider eBay Germany the standard to which other international sites should rise.

Still, "after migration" was a new world for eBay Germany. Rapid turnaround by the corporate group became a growing challenge as eBay matured into a sprawling global enterprise, one of the largest online applications in the world. eBay managed more transactions every day than NASDAQ, and the number of searches conducted on its site was second only to Google's. At the end of 2003, eBay had 95 million registered users globally, 5,700 employees, and gross merchandise sales of nearly $24 billion.

The result was that the speed of innovation at eBay Germany gradually slowed and with it, growth. The Germans struggled to continue generating and testing new ideas locally—discovery-driven learning—while running the business as part of an increasingly complex global platform. Once accustomed to making frequent site changes to try new promotions or respond to user needs, they felt increasingly limited by corporate constraints. "To many of us in Germany," said a German manager, "it was hard to understand why it took a time frame like six to nine months to ship a medium-size project. Our biggest frustration from the business side was that we felt we didn't have the flexibility to move fast to react to market changes."

A crucial ongoing issue concerned eBay Germany's home page. German staff members were pleased when they learned it would contain a section dedicated to promotional content selected and developed locally. They were dismayed to discover that even these changes had to go through San Jose and could often take up to seventy-two hours to implement.

"We ran so many up-to-date promotions on the site, we felt that a three-day response time wasn't appropriate," said a German manager. "With the Alando system, since we did not have so many strict internal processes, it took us about half an hour from the time we decided to change something on the home page to the time it was implemented."

This was the situation in 2004 when Whitman and Justus, newly promoted to head all of eBay Europe, visited Germany and challenged Groß-Selbeck and his team to reignite growth in the core business.

eBay Germany's Micro-Projects

The first German micro-project began on a Saturday just after that visit. It didn't happen because of strategic thinking and planning. It was simply something a young product manager and his marketing colleagues wanted to try. Tossing around ideas, they decided a treasure hunt would make a promising holiday promotion. With a €1,000 Christmas bonus awarded every hour, it seemed a surefire way to generate publicity and attract users. That same night, the product developer tested the idea with friends who were not eBay employees. Based on their enthusiastic response, he hurried back to the office and rounded up his team. They all worked nonstop until Monday morning creating registration pages, clues, an hourly countdown clock, and other elements needed for the treasure hunt.

The eBay Germany site had long before migrated to California, and so normal procedure required the Germans to put up the promotion through the corporate HTML group. Except they had to do it right away; the holiday was looming and there was no time to spare. Then a group member realized they could do it by using legacy servers from Alando's start-up days, in violation of eBay's corporate processes for changing the site.

On Monday morning, Matthias Schafer, then head of products, came in for a surprise:

Everyone was totally jazzed about the work that'd happened over the weekend. I said, "What are you guys talking about?" When the promotion was explained to me, I took the product developer in a room and said "Are you crazy?!? This is so risky—do you know what you guys are doing?" But because they had already put the word out, there was no way back. In retrospect, that was a good thing because if there had been a way back, I probably would've pushed the SOS button. I would have agreed to do it, but with a lot more security and scalability.

In spite of the risk—there were valid technical and security reasons the company wanted changes to go through the corporate HTML group—the leaders at eBay Germany didn't shut the effort down. Besides the fact that the holidays would be over by the time the promotion survived the corporate approval process, the fundamental reason they didn't was cultural. Even after four years as a part of eBay, the German team retained the willingness to try new, untested ideas that seemed to make sense. The treasure hunt was an echo of Alando's early days of free Big Macs and selling a Ferrari for €1, another of their zany promotions.

When the Christmas treasure hunt began, 10 million contestants logged on, and the promotion site, hosted on local servers, went down. The German team was able to secure more machines to compensate, but then other problems popped up, not least that hackers wrote scripts to win each hunt. German engineers worked nonstop to keep the hackers out, make quick adjustments, fix technical problems, and keep the site functioning and stable. "It was totally crazy," said one of those involved. "We learned every second. The great thing was that even though the promotion wasn't perfect, it still was a success. We did get a lot more traffic."

Weeks later, eBay Germany launched its second micro-project, this one a "get rid of your unwanted Christmas gifts" promotion. That also increased traffic. To Groß-Selbeck, the experiments were proof positive that his people could pursue new ideas quickly and effectively without going through an arduous corporate development process. And it could be done with manageable risk if it was contained on a small part of the site.

Justus Makes a Choice

When he finally sat down with the German team, Justus could hear the excitement in their voices as they explained their adventures in the first micro-projects. He was pleased to hear their big ideas for additional projects. After all, he had run this group until recently and had worked to keep alive some of its start-up DNA. He understood people's enthusiasm and willingness to try virtually anything to build the community of German eBay users.

But in his new corporate role, he had to consider pulling the plug. Micro-projects may have been a throwback to the early days of Alando, but this wasn't a quirky start-up anymore. Not only was there the risk of local chaos, as nearly happened with the treasure hunt, but eBay Germany's activities were now taking place in the much larger context of the global eBay platform and exposed that platform to unpredictable risks. Wasn't it his role to protect the company?

What if eBay Germany engineers hadn't been able to stay ahead of the hackers? Groß-Selbeck himself admitted that "this was risky because there are safety precautions you usually need to take. We kind of did this very quick and dirty." What if every eBay country created micro-projects and the company ran amok, focusing too much on fun, short-term promotions while neglecting key strategic initiatives that took on dangerous competitors like Amazon and Google?

The development process at eBay was fairly centralized and structured for good reasons, Justus understood, given the complexity of the company's systems. But he remembered when Alando had merged into eBay. He understood the problems of being part of a massive global platform and the toll it took on local agility. He knew that "when you're sitting in a country and you have great ideas, and you have to go through the central development pipeline that sits five thousand miles away, that was hard."

Justus had the power to end micro-projects and avoid the inevitable risks and problems they could create. But he loved them and told the German staff to pursue them further. "I thought these small, quick experiments were exactly what we needed," Justus said. "It was a way to build something fast, without going through the usual development process, but have it be robust enough so as to provide a good user experience." The kind of exploration, improvisation, experimentation, and rapid iteration that micro-projects once more allowed, he believed, were what had made eBay Germany one of the innovative engines of the entire company.

Justus also liked micro-projects in his new corporate role. They were more than just a way to try lots of things, to be creative. They actually generated data that could be analyzed, and they were a way to test ideas that emerged from analyzing the massive amounts of information the eBay site generated every day. Even better, what was learned in one location could be spread to others in Europe and elsewhere.

What eBay Germany Did with Micro-Projects

German staff members were delighted to move ahead with micro-projects. Through the spring of 2005, fully a quarter of them suggested ideas, from which a dozen were selected for launch. Over the next two years, eBay Germany completed over eighty micro-projects. Examples included a shopping tips site developed by the marketing team that attracted users at no cost who were doing searches on Google; an app that gave mobile phone users access to the core eBay system; and EasyLister, a more convenient way for users to provide information when listing items for sale. Germany was also the only eBay country to install a separate registration process for business versus private sellers. That allowed it to introduce a differentiated pricing scheme for business sellers.

Yet, as the number of projects grew, the process quickly grew unwieldy and left little time for reflection and examination of results. It needed more structure. In the beginning, a micro-project could be about anything, but the staff quickly realized that not every off-the-wall idea was worth trying. Hard questions needed asking: Is this consistent with our purpose and values? How will we know if it's succeeding? Can we scale it if it works?

In response to these questions, the staff created a system for prioritizing projects, monitoring them, scaling some, and terminating others. It was the structure-versus-improvisation paradox that's built into the nature of organizational innovation. Creating and using such a system required fine judgment. Too much structure would stifle ideas and defeat the purpose of trying lots of things, including some that might seem slightly odd. The goal was to add some method to their madness without losing the madness entirely. A key decision was to choose and evaluate projects according to their impact on core trading activity, that is, to ask the most fundamental question: would a project improve the experience of users as they bought and sold items on the eBay Germany site?

Eventually, micro-projects were incorporated into a mini-product-planning portfolio as part of Germany's product planning. An eight-member product planning council created two tracks: one for core activities and the other for micro-projects.

All these steps, by adding just enough system and process, improved micro-projects. In the beginning, the people who worked on projects were completely overworked because there were too few people and so many unfiltered ideas. Prioritization forced a bit more thought in the beginning about how a project would drive core activities on the site. As a result, people with ideas became better at making a business case for them, which led to a better portfolio of ideas, and that fostered a much better use of available resources.

An important feature of this process was its transparency. Openness and idea sharing at every stage produced a sense of fairness among everyone involved. As one of the German leaders said, "Everyone had some value to add. We got great ideas from customer service. They would tell us what the community was saying. We ensured that everyone had a seat at the table."

German Results

Not every micro-project succeeded, of course. To protect sellers against nonpayment and buyers against nondelivery of goods as advertised, a third-party escrow service was added to the eBay Germany platform. It worked as planned but attracted neither buyers nor sellers. Users obviously thought the traditional system based on trust worked just fine. Another micro-project enabled bidding via SMS text messages. Since most bids on an item were placed in the last minutes and even seconds of an auction, this feature meant bidders didn't have to stay glued to their computers. Again, the system worked as intended, but it was the early days of smartphones, and the technology didn't yet allow full customer-friendly mobile web access.

Even the failures were instructive. As technology improved, they provided important clues about what users wanted and didn't care about. For example, eBay Germany's failure with the escrow service kept eBay from going to the expense of adding that feature to its global platform.

Through its ability to experiment over and over—sometimes succeeding, sometimes not, but always learning—eBay Germany solidified its reputation as one of the most innovative parts of the company. For a long time, it was the fastest-growing eBay market, driven in significant part by local adaptation and innovations. By 2007, with 24 million registered users, Germany was eBay's second-biggest market by trade volume. It was 40 percent the size of the US site, even though Germany's population was only 28 percent that of the United States. Half of all German Internet users were registered on eBay.[2] Roughly half the German population going online in any given month visited the eBay Germany site at least once, a claim no other eBay market and few other web commerce sites could match. It accounted for roughly 30 percent of online retail commerce in Germany, the largest of any eBay country. Its unaided brand awareness among Germans was 70 percent, a result in part of strong press coverage that included repeated cover stories in some of the biggest German weekly magazines. And its advertising slogan, *3 ... 2 ... 1 ... Meins*, became, with eBay Germany itself, a part of national pop culture.*

Spreading Micro-Projects

In the early days of micro-projects, eBay Germany took pains to fly under the eBay corporate radar. "Nobody in San Jose knew what we were doing," said one manager. "We were afraid that if they learned about micro-projects, they'd shut the whole thing down. We felt this had to grow like a little plant, and once we were sure that it was a strong plant, then we could go out and socialize it."

Once a more robust process was in place, Justus decided it was time to talk about micro-projects with other European countries. At one of the Europe-wide summits, he asked Germany's leadership to explain

---

* *3 ... 2 ... 1 ... Meins* makes sense because in German the last two words rhyme: *drei, zwei, eins ... meins. Meins* means "mine."

the projects and what it had learned about managing them well. Within months, micro-projects were popping up across the continent. Eventually, European sites were doing almost fifty micro-projects in various countries per quarter. They were a key way, according to Justus, of "sustaining our speed as we grew."

Countries sometimes adapted and improved what another country had already done. A good example was EasyLister, the early German micro-project already mentioned. An unpopular feature of the German site (and many other country sites) was the lengthy form a seller had to fill out before listing an item. It required so much information that it discouraged potential sellers who went to other sites, such as the local equivalents of Craigslist, where listing was a snap. So the German group developed a much simpler form it called EasyLister, which proved to be popular. About a year later, eBay UK picked it up when someone there said, "I can do this better," and made it even simpler. That version was so successful that eBay corporate adopted it into the core sites for the United Kingdom, Germany, and the United States.

Justus showcased some of the innovations happening in Germany to Whitman and her team in San Jose. When she asked how the Germans had come to develop such new and useful ideas, Justus explained micro-projects and how eBay Germany had used local servers and outside developers to get around corporate limitations and pursue a multitude of new ideas.

Whitman was so pleased with what she heard that she invited eBay Germany to make a presentation to the technology and product teams at headquarters. That led to the development of a global micro-projects strategy. She recognized that this approach was a way to try out new ideas rapidly, reflect on their impact, and make necessary adaptations—in short, a way to innovate vigorously and proactively.

Groß-Selbeck, who headed eBay Germany after Justus had been promoted, said of Whitman, "In many organizations, you'd get fired for not following the rules. But Meg really tried to drive this sort of thing, recognizing the value in creating paths for innovation. Of course, though, when an operation was built on site stability and safety, you didn't want people breaking the rules often. It was a fine balance."

It was a sign of the company's high regard for its German arm that it promoted some of its leaders to larger strategic global roles. As Whitman told us, Germany's success was no accident, because the leadership team was first rate. (See the box, "The Paradoxes of Creative Agility.")

The Paradoxes of Creative Agility

As they encouraged micro-projects, Phillip Justus and his successor Stefan Groß-Selbeck had to address the twin paradoxes of creative agility.

Learning and Development versus Performance

While learning and development are important, performance—*Did you solve the problem?*—is what ultimately matters. Thus, leaders of innovation encourage people to test and learn from new ideas. But they also demand that people be data driven in their experimentation and performance focused in evaluating results. They want people to try new things, and they set high standards for how carefully the experiments are done and analyzed. They take outside-the-box ideas seriously and do things outside normal channels, as Justus and Groß-Selbeck allowed eBay Germany to do. Above all, they expect experimentation, continuous learning, *and* ultimate results.

Improvisation versus Structure

Too much structure—rules, hierarchy, planning, and the like—will stifle innovation, but too little will produce chaos. As we noted elsewhere, even improv actors and musicians don't say or play whatever they want. They work within constraints and themes that guide them. Complete anarchy rarely produces anything useful. In every setting, some degree of structure seems to help a group produce something worthwhile. The question is, how much? It is the role and burden of the leader to wrestle with this question constantly. We saw at eBay Germany how some structure "made playing around more powerful," in the words of a German team member.

---

eBay Today

Since these events, the world has continued to change and eBay has adapted with it. The move from "being a small community to a big city," as Whitman put it, has not always been smooth. Like other organizations passing through a similar transition, the company has worked to find the right balance of structure and improvisation, to use the terms of one of our paradoxes.

eBay Inc. has expanded beyond online auctions where growth was slowing and currently focuses on:

- *eBay*, which is the direct descendent of the original auction business. With more than 124 million active users globally and more than 500 million items listed, eBay is one of the world's largest online marketplaces for individual buyers and sellers, as well as small businesses.
- *PayPal*, which enables individuals and businesses to send and receive digital payments easily and quickly without disclosing financial information. With 137 million active accounts in 193 markets and 26 currencies, it processes almost eight million payments every day.
- The company's newest effort, *eBay Enterprise*, which provides commerce technologies, as well as multichannel operations and marketing support, for global businesses that seek to reach and do business with online buyers.

Apropos our story of eBay Germany, it's interesting to note that a piece of this transformation actually began in that country. Based on a deep understanding of its users, eBay Germany experimented with a new feature called "Buy It Now" that let buyers end an auction early by purchasing the item for a predetermined price. Encouraged by buyers' response, the Germans took the concept one step further and introduced a pure fixed-price format no longer tied to an auction. They were the first eBay market to try this approach, and it was a hit that eventually morphed into such a major business line for eBay worldwide that fixed-price sales currently surpass auction sales.

eBay's marketplace businesses are expected to grow in the mid–single digits annually, while PayPal is expected to produce double-digit annual revenue growth.[3] Reflecting this evolution, company slogans have shifted from "World's Online Marketplace" and "Connecting Buyers and Sellers

Globally" to "Whatever It Is, You Can Get It on eBay" and "Buy It New, Buy It Now."

In a real sense, the company is going about reinventing itself through a larger version of the micro-projects first pursued by eBay Germany nearly a decade ago. Through multiple experiments, trial and error, it's building on and expanding beyond eBay's original auction platform. In 2008, Whitman left eBay, saying that no one should hold a position like hers longer than a decade. Her successor as CEO, John Donahoe, has described eBay's challenge in a familiar way:

> In many ways, eBay was the first social network. It's a highly engaged com-
> munity-based shopping experience and we are trying a variety of things ...
> You're going to see a tremendous number of innovations and experiments.
> Our job is to drive them and see which ones consumers really respond to.

eBay can only win if it out-innovates its competitors—global online behemoths like Amazon and Google and up-and-comers like Rakuten and Alibaba, as well as the increasingly sophisticated Internet operations of traditional brick-and-mortar retailers.

The Leader's Role in Creative Agility

Above all, what we saw in eBay Germany was the power of constant, rapid experimentation to fuel innovation. The German experience confirmed that innovation most often comes from learning by discovery, from trial and error, rather than careful, detailed planning.

Leaders foster the three elements of creative agility

In our research, we found that leaders of innovative organizations fostered the three key phases of creative agility (see figure 7-1).[4] Creative agility is the ability to:

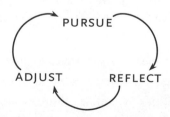

Figure 7-1 Three Elements of Creative Agility

1. **Pursue** new ideas quickly and proactively through multiple experiments
2. **Reflect** on and analyze the outcomes of their experiments
3. **Adjust** subsequent actions and choices based on what they've learned

It's important to note that these phases are iterative and recursive. They're iterative because in reality they're often done over and over when exploring an idea. Instead of *pursue-reflect-adjust ... done*, the process more likely is *pursue-reflect-adjust-pursue-reflect-adjust-pursue-reflect-adjust ... and on and on* until a solution emerges or it's clear the core idea won't work. Each iteration is recursive because it embodies adjustments learned from reflecting on the outcome of the previous iteration.

The number of iterations a group must go through to develop a breakthrough idea will depend on the complexity of the problem. Some problems require only a few iterations to solve; others take many iterations, sometimes spread over years.

Pursue new ideas quickly and proactively

Pursuing new ideas—vigorously, proactively, again and again—is not something most organizations do naturally. As we noted in chapter 2, they prefer to eliminate quickly as many alternatives as possible and commit to only one or two, rather than leaving their options open by testing several. They prefer planning over acting, in the mistaken belief that thorough planning will more likely produce real innovation. They try to define what the innovation will look like, often through something like a list of requirements or characteristics, and then lay out the steps that will produce such an outcome. But, virtually by definition, a real innovation cannot be identified in advance.

The most innovative teams proceed neither by detailed plans nor by no plans at all. Instead, they alternate brief periods of planning with longer periods of execution and improvisation. They scope out the problem or challenge, define a general direction to pursue for a solution, pursue it—if possible, by building a prototype to test in the real world, adapt it, learn, pause to do some brief replanning, and then try again, over and over.[5] As revealed by research, groups that took this approach turned out to be far more successful at innovation than groups that spent most of their time planning, rejecting options, and then betting on one approach. Innovative teams do some planning but focus on *acting* their way to the future, while less innovative groups focus on thinking their way ahead.[6]

The faster a group takes action and tries new ideas, the more ideas it can test. The more ideas it tests, the faster it learns. The faster it learns, the faster it can winnow out what doesn't work and find what does. The key to success for eBay German's micro-projects was that they could be developed and hosted locally, and that enabled the German team to try several ideas quickly. Speed is important, though—recalling the paradoxes—it must always be balanced by patience.

Leaders of innovation and their groups are willing to take calculated risks, tolerate mistakes and failure, and consider such outcomes not just inevitable but necessary for learning. If they don't experience some failure, they think they aren't trying enough options. Instead of eliminating variation, they consciously introduce alternatives, test assumptions in multiple low-risk experiments, and actively seek rich, real-time feedback. They are willing to proceed in new and unexpected directions based on what they learn. Sometimes leaders even create multiple teams to work on the same problem independently and then bring them together to foster cross-fertilization of ideas and approaches. Of course, they avoid any tests that might fail catastrophically and produce deep or lasting damage. This was why Justus and his colleagues agreed on a common set of security and safety standards that had to be met by all micro-projects.

Effective leaders of innovation are careful not to assign blame or punish anyone when something does fail. Conversely, leaders and groups that insist on thinking their way into the future usually fear and punish any efforts that don't succeed. They usually follow anything that doesn't work with a search for the guilty. It's no surprise, then, that they and their members are reluctant to try anything not certain to succeed.

Experiments are not pilots, though many people think they are. Pilots are usually the first phase in a course of action to which an organization has already committed itself. It's a test run, a chance to iron out the bugs, the first step in full implementation. Everyone expects that a pilot, with some tweaks and adjustments, will quickly morph into the full-blown new direction more or less as planned. And those running pilots are usually precommitted—deeply and personally—to their success because their careers and reputations are often on the line. Thus, the goal of a pilot isn't so much learning as it is making sure the pilot works, no matter what.

On the other hand, experiments like eBay Germany's micro-projects are about open-minded exploration. While those doing them certainly hope for and may even expect success, no one is personally committed to them and no one is deeply disappointed—or punished—when they don't work or when they point to a different direction. Hence, those running experiments can remain open to learning whatever the experiments tell them.

Reflect on the outcomes of experiments

Reflection or postaction analysis and review is where knowledge is harvested. It is what makes experiments valuable sources of learning, even when they fall short. Leaders of innovation not only encourage people to pursue new ideas but also demand that they reflect on the results, because only reflection will reveal the adjustments needed to make further progress toward a solution.

Reflection includes but goes far beyond a simple review of what happened. It should include active gathering of data, solicitation of feedback, and the rigorous, objective analysis of that information. Experiments should be conducted in a way that produces as much data and feedback as possible. Such a disciplined approach is part of the "how we think" rules of engagement discussed in chapter 5.

Reflection should also be done consciously, collaboratively, and openly. Critical metrics and key information should be readily available to everyone involved. Many groups skilled at innovation conduct formal postaction reviews in which all group members review the data, discuss the lessons to be drawn, and decide on adjustments and other next steps. There's nothing secret or exclusive about the process or the decisions that emerge. As Whitman observed, it's important to expect "excellent analysis."

Group discussions can, of course, grow heated; people can disagree about the interpretation of outcomes and data. The goal is to try to create a no-penalty culture, where people are free to change their minds or be on the wrong side of an issue with no penalty. "We're just different in the way we go about making decisions," Whitman said. "We have heated debates. We reach consensus or I make a decision. If I am wrong, I change it, and I don't take myself too seriously. But we made a pact that when we leave the room, you support the position. Very early on, we were explicit about that."

Adjust subsequent actions and choices

The goal of this phase is to identify the next steps in seeking a solution. Here the group identifies what actions to take next, based on the lessons that emerge from reflection. Many times, the adjustment will be a modification in the action just taken and another iteration of the pursue-reflect-adjust cycle. But adjustment may also include a determination that the experiment succeeded and should be rolled out or scaled up. It may also include a finding that the core idea won't work and should be either abandoned or set aside for the moment. Or it can even mean stepping back and using the new information to ask this fundamental question: is the problem really what we thought it was, or do we need to understand it in a new and different way?

Creative agility requires a leader who consciously creates and maintains a context in which the group can proceed through the pursue-reflect-adjust cycle quickly and effectively, over and over, until ultimately finding a solution. In short, a leader who expects both experimentation *and* progress.

As we saw, Justus and his colleagues recognized that sometimes structure and constraints can enhance creative agility. As they gained experience with the micro-projects, they realized the value of a certain amount of process and focus. Thus, they evolved the mini-product-planning process that encouraged experiments, while discouraging activities that obviously added nothing to the user experience. At the same time, they were able to apply advances in technology and statistical modeling to assess and learn from the results of the micro-projects.

Finally, to work well, creative agility requires a community. Common purpose and shared values provide a framework for creating and assessing experiments. And rules of engagement guide how a group thinks about problem solving and how it handles the potentially negative side effects of disagreement and conflict as results are assessed and new approaches planned.

We hired innovators, and if I were to forbid a passionate team to do something, it really would have misused their talents. I wanted people with a vision, and the ambition to build the next great thing. We needed to let teams go far enough so they could in fact discover this great new thing. Or, in another scenario, they'd recognize it was not quite right, then decide to work on something else, in the best-case scenario integrating their knowledge into another solution.

—**Bill Coughran**, then senior vice president of engineering, Google

CREATIVE
RESOLUTION

Many people believe that once solutions have been generated and refined through discussion and conflict (creative abrasion), then tested and further evolved through trial and error (creative agility), only one simple step remains: choose one of the solutions and run with it.

In fact, this third phase of the innovation process—creative resolution—is far from simple because the best innovative solutions often combine ideas, including ideas once considered mutually exclusive. Even if an organization has mastered the first two capabilities, without the ability to make integrative decisions innovations solutions will remain elusive.

To see this third capability in action, we turn to Google a few years ago and its then senior vice president of engineering, Bill Coughran. As he dealt with the mission-critical task of meeting Google's burgeoning need for data storage, we can see in some detail how he led his infrastructure group in a way that fostered its ability to innovate and, in particular, make integrative decisions.[1]

We will take a fairly in-depth look at how Coughran led his group because, to understand what he did to encourage this key capability, we must see his actions as part of the innovation leader's overall task—to create a context in which people are willing and able to innovate. Coughran was soft-spoken and rarely said, "Do this!" or "Don't do that!" But every day in virtually all he did, he was shaping the work and focus of the people in his group and the setting in which they did it.

The Storage War at Google

In early 2006, Coughran needed to resolve a storage war between two groups of passionate engineers. For two years, the groups had been pursuing two alternate ways of satisfying Google's voracious and rapidly growing appetite for storage capacity. The need to implement a new storage system was at hand; it was time for a decision.

Google's storage needs were both mission-critical and cutting-edge. The company obviously could not achieve its mission of organizing the world's information and making it "universally accessible and useful" without the right storage capacity and capability. Yet the requirements of the company, still only a few years old, already surpassed anything readily available off the shelf. No one had ever tried to build storage capacity of the scope and scale that Google required. The company was pressing on the edge of data storage technology and by its own efforts pushing that edge further and further out.

When Coughran joined the firm in 2003, Google's gross revenue was $1.5 billion—almost entirely from paid listings linked to searches—with an operating profit of $342 million.[2] Through its own website and portals like Yahoo! and AOL, Google powered over 75 percent of the 200 million searches conducted daily in the United States, and a similar share of the more than 300 million searches conducted daily outside the US.[3]

Developing storage systems to handle this enormous and growing volume was one of the key responsibilities of the one-thousand-person infrastructure group that Coughran led, along with web search infrastructure, web crawling, web search indexing, image search, and front-end serving.

Primarily a development group, the infrastructure group built the engine room, as Coughran put it, that not only allowed Google to do what it did but also provided a key part of its competitive advantage.

Coughran, age fifty, was one of several seasoned leaders Google brought in to help guide its explosive growth. He had headed the famous Bell Labs Computing Sciences Research Center, which created both the popular languages C and C++ and the near-universal UNIX operating system. He had also cofounded and served as CEO of Entrisphere, a Silicon Valley company ultimately acquired by Ericsson that developed hardware and software products to streamline and simplify data. He held bachelor's and master's degrees in mathematics from Cal Tech, as well as master's and PhD degrees in computer science from Stanford.

Google's evolving storage needs

When Coughran took over the infrastructure group, one of the most critical teams he managed was a group of engineers responsible for the Google file system (GFS). Specifically designed for Google's web searches, this then-new, highly sophisticated storage system provided unprecedented fault tolerance, ran on inexpensive hardware, and could deliver high aggregate performance to a large number of clients. It could handle the rapidly increasing number of web pages indexed, a critical component of the searches Google conducted for users. In Coughran's words, it was "designed to store large amounts of data ... incrementally adding more and more to one large collection of data and then ... streaming [it] ... back at massively high rates."

The problem was that new and different storage demands were emerging every second, largely because of applications, which were both a technical and a strategic expansion beyond Google's original exclusive focus on search. A key example: Gmail, Google's free e-mail system that offered users a gigabyte of storage, many times the amount then provided by rivals (for example, fifty times more, on average, than Hotmail and Yahoo!).

The success and rapid growth of Gmail—along with the steady expansion of other Google Apps, such as Google Talk and Google Calendar—put pressure on the company's storage systems. It was more than a simple need for more storage, though that by itself was a significant problem. Storing data for search and storing data for user-facing applications were very different, and GFS was optimized for search. There the technical challenge was storing large chunks of data in one massive file. But with applications like Gmail, the challenge was storing small pieces of data that were being generated asynchronously all over the world in millions of small files. It was the difference between streaming billions of web pages through processing engines and, as Coughran put it, "your aunt sending you a 300-character Happy Birthday message and being able to store just that."

What Google needed in a new storage system may not have been apparent, but it was clear that the current system, GFS, would soon require significant modification or replacement. This was not a one-time problem. Whatever replaced GFS would itself almost certainly need to be replaced in a few years. That was the long-term reality, though the immediate problem Coughran faced was to find the next system.

The infrastructure group

Like much of Google, the infrastructure group was then organized around three basic types of teams. First, there were small, self-selecting teams that emerged in response to some challenge or problem, or simply because one or two engineers had a great new idea. These start-up teams were typically small by design because Coughran preferred to keep groups at a more human scale. They rarely comprised more than five or six members, who often sat together in large rooms with cubicle clusters.

If and when such a project began to scale into a larger, ongoing activity—the GFS, for example—the team would grow in size, form subgroups to work on specific features, develop customer dependencies, and generally turn into a more conventional team.

The third type of team was not self-selecting. Rather, it was one Coughran created to fill some specific need. "Where I see strategic gaps," he said, "I will sometimes ask a specific set of engineers to come together and figure out how to build something." He might say, for example, "We have a problem here because this system is not, in my opinion, going to make it to the next stage of evolution, and we need a set of people to step back and think about some great new thing." Then he would handpick a new team to work on it.

Two storage teams emerge

As Coughran expressed concerns within the infrastructure group about storage needs, various teams began to self-select spontaneously around different solutions. In situations like this, Coughran and his senior people would look at the emerging alternatives and encourage the disparate groups to coalesce around a few promising approaches. In this case, they encouraged those interested to form two teams.

The first, said Coughran, "wanted to add systems on top of GFS. Adding software stacks like this—also called middleware—was common in the software world. The layers on top were designed to provide services that the layers underneath did not provide. The idea was for the software stack to support Gmail." This group was called the "Big Table" team.

The second group coalesced around three senior engineers in storage who were working on Gmail's back-end infrastructure. Younger and less experienced than those on the Big Table team, these engineers believed that the storage requirements of applications were so different from those of search that GFS could not be adapted; it needed to be replaced. They wanted to build a whole new system tailored for both search and applications. Hence, this group came to be called the "Build from Scratch" team.

Coughran let both teams spend their full time pursuing their ideas, a process that likely would take one or two years, even though he knew the teams would be working at breakneck speeds. "I thought they both had some very interesting ideas that were worth exploring, so I encouraged them to build prototypes," he said. He had a hunch, based on deep experience, that the Big Table approach was more likely to address Google's needs and that the Build from Scratch team would struggle to make its ideas work at the scale Google required. "But I did not know for sure," Coughran said. "I knew we didn't have all the data yet. No one in the organization ... could know for sure which system would be best in the future. Engineers on the Build from Scratch team were excited about building the next great thing, and ... they needed to experience firsthand the challenges their system would have. I did not want to be top down about this."

How Bill Coughran led the infrastructure group

Coughran naturally led his group in the deliberately loose way then encouraged by the founders, Larry Page and Sergey Brin. His nearly one hundred direct reports frankly made it virtually impossible to lead any other way. "Google always had a very bottom-up culture," he said, "and I wanted to nurture this." He gave as much freedom as possible to his engineers, "keeping the reins in enough so that we didn't degenerate into chaos."

It was a style he had developed at Bell Labs where innovative, ambitious engineering teams required a leader who could create a context for them to get their work done, not to set a vision for them to follow. At Google, he said, "I could have tried to control everything and walk around saying, 'No, you can't do that' when I saw people running astray. But that would have destroyed the organization, because it would have trained people to not make decisions until they got approval from me."

The loose management Coughran practiced was almost certainly necessary given the kind of people who worked at Google. Not surprisingly, the company attracted world-class technical minds, and the infrastructure group comprised some of the most experienced engineers in the company. As one engineer explained, work in infrastructure "wasn't all that sexy." It required a person "who genuinely loved the work for what it was; someone who loved to tinker with complex systems and maybe even love the process itself more than the end product." Because many engineers came from research labs and had PhDs, the group developed an academic feel, and its people expected to operate with considerable autonomy.

Google offered dual-career tracks—technical and managerial. Managers were not necessarily more senior than those on technical paths. In fact, the most respected leaders were usually technical leaders. To be accepted by engineers, a manager had to be seen as someone who could enter fully into a technical debate.

In addition, according to an engineer in the group, "Many people at Google made tons of money with the Google IPO, or from other Internet companies. Plus, for all of the talented engineers, it was easy to move to the hot new company next door if you weren't happy." Consequently, he said, leading at Google was like leading a "volunteer organization."

During his first two years at Google, Coughran assembled a "well-rounded portfolio" of leaders, his "brain trust," that helped him run infrastructure. It was a flexible system rather than fixed layers of permanent managers. His reports consisted of both technical leads (TLs) and engineering directors (EDs).

Tech leads were top engineers. One was assigned to every team and served in that function only for the duration of the project. They remained individual contributors, and their role was to provide technical guidance. "We needed to appoint one person as the tech lead," said a senior engineer, "because we needed someone to serve as a benign dictator in settling technical disputes. Of course, if tech leads wanted their teams to function well, they'd solicit lots of feedback from the team before making decisions."

Engineering directors, a common title in high-tech companies, were skilled engineers who served as managers. They were responsible for people management, keeping the team on schedule and budget, helping clear roadblocks and get decisions made, figuring out when more resources were needed, and providing coordination between teams whose work somehow overlapped. They were more long-term and big-picture focused, and they made sure the work of their teams stayed aligned with infrastructure's and Google's overall priorities.

The key difference between TLs and EDs, according to Coughran, was that TLs were strong technically "but perhaps a bit less patient." They were leaders without direct reports. EDs, on the other hand, were better on people issues and strong technically, though not as strong as TLs. Coughran wanted to avoid the mistake of many research organizations, which was to make the best technical people managers of people, a job they often didn't perform well.

Each ED had about thirty direct reports and was responsible for a particular aspect of the infrastructure group. The EDs met as a group every two weeks to update each other on the progress of their teams. These gatherings helped them perform one of their key functions—to act as connectors, the organizational glue, between groups within and outside infrastructure and to be sources of information about corporate and group priorities.

Coughran sought diverse EDs who could command the technical respect of engineering team members; who could attract, motivate, and retain the right kind of talented engineers; who could actually deliver systems; who could develop engineers and other managers; and who could deal with the ambiguity of innovative problem solving. But he looked for even more: "I needed leaders who were okay with not always having the last word in a conversation. That only resulted in a competition about who can talk fastest and loudest. I also needed leaders who could allow subordinates to make their own decisions, and even mistakes."

Management structures in the infrastructure group

While Google lacked many of the control mechanisms typical of a more traditional organization, it did institute a number of management structures and practices that eased the work of innovation. It provided yet another instance in the organizations we studied of finding the right balance between improvisation and structure.

A centralized group, for example, handled many aspects of locating and hiring new employees, all of whom had to pass interviews with at least six Google engineers. As a result, the company tended to hire people who were both smart engineers and driven personalities, who, as one engineering manager said, "loved the work they did, desperately wanted to succeed, and craved peer respect."

Though managers weren't directive, the organization was very clear about priorities. People were often asked to make the link between their ideas and those priorities. "As an engineer here," said one of the managers in infrastructure, "to a large extent you could do whatever you wanted. The trade-off was, there were a few things you absolutely had to do on time, and could not be screwed up."

To provide necessary guidance, dissemination of information, and social glue, Coughran established a quarterly summit that focused on particular topics. In these meetings, engineers and teams working in the same broad area met for a few days to share and discuss what they had learned and were planning next.

Above all, he expected his managers proactively to make links between groups with similar interests. With Google's dramatic growth and dispersion of groups worldwide, he was especially concerned that a team too focused on its mandate would "have blinders on." EDs had an important role in sometimes making more than connections. In some cases, teams were so heads-down driven that the manager had to "bump" them together to keep "insulated pockets from forming," Coughran said:

> I use the word bump [because] making an introduction's not enough. You start with the introduction but sometimes you have to say "Yeah, I know the two of you know each other, but have you actually talked to them about this particular failure mode they've seen?" That kind of thing. And then you have to make sure the conversation goes deep enough.

Engineering reviews

Perhaps, though, the key management practice in the infrastructure group was the engineering review. Such meetings were done either face-to-face or by video conference and occurred weekly, usually attended by Coughran and many of the EDs. For any one team, however, the reviews came less often. This was a key forum where creative abrasion could occur as teams discussed their work and responded to the questions, issues, and ideas of other engineers.

For the two storage teams, Build from Scratch and Big Table, Coughran conducted separate engineering reviews roughly every six weeks or twice a quarter. In fact, there was little contact between the two groups. This was partly a result of the physical distance between them (one in California and the other in New York), but it was also because their mandates were to explore separate, competing approaches, not to work jointly. Because they each knew something of each other's work, a sense of healthy competition had inevitably emerged.

In the reviews, a team reported on its current status and some of the challenges it was facing. Coughran would respond with guidance rather than direction. If he or his EDs had known what the teams should do or precisely the solution they should develop, there would have been no purpose in creating a team. So, teams like the two storage groups were given great freedom to pursue their competing ideas.

Yet an engineering review was anything but a simple update. A key purpose, in Coughran's words, was "to force teams to assess their progress relative to their goals." By asking penetrating questions in his soft-spoken way, he sought to "inject tension" and "intellectual reality" and encourage teams to push their thinking and challenge assumptions. He wanted to drive debate and intellectual honesty to make sure teams didn't get stuck and "the pieces were going to fit together."

To do this, he often drew on his own extensive experience. He frequently knew when a team was pursuing a path likely to encounter problems. As one of his EDs said:

> Bill would say something like, "I worry about ..." The concern could be related to cost, performance, latency, scalability, security, and so on. This had a way of conveying his concern in a nonthreatening way and allowed people to respond with the data or to leave knowing what data they needed to obtain.

Coughran rarely (though not never) said, "Don't do that" to a team. "You misuse their talent," he commented, "if you say, 'You can't do that.'" He wanted people to have a vision, an idea, for the next great thing and to go far enough that they recognized it was the next great thing—or it wasn't. "The thing I try to do," he said, "is get them to argue with each other and surface the data. We try to let data drive our decisions ... and make objectively based decisions." He also refrained from giving people answers when they asked questions. "You want to challenge people to think for themselves," he said. "You don't want a situation where they defer to you, because that, in my opinion, undermines the fundamental health of the organization."

Consequently, he was usually vague about what he specifically wanted from the engineering reviews. "Ninety percent of the value of having the engineers speak with me was the fact that they didn't know what I was going to ask," he commented. The uncertainty, he believed, created more value than any questions he might actually ask because it forced them to ask themselves such crucial questions as, "Are we doing the right thing?" or "Are we really making progress?" Equally important to him, it also forced them to speak with other groups as they tried to anticipate his questions.

This was the basic approach Coughran took in engineering reviews with the two storage teams. For example, with the Big Table team members trying to build software stacks on top of GFS, the company's current storage system, he questioned them about how well they could meet the performance needs of applications, such as Gmail, with its millions of individual e-mail transactions. And with the Build from Scratch team members who wanted to rethink and rebuild Google's storage systems from the bottom up, he continually pointed out the scale at which their system would have to operate—hundreds of millions of users generating massive amounts of data.

What he did not do was bring together the two competing teams to confront each others' ideas. Each team created its own marketplace of ideas where creative abrasion could occur. Then he and his EDs acted as cross-pollinators who carried ideas and challenges from one to the other.

He avoided direct debate because he believed that engineers tended to be highly opinionated and liked to be right. "If one team was building the perfect left-handed thing," he said, "and the other was building the perfect right-handed thing, and you put them in the same room, you may not get anywhere, even with a respected mediator."

Coughran much preferred to sort out conflicts with objective data. To do that, he had to let the teams develop their ideas to the point that they could be rigorously tested. But that required more patience than even some of his own engineers could muster. One of them, a twenty-six-year-old new hire working on GFS, came across the two competing storage teams and could not understand why Coughran would let the teams keep working if only one solution could be implemented.

So he found Coughran in his office one day and confronted him with the question. "I left the conversation understanding Bill's logic," said the engineer. "Allowing two different solutions to a problem to be worked on wasn't as crazy as it first seemed." Nonetheless, he still didn't understand why "the projects were being allowed to go on for such a long time."

Coughran understood the young engineer's concerns, but he felt any duplication of effort was trumped by larger considerations. "I needed to take the risk of letting them run" he said, "so that they could come to the realization, 'Oh, this isn't going to do what I thought.' I exercised personal judgment about when they would be ready to listen to a data-driven argument because people are not always ready for those arguments. You have to know when to cause a decision to happen. If there's an art to this, that's where the art is."

Time for a decision

After two years of letting the storage teams develop their ideas, it was time "to cause a decision to happen." By that time, Coughran had arrived at two conclusions: first, that neither team had found a long-term solution, and, second, that the Big Table approach, a software stack on top of GFS, was the better solution in the short term. He also believed, however, that the Build from Scratch team had made many interesting discoveries that would be useful in the future, even if its approach wasn't ready for implementation. His problem was that the Build from Scratch team was still charging ahead. In spite of encountering many perplexing failures when it tested its ideas, team members remained confident their methods would ultimately succeed.

About this time, Coughran hired Kathy Polizzi, an ED who would focus on storage, and shared with her his thoughts about the two teams and their approaches. "I did not just want to kill the [Build from Scratch] project," he told her, "because I only wanted to pull rank in extremis; I did not want to undermine future creativity. In cases when I did have to be dictatorial, I viewed it as a failure on my part."

The two of them spent much time discussing how to bring the New York (Build from Scratch) team to recognize that its approach was "not quite right." For that, they felt, the team had to "bump up" (clearly one of Coughran's favorite metaphors) against reality, and so Polizzi pressed it to bring its system to a semi-operational state and run performance and scalability tests. She set a time frame within which it had to eliminate concerns about the ability of its system to handle the massive scale at which Google operated. To do this, she and Coughran exposed the team to problems the current GFS had actually encountered. Showing the team "real use cases and real failure cases at full ... scale," she said, "made it clear to them what some of the challenges were."

Polizzi also put team members in joint meetings with the operations teams responsible for keeping Google up and running. These were the people whose pagers went off in the middle of the night when there was a problem. As she said, they "put a human face" on the problems, issues, and priorities that any new storage system would have to deal with.

Finally, she said, "the team started to see the limitations of the system they were building." By the fall of 2006, it had reached its own conclusion that its system, while it embodied many worthwhile ideas, could not yet fulfill Google's requirements.

On to next steps

In late 2006, the storage stack the Big Table team developed that sat on top of the GFS was implemented throughout the company. It was a distributed storage system designed to scale to huge sizes—petabytes (one thousand terabytes) of data across thousands of servers. In addition, it could support workloads that ranged from throughput-intensive web crawlers to latency-sensitive end users. It featured high availability even in the event of disk, server, and network failures, and it could handle the needs of both search and applications.

Meanwhile, Google's storage needs were expanding even faster than anticipated. For example, in October 2006, the company spent $1.65 billion for YouTube, a highly popular website for posting and watching videos. It was yet another type of application that added even more levels of complexity.

Coughran was convinced that, in the next few years, Google would clearly need a new storage system that surpassed the capabilities of both the Big Table and the Build from Scratch systems. In fact, he had already asked Google's two most-senior engineers, Jeff Dean and Sanjay Ghemawat, to start experimenting with prototypes for such a system, called the "next-generation system," and that work was taking on greater urgency.

After implementing the Big Table solution, Coughran and Polizzi faced another task: deciding what to do with the Build from Scratch team. It could join other projects already under way in the New York office or seek out other projects outside storage infrastructure. But Coughran and Polizzi chose a third option. They folded the Build from Scratch team into the team working on the next-generation system.

As Coughran said, he wanted to "orchestrate a solution to ensure that the knowledge they had gained got integrated in future systems." For Polizzi, the move was a way "to incorporate the Build from Scratch team into a mainstream, high-priority project" where the company could take advantage of the lessons it had learned. It would be a setting where its ideas had a greater chance of succeeding. "Part of the problem with their [original] system," she said, "was it was too focused on solving the specific application problem and thus not general enough." The next-generation system "would enable them to work on a more generalized, longer-term solution to a problem similar to the one they had been working on."

As it turned out, many of the discoveries of the Build from Scratch team did get incorporated in the next-gen system. "The original storage system," Coughran said, "had limitations in the number of files or data items it could handle," which was a problem for handling the requirements of Google's new, nonsearch applications. The design developed by the Build from Scratch team "allowed a much larger set of data objects or files than had been possible before ... That was a major advance." Other technical ideas about safeguarding data in the face of disk drive or server failure were also incorporated.

From one point of view, this story was about a contest between mutually exclusive approaches, only one of which would become the next storage system. From that perspective, it wasn't a story of integration at all. But from the larger perspective—obviously the more important one, given Coughran's mandate—it was indeed about integration: valuable ideas were developed by the team whose ideas weren't used right away in the next storage system. But Coughran recognized their potential value and made sure they remained in consideration for solutions even further down the road. As one manager observed, "Bill always kept his eye on where we needed to be at some point in the future."

By following the course he did, he achieved three important outcomes. First, the company found the better solution to its near-term problem. Second, it made progress on developing even more capable storage systems in the long run, so the company would be ready with new technology when it was needed. Third, and just as important, he developed an organization even more willing and able to let multiple ideas, even competing ideas, develop and mature.

As we look more closely at Coughran—how he thought and what he did to address an urgent, mission-critical problem Google faced—you may be thinking, "That's interesting, but what can we learn from a company like Google that had money to burn?" True, Google had substantial financial resources, but it didn't have a surfeit of superb storage engineers. They were the precious resource, and Coughran fully understood the value of their expertise to the firm. He also understood their need for autonomy and their desire to use those talents and expertise to solve challenging problems. As we've said, many did not have to work at all and virtually all of them could find other work inside or outside Google. The challenge for Coughran was to create a place at Google where they could do the work they wanted to do, in the way they wanted to do it. (See the box, "The Paradoxes of Creative Resolution.")

The Paradoxes of Creative Resolution

As he led the two competing teams in their search for the next storage solution, Coughran grappled with the two paradoxes that distinguish this capability.

Patience versus Urgency

The right balance between patience and a sense of urgency can spur innovation. But too much tilt in one direction or the other will produce the opposite outcome. Again, the leader of innovation must find the delicate balance that fosters new ideas and ultimate results. This was a key piece of Coughran's dilemma as he sought to give the two teams the time they needed to develop their ideas, all while urging them forward as quickly as possible to satisfy Google's pressing needs and bold ambitions.

Bottom-Up Initiative versus Top-Down Direction

Innovation most often comes from bottom-up initiative. Ideas emerge and people gravitate to them and seek to make them work. They stumble and learn from their mistakes and failures. Yet no organization can survive if its people work forever on anything and everything willy-nilly. Some boundary conditions and some degree of direction are necessary. But how much? When do you let proponents proceed with developing their ideas and when do you step in? This was Coughran's dilemma because Google could eventually only pursue one of the two teams' solutions. Yet Coughran didn't want to lose the ideas developed by the other. He had to find some way of integrating those ideas into the company's long-term storage strategy.

The Leader's Role in Creative Resolution

Brilliant solutions don't occur spontaneously, especially for the kind of complex problem we saw at Google. They come from working through ideas, options, alternatives, even failures and mistakes, and combining them in new ways to find the best solution. Indeed, the ability to see a problem whole and then integrate a variety of perspectives and ideas is a crucial part of the innovation process. It was a key concern of all the leaders we studied.

Unfortunately, real creative resolution happens infrequently. Most decisions are little more than the simple selection of one option, to the exclusion of all others, or some sort of splitting the difference between alternatives. What's needed, instead, is a healthy decision-making process like the one we saw in the infrastructure group at Google.[4]

It's easy to misread what a leader like Coughran was doing. His approach could seem too soft-spoken, too easygoing, too laissez-faire. Certainly it seemed so to the young engineer who questioned him about the two teams. Though he wasn't barking orders or making preemptive decisions, Coughran was carefully creating and shaping an environment in which his engineers were able and willing to innovate. He was proactively playing the role, in Vineet Nayar's words, of "social architect." We described his actions as a leader in some detail to show how he did that. Now we want to highlight a few of those actions that can help guide anyone leading innovation and trying to foster creative resolution.

Leaders guide their organizations to keep multiple options open

The best solutions appear when groups practice "both-and" thinking, rather than "either-or" thinking, when they're able and willing to work through the complexity of many possible solutions without choosing one prematurely.[5] To help them do this, leaders of innovation make sure there are community practices, values, structures, and rules of engagement that foster this kind of integrative decision making.

The ability to keep multiple options open requires what has been called an "opposable mind." Leaders and groups with this ability are able to "hold in their heads two opposing ideas at once." Then, "without panicking or simply settling for one alternative or the other," they're able to create a new idea that combines the two and is superior to both.[6]

This notion of the opposable mind helps explain why creative integration is so rare. For individuals and groups alike, working through complexity creates anxiety because it requires holding incompatible ideas without resolving them right away. We react to this internal tension by immediately trying to simplify it. We respond to complexity by converting its components to simple, stark alternatives; dealing with them separately; and eliminating all but one or a few. To ask people to keep thinking holistically, to forgo rapid simplification and reduction, is to ask them to live willingly in a state of tension and ambiguity.

Leaders who press this approach and expect it of their groups risk the ire of their people, because it flies in the face of what we often expect of those in charge. We want leaders to provide clarity and direction, not allow and even encourage confusion and turmoil, even temporarily. We expect our leaders to decide, to "pick one," as soon as possible. Indeed, we consider rapid and clear-cut decision making a hallmark of good leadership. Those who seem to put off choices are likely to hear people grumble, "What we need around here is some real leadership."[7]

Many leaders hold themselves to the same expectations. They're more comfortable in the role of visionary or expert, the one with the most foresight and insight who is prepared to act boldly. Integrative decision making provides no individual glory or thrill of victory and little sense of personal accomplishment. When it works, people find it hard to ascertain where a solution originated, let alone assign credit for it. It emerges, which is why so many people think it just appeared.

Integrative decision making also flies in the face of "chunking," a widely used approach to complex problems that involves breaking them into pieces and solving each piece separately. The problem with chunking is that it leads a group to lose any sense of the whole, of how the parts fit together, which reduces the possibility of recombining the parts in new and better ways.

Leaders and groups good at keeping options open are able to resist the pressure to make quick choices and move on. They're patient enough to cope with the messiness and complexity, and they're strong enough to admit they don't have immediate answers. They're confident the best solution will eventually emerge. They trust that the process will produce something better.

Leaders of innovation help build people's ability to do integrative decision making by the expectations they set. They don't tell people what direction to take, but they also don't hesitate to send teams back to keep looking for a better solution or to study a situation more closely. They create delays. They make clear that people must grapple with the complexity, not avoid it with simplistic choices. For example, Pixar CEO Ed Catmull, when presented with the choice between "buy more computers or delay *Cars Toons*," refused to accept such an either/or choice. And Bill Coughran at Google pushed each storage team to grapple with the kinds of problems the other team was addressing. Such leaders are willing to seem indecisive for a period of time—to endure the anxiety and tension of their people—in order to create time for ideas to develop and integration to occur.

Obviously, not every option can stay open forever. Some judgment is required. In the Google story, when Coughran socialized the storage problem, not two but four or five small groups emerged with different ideas. Coughran and his senior people believed that was too many to pursue simultaneously, and so they picked the two that seemed most promising.

After two years of study, it was time to choose the next-generation storage system. But instead of simply making what might be perceived as an arbitrary choice, Coughran and his manager guided the engineers to recognize the shortcomings of their own approaches. Even then, they made sure the team's cutting-edge but unused ideas—and the people who developed them—were fully engaged in the ongoing effort to create future generations of storage.

Leaders create the space for integration by keeping things simple, flexible, and open

Highly structured organizations with closely defined position descriptions; voluminous rules, policies, and procedures; and a rigid hierarchy tend to discourage the cross-role thinking and communication that foster integration. In contrast, effective leaders of innovation view structure in all its forms as a flexible tool for fostering the process of collaborative discovery and creative resolution. The storage group within infrastructure at Google was an example of this. Responsible primarily for the development of new systems and products, it comprised flexible teams that appeared and disappeared as needs arose and were satisfied.

Many leaders in our study had an aversion to excessive rules. Like Coughran, they preferred to manage by exception and to step in only when necessary. Instead of relying on formal structure to guide and control behavior, they found that informal or social structure (shared values, norms, social networks, and peer pressure) was more effective in most circumstances. They didn't hesitate to rearrange groups as needed, to change work assignments, and even to adapt seating arrangements to meet current needs for problem solving. In short, they viewed structure as a tool, a means to an end, not something that, once done, was done forever.[8]

They also paid much attention to physical work space. First and foremost, they created work and common areas that encouraged random interactions among people from all parts of the organization. They also created spaces that were easily adaptable. Furniture was portable, so that people could move around and work face-to-face. And technology, ranging from a rich social media environment and multiple means of interacting, was available to encourage engagement and relationship building. At Google, when high-priority activities spanned multiple groups, they would take over some large, open seating area and create a "war room" where people could wrestle together with a problem or project for weeks or even months.

Leaders of innovation lead differently

Coughran never tried to be the visionary, the expert, or the decisive "I'm in charge" leader. He and others tried to keep conventional management to a minimum. In the words of then CEO Eric Schmidt, managers at Google were intended to be "aggregators of viewpoints, not the dictators of decisions," because the company favored consensus and data-driven decisions in the belief that "the many are smarter than the few."[9]

That hardly meant that leaders like Coughran remained uninvolved or exercised little influence. On the contrary, in his inquiries during regular review meetings with each team throughout the storage project, for instance, he asked difficult and probing questions, raised points of view that needed more attention, shared information about what the other team was doing, and ultimately required each team to demonstrate that its ideas could work in real world settings. But he also gave the teams autonomy and responsibility. "One of the ways to preserve this culture of bottom up and people being able to take risks," he said, "is you've got to let people make choices, and make mistakes."

These were some of the key ways Coughran proactively and strategically created an environment for innovation. He specifically took this approach not just because he wanted a solution to Google's storage challenges. He also wanted to foster the ongoing ability and willingness of his organization to innovate beyond the current problem. "I never wanted to pull rank and tell a team to stop working on something they were passionate about," he said. "We hire innovators, and if I were to forbid a motivated team to do something, it really would misuse their talents."

Some engineers at Google pursued exploratory projects up to 20 percent of their time. Once an idea required further investment, however, it needed approval, or, as Coughran said, he and other senior leaders had "to figure out which ones to nurture." It was a fine balance between top-down direction and bottom-up initiative. Top-down direction worked when it was necessary because the decision-making process was clear and, whenever possible, data-driven, rather than arbitrary, and decisions were made in the context of the group's and company's purpose and goals.[10]

This kind of leadership also required patience. Google faced storage challenges of a scale never seen before, and everyone knew the problems would only grow even larger. What could be more urgent? Yet Coughran allowed the teams sufficient time to explore their ideas fully, calling for resolution only when necessary.

Managing those tensions, he found, was an ongoing challenge. While the technical dilemmas were unprecedented, Coughran believed the real issues of innovating at the scale and pace required were "people issues." "They're very hard to deal with," he said, "because you don't want an organization that just salutes and does what you say. You want an organization that argues with you. You want to nurture the bottom-up efforts. Occasionally, I have to say 'Whoops, you can't do that!' But I deliberately try to do that only once a month, on average, in my whole organization. I avoid that like the plague."

By avoiding a top-down decision and by forcing each team to experience for itself the strengths and shortcomings of its ideas, Coughran created a setting where each team could develop its approach fully. The outcome was more than a solution for the next generation of storage. It was even more than a major contribution to storage generations beyond the next. Members of both teams also emerged more able and more willing to take on the next innovative challenge.

With creative resolution, we complete our discussion of the three organizational capabilities—creative abrasion, creative agility, and creative resolution—that constitute the *ability* to innovate. We hope we've shown how they work together, iteratively and recursively, to help a group generate new and useful solutions. And we hope it's clear how all three depend on a group's sense of community based on common and compelling purpose, shared values, and common rules of engagement—the key components of the *willingness* to innovate. The innovation leader's role is to make sure all these elements are alive and well within his or her group.

Part III:
Collective
Genius 2.0

INVENTING THE FUTURE

I n researching and writing Collective Genius, we were privileged to meet and observe a number of leaders who had demonstrated their ability to lead innovative organizations. Our goal in working with them was to distill from what we saw a framework for leading innovation that was robust enough to capture the challenge but simple enough to guide action.

In chapters 1 through 8, we presented not only the framework but also a series of stories and portraits that, we hope, let you see leaders of innovation in action. We want you to learn from their experience.

We hope the lessons came through loud and clear. You can't plan for innovation or tell people to innovate, but you can organize for it. Leading innovation is about building an organization where individual slices of genius come together to create collective genius through collaboration, discovery-driven learning, and integrative decision making. To do that, you as the leader face two basic challenges.

First, you must create a place where people are *willing* to do the hard work of innovation with its inherent paradoxes and stresses. For that, you need to build a community with a sense of shared purpose, values, and rules of engagement. (See figure III-1.)

Second, you must create an organization in which people are *able* to do the work of innovation. You do that by building three organizational

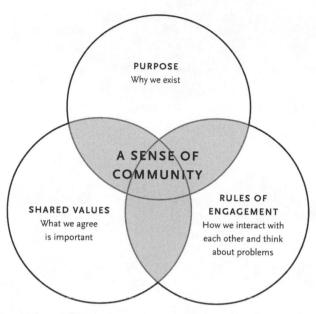

Figure III-1 The Willingness to Do the Hard Work of Innovation

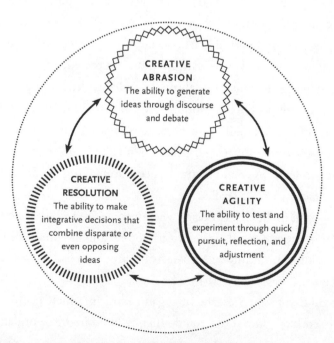

Figure III-2 The Ability to Do the Hard Work of Innovation

capabilities essential to innovative problem solving: creative abrasion, creative agility, and creative resolution. (See figure III-2.)

As the stories of our leaders made clear, this is not easy, though the effort certainly pays off. Imagine what your organization could accomplish if it were able truly to unleash and harness the slices of genius of all organizational members to produce breakthrough innovations again and again.

A Living Laboratory

But our journey isn't quite done. In our research, we came across some windows into the future that gave us a sneak preview of what's ahead for leading innovation.

We saw a handful of leaders who were conducting experiments to learn how to address a changing world. They were trying to create what we call "collective genius 2.0." The problems they aspired to solve, they found, required reaching outside the firm to locate collaborators, in some cases even across sectors. These leaders found what research confirms: problems no longer fit neatly into the ways companies and institutions, and even knowledge, have been typically organized. Finding solutions, these leaders realized, would increasingly depend on their ability to combine organizations and categories of expertise that had previously been separate and, in some cases, in competition.

These leaders were building ecosystems that broke down the traditional boundaries between organizations and even sectors. The challenges were obvious. Given the problems fostering innovation within the same organization, it's not hard to imagine the huge obstacles confronting a group of organizations that have never collaborated before.

In chapter 9, we follow along as Larry Smarr and his colleagues at the California Institute for Telecommunications and Information Technology (Calit2) figure out how to build the university of the future. Smarr had to make Calit2 "collaborative-ready," as he said, so that it could serve as a catalyst for the cross-sector innovation needed to improve the livelihoods and lives of California citizens.

We also introduce you to Amy Schulman, the executive vice president and general counsel, as well as the head of consumer health care, at Pfizer, the world's largest research-based pharmaceutical company. To produce the innovative and cost-effective solutions their rapidly evolving industry needed, Schulman and her colleagues set up the Pfizer Legal Alliance. In this ecosystem of outside law firms, longtime competitors had to collaborate, learn through discovery, and do integrated problem solving as if they were a single law firm.

In the epilogue, we turn to this critical question: where will we find tomorrow's leaders? The future depends on our ability to create the next generation of leaders of innovation. But if effective leaders of innovation don't think and behave like conventional leaders—as we've argued throughout *Collective Genius*—how will we identify and prepare tomorrow's innovation leaders? Once identified, what are the stretch assignments and social networks they need to be exposed to?

To consider these questions, we show how Steve Kloeblen, vice president of business development at IBM, went about building an ad hoc virtual community, the World Development Initiative (WDI), as a way to encourage values-based innovation at IBM. As that effort moved forward, Kloeblen found he was also building a boot camp for leading innovation and a cadre of leaders willing to work on new ideas beyond their regular jobs.

Next we present the story of Jacqueline Novogratz, CEO of Acumen Fund, a pioneer of the social enterprise movement that advocated a market-based approach to eliminating poverty. In the end, she and her team concluded that Acumen Fund had to get into the business of leadership development. With partners, Acumen developed the Regional Fellows program to build ecosystems of leaders at "the merger between business and society, with the 'moral imagination' to create solutions to global poverty."

Finally, we introduce Sung-joo Kim, chairperson and chief visionary officer of Sungjoo Group and luxury brand MCM Products AG. Kim's life story could be a blockbuster movie. Everyone told her she was crazy when she started a company, composed predominantly of Korean women, with the goal of building a billion-dollar fashion enterprise. But Kim and her small organization were able to beat the odds and compete successfully head-to-head with leading luxury brands like Louis Vuitton and Prada. Her experience reminds us that many talented people in all parts of the world—such as women in South Korea—have been largely invisible because of stereotypes based on age, gender, cultural, and other differences. Identifying—despite these stereotypes—who really has the right stuff and offering them developmental opportunities to become leaders of innovation are the matters to which Kim has devoted her life.

We end with these short stories about collective genius 2.0 to inspire you to start experimenting and creating your own collective genius. You needn't be a genius yourself. All of the leaders we studied recognized their own shortcomings and were the first to admit that they were far from perfect. They feared and disliked being put on a pedestal. They constantly experimented to improve the way they led their organizations. They understood that taking the risks necessary to break new ground would inevitably produce missteps, "leadership breakdowns," and "unspectacular results," as one leader described them. That didn't deter them.

Will their organizations be able to sustain innovative success? Only time will tell. Leading innovation requires constant nurturing and adaptation.

WE'RE MAKING STUFF UP AS WE GO ALONG. WHAT WE'RE DOING NOW WOULD'VE BEEN IMPOSSIBLE A YEAR AGO. THERE ARE NO MODELS, NO BOOKS. IN FACT, WHEN WE STARTED THE COMPANY, WE LOOKED THROUGH BUSINESS BOOKS BECAUSE WE HAD NO IDEA HOW TO RUN A BUSINESS. THEY WERE OF NO USE WHATSOEVER. IMPORTANT IDEAS LIKE "VALUE YOUR PEOPLE" ARE BOILED DOWN TO THESE CATCHPHRASES THAT EVERYONE SAYS BUT NO ONE REALLY KNOWS WHAT IT MEANS TO LIVE BY. THE ESSENCE OF THE LESSON OFTEN MISSES THE LESSON. WE'RE NOT JUST MAKING UP HOW TO DO CG MOVIES; WE'RE MAKING UP HOW TO RUN A COMPANY OF REALLY DIVERSE PEOPLE WHO CAN MAKE SOMETHING TOGETHER THAT NO ONE COULD MAKE ALONE.

—**Ed Catmull**, cofounder, Pixar, and president, Pixar and Walt Disney Animation Studios

CULTIVATING
AN INNOVATION
ECOSYSTEM

Many of today's toughest challenges are so big and complex that they don't fall neatly within the boundaries of existing organizations or traditional ways of structuring knowledge. Solving them requires the expertise and perspectives of multiple disciplines.

That calls for new ways of innovating across traditional boundaries—fields of knowledge, organizations, public institutions, governments, and even nations. It calls for innovative ecosystems or what we term collective genius 2.0—open innovation across organizations, networks, or sectors.[1]

More and more organizations are now experimenting with this approach.[2] They're trying to tap into pools of insight and expertise both inside *and* outside their borders.[3] As the size, complexity, and consequences of problems keep growing larger, these efforts and experiments will surely increase as well.[4]

Unfortunately, innovative ecosystems often fall apart, in spite of everyone's best intentions. Reasons aren't hard to find. Competing goals, self-interest, past practice, different operating methods, clashing cultures and values, a history of competition, a lack of experience with such collaboration—all these negative forces simply overwhelm whatever positive forces brought the group together initially.

A growing number of practitioners and researchers are working to understand what it takes to build such border-jumping ecosystems. Most of what's known so far has emphasized structure and governance, which are important, but not, from what we've observed, the only ingredients needed for them to succeed.

The role of the leader has received only limited attention. Leaders face many challenges simply trying to foster the willingness and ability of their own organizations to innovate. Add the extra complications of fostering collaboration among separate and diverse organizations and the process becomes all the more complex, difficult, and even chaotic. When partners outside the boundaries of a single organization must collaborate, leaders must create collective genius across external boundaries higher and wider than any they've faced internally. The implications for leadership would seem to be profound.

Because of the nature of the problems they hoped to address, two of the leaders we studied found themselves building such innovative ecosystems. Both were not only surviving, but thriving. It's reassuring to know that, though many ecosystems fail, some have been able to flourish for years. They can provide valuable insights.

In this chapter, we briefly profile two particularly ambitious ecosystems and share some of our thoughts about the critical role of the leader. It is certainly too simplistic to assume that leading innovation in an ecosystem is the same as leading innovation in a single organization, and we don't claim to have all the answers.

But it's worth asking the question, what do leaders of innovation ecosystems do? How do they foster a group's willingness and ability to innovate when that group comprises a collection of disparate organizations not accustomed to the kind of collective, close, creative collaboration that innovation requires—groups that previously pursued different interests and may even have been competitors?

The answer is important because whatever it takes, that is what break-throughs will require in the future.

Calit2

Over a decade ago, the state of California created four research insti-tutes intended to ensure that the state, in the words of then Governor Gray Davis, would "maintain and expand its role at the leading edge of technological innovation in the twenty-first century."[5] The chancellors of the University of California, San Diego (UCSD), and the University of California, Irvine (UCI), two state university campuses located about a hundred miles apart, applied as partners to establish one of these organi-zations, the California Institute for Telecommunications and Information Technology (Calit2, or the Institute).[6]

The goal was to create an environment outside normal institutional boundaries where researchers could move quickly to pursue large, complex projects that cut across multiple departments, campuses, and disciplines. Through the Institute, faculty would connect with partners around the world, including global companies and industries; local, regional, and state governments; and researchers at other universities and institutions.

While the development of the proposal for Calit2 was underway, Larry Smarr was recruited to help set up and head the Institute. A PhD in physics, Smarr had been founding director of the National Center for Supercomputing Applications (NCSA), which later evolved into the National Computational Science Alliance, a coalition of over fifty colleges, universities, government labs, and corporations whose purpose was to prototype the information infrastructure of the twenty-first century. In that and other positions he had played a transformational role in many of the key IT developments of the previous decade, including the Internet and the web.

Several features of Calit2 attracted Smarr. At NCSA he had already seen that powerful innovations could emerge when researchers from dif-ferent fields worked together. He believed collaborative models of research and innovation were better suited for addressing today's complex prob-lems and opportunities. Calit2 would be a place where those models could be explored and developed. Between the two schools, he said, the

Institute could "field a team of experts for every problem." That would give it the potential to make "unique, substantial contributions" to the great challenges of the twenty-first century in such fields as health care, energy, climate change, water sources, and digital culture. Finally, he felt that universities needed to fill a growing and troubling void—to perform the long-term research that companies no longer did because heightened competition forced them to focus on the near term.

Smarr knew the leadership challenges at Calit2 would be great. "We are disruptive in principle," he said. "We cut across twenty-four departments and many different schools on two separate UC campuses, and we can do things at a faster speed than almost any other part of the university." To fulfill Calit2's role as a catalyst for research that brought together engineering, physical sciences, digital arts, medicine, and public health, as well as the biological, behavioral, and social sciences, he had to get individuals who were used to great autonomy to collaborate *voluntarily*. He would have no formal authority to push them together. They would come together at Calit2 only because of their shared interests and passions.

As the UCI chancellor Michael Drake said:

> As much as we say we want to do things in a new way, the fallback is to revert to our traditional patterns of working alone. Collaboration takes energy. We also have to convince our faculty that investing in multidisciplinary projects is a good use of their time. At research universities such as UCI and UCSD, faculty are rewarded for their individual contributions to their field. Assistant professors are granted tenure for original work that tends to be narrow and focused in one discipline. Then we turn around and encourage these faculty to work with other departments on wide-reaching projects. It's a bit of a leap of faith for them.

Pfizer Legal Alliance (PLA)

Most people don't think of the law as a profession ripe for innovation. But Amy Schulman, general counsel and executive vice president of Pfizer, the global pharmaceutical company, didn't share that perception. When she joined Pfizer in 2008, she believed that her legal department had a strategic role to play at Pfizer, given the revolutionary changes—scientific, technological, and regulatory—sweeping through the health-care industry.

But to play that role, she believed her group had to reinvent how it partnered with Pfizer's business units and how it worked with the company's extensive network of outside counsel. Not only did she undertake a major reorganization of her division, but she also, to the surprise of many, created the Pfizer Legal Alliance (PLA), an ecosystem comprising nineteen of the company's external law firms that would perform the lion's share of its legal work. Perhaps the most striking sign that the PLA would take a different approach was that it abandoned the traditional, almost sacrosanct, "billable hour" for paying outside counsel and replaced it with a structure of flat fees.

Schulman wanted a new approach to legal collaboration and was saying to outside firms, in effect, that she wanted them to be a hybrid between an outside lawyer and an inside lawyer. As cases grew more complex and dispersed over multiple jurisdictions they required more collaboration among different firms. This pressure was making clear to many in the legal profession that the old model of "every firm for itself," based on the billable hour, no longer produced the best legal work for clients.

A firm like Pfizer relied on a national network of outside firms. A single blockbuster drug could spawn thousands of suits, filed in thousands of different jurisdictions around the country. Many of these cases revolved around the same or similar legal issues. They often required highly specialized expertise and in-depth research about particular legal or scientific matters; expertise that was difficult for any single firm to acquire and provide. Because "litigation is local," as one lawyer explained, Pfizer couldn't send corporate lawyers from one state to argue cases before judges and juries in other states, where they might be viewed with suspicion. Consequently, Pfizer often had to hire a cadre of firms across the country to meet their legal requirements.

Schulman knew that if companies like Pfizer could transform its network of law firms into a true collaborative community, the potential advantages would be enormous: for any specific case or type of case, the network could combine representation by different firms, each bringing its own strengths. It would be more efficient and less costly to have firms share knowledge, expertise, and research. Over the long term, it would allow deeper relationships to develop between Pfizer and the various firms, and as the firms got to know Pfizer better, they could deliver more proactive legal advice. Such a community would also give Pfizer access to the best of the best lawyers from a collaborative collection of top law firms, allowing the company to assemble teams quickly that could deal most effectively with highly complex issues involving litigation, regulatory, compliance, securities, and health and safety components.

All this depended, however, on getting the outside firms to function as a single law firm. The traditional system of building a network of outside firms competing for a bigger share of the billable-hour pie could not produce any of these benefits. With the growing complexity and size of today's legal cases, that was a fatal shortcoming. Changing the system began with replacing the billable-hour model with negotiated flat fees. But the goal wasn't just to save money. It was to produce the best possible legal work, work that demanded innovative solutions, for Pfizer.

Figuring out how to turn the PLA into a community *willing* to work together and do innovative problem solving was Schulman's first order of business. All the firms shared the same client, Pfizer, and subscribed to a common professional ethic—that the client needed and deserved their best legal work—providing the basis for a sense of shared purpose. But the core question she had to address was this: can the practice of law across competing firms be a team sport when that's not how the legal profession has always operated? Schulman had to bring together lawyers from competing firms and lead them not just to cooperate but genuinely to collaborate, which required unprecedented trust.

Virtual law firms were notoriously difficult to manage. As a colleague of Schulman explained:

> In a virtual firm, a client asks you to work with lawyers from other firms, but it's rare that a real team ever develops. All the lawyers look out for their particular firm's interests. People are reluctant to share information. People are paranoid that others are going to get more credit and therefore more business. It's the opposite of collaboration.

Community Is the Key

Given such enormous obstacles, how have Calit2 and the PLA both survived and succeeded over several years? We don't have definitive answers, but comparing what we saw in them with what we saw in the innovative organizations we studied leads us to some observations.

What we saw did confirm the importance of structure and governance. As they gained experience with Calit2 and the PLA, both Smarr and Schulman found they needed strong governance structures. Where multiple distinct organizations needed to collaborate, clear boundaries and roles, along with standardized processes—ways of working together—became even more important. And, certainly, their ecosystems required a robust infrastructure of processes and tools that facilitated the work of collaboration and innovation.

However, the major challenge for Smarr and Schulman, as we observed, was not simply to create capability, but also to cultivate willingness among the different, often competitive and contentious individuals and groups that belonged to their respective ecosystems. Innovative groups inside the same organization at least begin with a rudimentary preexisting bond—their connection to the same firm or institution—but those in an ecosystem don't even enjoy that small advantage.

Given ecosystems' inherent complexity and high potential for conflict, it's no surprise that a leader's initial impulse is often to begin with a legalistic focus on structure and governance, that is, to define the relationships among members, their relative rights and privileges, and the rules that govern who gets to do and decide what.

Those are important considerations, but the flaw in focusing on them exclusively or primarily becomes apparent when you recall the first and most fundamental task of an innovation leader. Since all innovation is ultimately voluntary, it must begin with the *willingness* of those involved to do the hard work of innovation: collaboration, discovery-driven learning, and integrative decision making. If that was true for innovation inside a single organization, it's especially true for innovation in an ecosystem of diverse organizations.

Rules of governance and structural clarity can remove obstacles that might block people's willingness to innovate, but they cannot create that willingness. Something more is required. That "something" is the same for an ecosystem as it is for a single organization. It is community: the sense of being joined in a worthwhile cause, of pursuing a common compelling purpose built on shared values. Without this social fabric, no ecosystem can survive long enough to accomplish much.

What we observed at Calit2 and the PLA were leaders who understood this reality and worked hard to create the necessary social fabric. They understood the need for rules and structure, but they also knew that these elements alone would not counter the forces of disintegration constantly working to pull their communities apart. That required the willingness of the individuals and groups in their ecosystems to innovate together. Without willingness, there could be no collective genius. And the key to willingness was to create a sense of community around a common cause.

Building Community at Calit2

For Smarr, the process of building community began even before Calit2 formally existed. To prepare the proposal for creating the Institute, the two campus deans of engineering repeatedly brought together a multidisciplinary group of researchers from faculty at both UCSD and UCI, while Smarr was still being recruited. The deans, and later Smarr, led these groups through multiple, often grueling meetings to generate a detailed statement of what Calit2 would be and how it would operate.

Agreeing on purpose

One of the first and most important steps they took was to identify the four strategic applications, specific areas where Calit2 would focus its efforts: environment and civil infrastructure, intelligent transportation, digitally enabled genomic medicine, and new media arts.

Identifying these specific areas was important because the state's mission for the four research institutes—to "maintain and expand [California's] role at the leading edge of technological innovation in the 21st century"—was necessarily broad and aspirational. It was, however, too general to attract faculty researchers. To succeed, Smarr and the group had to translate it into specific areas that would attract academics interested in doing specific and real research that interested them. The four specific areas created the purpose that aligned the Institute's broad mission with researchers' passions and interests. As Smarr recalled, putting together the proposal was an important "forced march," a way to "identify and bring together the right faculty and collectively develop a common purpose," which could serve as the foundation for a vibrant innovative community.

Leading in this way from the very beginning was critical for Smarr because he had virtually no formal authority to compel cooperation and participation. For that reason, he had to respect and work within the universities' existing and jealously guarded systems of rights, privileges, and infrastructures. Faculty retained their offices in their home departments. The Institute could not make academic appointments, and faculty reviews for promotion remained the prerogative of the departments. It would always be the faculty who ultimately chose their projects and partners. Smarr and the Institute would not dictate their research or the problems they addressed. He and the Institute would provide the necessary tools and resources, bring people together for fruitful collaboration, and act as a bridge between Calit2 and others around the world. Their role was to create a place where people from diverse domains could gather and innovate without determining or directing what they did.

As one of Smarr's senior Calit2 colleagues said, "Faculty work with Calit2 because we offer resources and a multidisciplinary collaboration environment that they don't find in their own departments. If we tried to tell faculty what to do, it would never work." From the very beginning, Smarr worked hard to foster the notion expressed by a UCSD dean of engineering: "Anything that helps Calit2 also helps us."

Agreeing on governance structures and rules for working together

Once the schools and faculty identified Calit2's purpose, Smarr could then work with them on the next step: creating governance structures that clarified decision-making rights, and developing the rules of engagement that guided researchers as they worked together and shared Calit2 resources.

The formal governance structure they developed was intended to allow and encourage inclusive decision making. Divisional councils with broad representation of faculty and staff were set up at both UCSD and UCI, each led by a division director who was a faculty member. Calit2 also had both internal and external boards. The internal governing board was composed of deans and the vice chancellors for research who made sure that Calit2's disruptive practices were executed in a manner acceptable to the rest of the UC system. The external advisory board was composed of distinguished individuals from the private, public, and government sectors that weighed in on matters with regard to possible future directions, long-term strategy, and how to diversify funding.

Early meetings and deliberations of the governing board often ran long. Smarr knew that detailed discussion sometimes frustrated people, but he wanted to ensure that all opinions were heard and none dominated. For people to become committed and responsible citizens of the Calit2 community, they had to feel they had a voice in what the community did and how it worked. In particular, he sought to avoid fissures along traditional lines—for example, departments or schools. University constituencies sometimes had differing priorities and concerns that could easily have torn at the fabric of the Institute if he had followed a less transparent approach. His goal in these discussions was not compromise but, as he said, "qualified consensus"—in other words, creative resolution.

Rules of engagement included a cost-sharing model and agreement about how much to spend in support of Calit2's extensive state-of-the-art facilities and how to govern use of those facilities. Another piece was an understanding that Calit2 wanted faculty to use widely available IT equipment and freely distributable software whenever possible. That saved money and, equally important, facilitated the dissemination and replication of ideas; in other words, it fostered creative agility. For example, Calit2 researchers built different versions of tiled visual displays out of dozens of large commercial PC flat-panel screens and created both the software for running the displays and a wiki where instructions and the software were freely available to anyone.

As one of the researchers who participated in all this preparatory work said, "It took more than a year to reach agreement, but the process laid the groundwork for collaboration among faculty." (See the box, "Future Patient.")

Fostering a sense of community

Smarr and his team shared a belief with many of the leaders we studied, that physical work space can play a key role in fostering a sense of community. They wanted work space that not only provided cutting-edge research tools

Future Patient

Future Patient is a Calit2 initiative that brings together computer scientists, clinical researchers, medical doctors, and patients to investigate "how the big data we are gathering across medical records, patient record symptoms, clinical measures and genomic and microbiome data can be used to foster a more scientific understanding of health," noted Jerry Sheehan, Calit2's chief of staff. The microbiome is the 10 trillion microbes that live and do crucial work in every human gut. Little understood, the microbes' crucial role in human health has only recently been widely acknowledged.

Future Patient uses software tools developed by Calit2 that display a patient's microbiome, clinical biomarkers, and other self-tracked data on the Institute's room-sized display walls. The hope and intent is that these large displays will allow researchers to compare visually healthy and diseased individuals' microbiomes, find correlations, and generate hypotheses that drive future research.

Data for Future Patient comes from Smarr's own personal data, along with anonymized data from subjects in the Human Microbiome Project at the National Institutes of Health. Calit2 runs the data through its supercomputer software to produce a visual breakdown of over three thousand unique microbe species that may be present in a person's gut.

After it had done this for an initial fifty-five individuals, the Institute began bringing in clinicians and researchers working on specific diseases to query the data on the displays. Based on their reactions, Calit2 refined and matured its software and then began working with actual health-care providers who were interested in seeing and helping develop the kind of medical information that is now cutting-edge but will be widely used in five to ten years.

but also expanded knowledge flows, physically encouraged connections, and increased the odds of serendipitous encounters.

At UCSD, San Francisco-based architecture firm NBBJ, with input from the Calit2 cross-departmental teams, designed a six-story, 250,000 gross-square-foot building (later named Atkinson Hall) with few walls and offices, an open environment where faculty and technical staff could share work space. The UCSD division director, Ramesh Rao, specifically chose office furniture that could be reconfigured easily and quickly to bring together groups of various sizes. A second Calit2 building of 120,000 square feet, this one on the UCI campus, was also designed so its spaces could be easily reconfigured to fit the needs of the teams currently using them.

"Having a building on each campus," said a Calit2 leader, provided "the opportunity to explore innovative uses of high-performance telecommunications systems—to tie the two buildings into a common 'collaboratory.'" This was made possible by one of many technology platforms provided by Calit2, a state-of-the-art fiber optic network that connected collaborators not only within and between the two schools, but also worldwide.

Calit2 provided office and lab space for researchers collaborating on projects, but no researcher or department was assigned permanent space. Calit2 was intended to serve as a project hub for faculty from different departments. Researchers were encouraged to share such specialized facilities as clean rooms, photonics labs, and media spaces at both schools. (See the box, "KAUST and State-of-the-Art Visual Displays.")

Creating such shared spaces was not always the obvious or easy approach; nor was it standard practice on campus. The Nano3 Lab, for example, Calit2's clean room at UCSD, was a shared facility that brought together for the first time at UCSD three fields of nanoscale research and development (nanoscience, nanoengineering, and nanomedicine). "Creating Nano3 was one of the formative cultural moments for the UCSD Division of Calit2," Smarr said. "Institute leadership had to resist the prior campus culture of dividing up the clean room space by faculty member or department. Instead, the UCSD division director facilitated discussions and encouraged the faculty to come back with an agreed upon open and shared facility with pooled equipment available to all." The result was a larger and better-equipped laboratory than anything a single department could have built on its own. It too was a space that encouraged connections and collaboration, as well as fostering a sense of shared purpose.

KAUST and State-of-the-Art Visual Displays

One of the Institute's more ambitious global partnerships was with the King Abdullah University of Science and Technology (KAUST) in Saudi Arabia. KAUST is an independent, merit-based, graduate research university of science and technology open to men and women from all cultures around the world.[7] KAUST aimed, like Calit2, to encourage bold and collaborative research that addressed both regional and global challenges.

Calit2 developed the KAUST Visualization Laboratory Showcase concept, then designed and deployed within the showcase large-scale LCD-panel-based collaboration and virtual reality systems, including the 3D NexCAVE, the REVE autostereo display, and a 40-megapixel tiled wall for SAGE and MediaCommons display, all the first and largest of their kind in 2009.

Calit2 worked with KAUST's Visualization Lab staff to install this technology on the new campus in Saudi Arabia, where it has been used to visualize huge biochemistry and earth sciences data sets, as well as to collaborate in real time with researchers worldwide.

Becoming a catalyst

The way Smarr and his colleagues led Calit2 was influenced heavily by the approach taken at AT&T's legendary Bell Labs where UCSD Chancellor Bob Dynes and several key Calit2 founders had worked.[8] (Recall that this was also true of Bill Coughran's group at Google.) The leadership structure there had been decentralized and relatively nonhierarchical. Formal leaders at Bell never felt it was their responsibility to set direction and get others to follow. Instead, according to one of the researchers who'd worked there, leaders acted as "the first among equals" whose principal role was to create an environment where talented people could work together to solve problems they were passionate about. Like Bell Labs, Calit2 was a fluid environment in which faculty could come and go based on their current projects. Research would be self-organizing, with researchers ultimately choosing each other as collaborators.

Instead of being the one guiding or directing the action, Smarr saw himself primarily as a catalyst. It was his boundary-busting job to bring together the right people, perhaps plant some ideas, and get them talking. The rest was up to them. Thus, in his frequent interactions with faculty, he made a point of asking questions and listening deeply so as to understand how he could make connections among them.[9] As one faculty member said, "Smarr doesn't start with preconceived notions. He is more likely to make introductions." Another colleague called him a "dot-connector extraordinaire." He was particularly good in that role because of his deep scientific knowledge and curiosity about many fields, which enabled him to talk with and gain the respect of specialists in many disciplines. It was an approach that helped him deal with hundreds of faculty across two separate campuses, as well as hundreds of industry and government partners. A small but telling example: over time, he moved his office at the Institute three times in order to be closer to the action and encourage chance encounters. (See the box, "The Wildfire Initiative.")

Building bridges to the outside world—and the future

Once the Institute was under way, Smarr's role as catalyst and connector took him beyond the two universities and led him to build bridges between the Institute and the wide world outside. Some of this was as simple as attending the best conferences in search of new ideas across a broad range of disciplines. The goal, in Smarr's words, was to "sense the emerging future before it's widely recognized" and give a head start to Calit2's innovation teams. He was also often on the road talking to diverse groups about the new ideas bubbling up at the Institute. "Getting more people aware of early-stage innovations and innovators," he said, was a way to attract the best talent and partners to Calit2.

Through faculty research, the Institute has connected with others around the world—including researchers in many locations such as Italy, Saudi Arabia, and Mongolia. Many projects have involved global partnerships that allow faculty to create and test solutions in real-world contexts.

The Wildfire Initiative

Smarr and his colleagues built strong local, regional, and state relationships. In the Wildfire Initiative, for example, the Institute worked with emergency first responders in southern California to develop information technology for crisis response.

Recent firestorms, considered in aggregate the worst natural disaster in that region's history, revealed the importance of reliable and timely information. To save lives and property, crisis responders—firefighters, police, county officials, health-care providers, and others—need good information about what resources (for example, police, firefighting, rescue) are available where, the state of civil and transportation infrastructures (for example, roads and bridges still open), and not only the current location of a fire but also the direction it's likely to take.

Calit2 experts took a multidisciplinary approach in working with responders to apply the power of IT to these problems. They put together teams of experts in IT, social sciences, organizational behavior, and disaster management. They built on the powerful infrastructure of the San Diego Supercomputer Center's High-Performance Wireless Research and Education Network. According to a description of the effort on the Calit2 website, its goal was "to radically transform the ability of responding organizations to gather, manage, use, and disseminate information within emergency response networks and to the general public."

The Institute also had major engagement with such industry partners as Qualcomm, Ericsson, Boeing, and Emulex. The nature of the private-sector relationships has varied. Some commercial partners have posed specific problems, and Calit2 formed a team with representatives from the university and industry to focus on finding a solution for each. Some industry partners have used the Institute as a center to test prototypes or commercial products. Still others used the unique facilities at the two buildings, such as clean rooms or telecom labs. Creating and maintaining these relationships quickly became an important aspect of Calit2's work and a growing part of the Calit2 leadership team role. These partnerships, in which both sides had much to learn from the other, allowed the Institute to investigate a wide variety of research questions and issues.

A key part of Calit2's and Smarr's roles was to be out on the edge. (See the box, "CineGrid.") Smarr commented:

> As a leader, it is important to be looking for new multidisciplinary emerging opportunities and then convene the faculty, staff, students, and industrial partners to discuss how to get a working prototype going before the funding calls come out. That way the team has gotten to know each other and a lot of the rough edges have been smoothed off. This "team-building before you need to" is one of the reasons Calit2 has been successful.

CineGrid

Calit2 helped to give birth to CineGrid, a public-private partnership with the US entertainment industry, especially that portion located in California, to explore how emerging digital technologies will transform that industry. In moviemaking, for example, it covers everything from the impact of ultrahigh definition to the way technology will change every stage of the process from conception to shooting, editing, and distribution.

Calit2 has played a double role in CineGrid. Working at the intersection of industry and academia, it was able to act as a convener that transcended the two worlds and could bring together both university researchers and Hollywood talent to talk about overlapping interests. Then, having created this forum, Calit2 could play its second role as a technology developer. In that role, it has showcased some of the emerging technologies it's working on that illustrate potential opportunities. "You get together a multidisciplinary group," said Sheehan, "and then you show them a new capability with data relevant to them, and that becomes a synergy for thinking about future collaborations."

Smarr's role as a bridge builder both inside and beyond the universities quickly became self-reinforcing, and people and institutions began to approach him. The CEO of a local organization dedicated to growing San Diego's innovation economy said, "I work in the research community every day, and yet when I have to really figure out some complex technology," she would go to Smarr because he was a "walking inventory of who's doing what." She commented further,

> The other great thing about Calit2 is how they are connected to lots of places around the world where we don't really have contacts. And so to be able to access the faculty's outside connections is hugely important. Calit2 is looked at favorably and has really become, in terms of the business community, the go-to place for looking at big problems.

Now more than a dozen years old, the Institute has clearly succeeded in what it set out to do. The number of researchers, industry partners, and federal grants, and the amount of money received from industry and government have exceeded initial projections. It has also captured the attention of academic peers around the world. UCSD and UCI faculty have been clearly engaged, judging not only from the number of projects initiated but also from the number of faculty who have simply shown up at Calit2 meetings and taken an interest in its work.

Even now, as we write this, the Institute continues to evolve and grow. It still focuses on the areas outlined in the original proposal. But to those areas, in response to events subsequent to its creation—for example, the 9/11 attacks, California wildfires, and Hurricane Katrina—Calit2 has added a new application area: public safety and disaster response. The Wildfire Initiative is an example of its work in that area.

Also based on its experience, the Institute recently revised its mission statement to read: "The mission of Calit2 is to unite faculty, students, and research professionals at UCSD and UCI with private and public sector partners to explore how emerging information technologies and telecommunications can transform areas vital to the state's economy and its citizens' quality of life."

Much of its ability to function and succeed goes back to its leader's wisdom in focusing from the very beginning on working inclusively with potential members to build a purpose-based community. One of Smarr's colleagues said:

> There was a critical importance to developing our strategic mission. The initial Calit2 proposal was developed by a community with faculty input from both campuses. It helped tease out what contributions they could make individually and collectively. The unique research projects that followed were then a virtual road map for achieving that mission.

Will Calit2 survive when its founding leader eventually departs? Former UC president Richard Atkinson commented on that question:

> Calit2's biggest challenge will be transforming itself from an experiment into an enduring part of the two campuses and the University of California as a whole. But great institutions continue to thrive after their founders depart. Calit2's track record and momentum will make it attractive for Larry's successors to continue the institution.

Building Community at the PLA

The Pfizer Legal Alliance was Schulman's second ecosystem. Before joining Pfizer, she had been a litigation partner at DLA Piper, one of the world's largest law firms with over three thousand lawyers in twenty-five countries.[10] Her client roster included a number of *Fortune* 100 companies, including Pfizer.

Like most large corporations, Pfizer had relied on hundreds of outside firms to do its legal work. But that approach had grown unsustainable, and in 2005 it announced that henceforth it would place nearly all its product liability work with a small group of external firms—preferred providers. It chose Schulman and her team at DLA Piper to serve as lead national counsel specifically to handle lawsuits involving COX-2 inhibitors. In this role, Schulman had to lead a group of hundreds of lawyers spread across twenty firms around the country in developing and executing a strategy for dealing with the lawsuits. She was determined to create a real law firm out of these diverse and competitive players, almost all of whom worked for traditional—that is, hierarchical and status-driven—law firms.

This approach hardly functioned perfectly all the time, but overall it was considered a great success. The number of billing lawyers decreased by over 60 percent. Assignments were better and more efficiently deployed, and the legal work was superior, Schulman thought, to that typically done by traditional collections of outside firms. Where there were problems, she found, the root cause was often the billable-hour model. Not only was it expensive, but it promoted inefficiency, discouraged proactive legal counsel, and was a barrier to building the client-firm relationships and cross-firm collaboration that clients deserved.

Joining Pfizer as general counsel gave her the opportunity to address this issue directly. When she set up the Pfizer Legal Alliance, building on her experience with her previous ecosystem of outside lawyers, a key part of the relationship was a system of flat fees that replaced the billable hour. Some outside firms balked at the arrangement and didn't apply to join the PLA.

Schulman and her Pfizer team were careful to accept only top-flight firms that were willing to experiment not only with a new payment system but a new way of doing legal work. As one team member said: "In addition to their skills and geographical footprint, a key criterion in selection was a willingness to collaborate with other firms, a willingness to experiment in how their fee was calculated, and an interest in being a pioneer."

That was only a start, however, in building a sense of community.

Inclusive leadership

Calit2 and the PLA differed in that the Institute was entirely voluntary, while outside firms in the PLA worked for Pfizer, the client, once they consented to join. Nonetheless, Schulman understood that a shared approach to leadership would be essential for the PLA to work. From the start, she clearly expressed her expectation that member firms should learn and work together to address Pfizer's evolving needs.

While Schulman technically headed the PLA, her position involved other responsibilities as well, and so she quickly concluded that the PLA needed a point person, a real hands-on leader to provide the nurturing and constant attention it required. She appointed Ellen Rosenthal as the

PLA's chief counsel. After a careful review, Rosenthal set up a steering committee that, besides herself, included the lead Pfizer lawyers for litigation, corporate governance, and research and development. Among other responsibilities, this steering committee set the annual flat fee for each PLA firm.

The flat fee arrangement, a key element of the rules that governed how the PLA worked, was so radical for all involved that it required careful and regular attention. Pfizer didn't dictate a fee for each firm and then work with it in traditional ways. Instead, the steering committee worked closely with each firm every year to understand its anticipated workload for the year ahead, including possible contingencies, and based the fee on that mutual assessment. As Rosenthal said:

> We spend a lot of time with our firms working on how to manage on a flat fee. In a land of unlimited resources, you just call a lawyer and say, "Do this project for me." Now we call the law firm and say, "This is how we think we should manage this together." We don't want a fifty-page memo that we're never going to look at ... We like the one-paragraph answer. Don't caveat it fifty different ways. Just say, "Our gut reaction is X, Y, Z. Should we go forward and do some more work on it?" So it's the kind of thoughtful work most helpful to our in-house lawyers and clients. It's more efficient. It gives us better, quicker answers. And it allows us to make decisions more intelligently. The PLA collaborative allows us to work closely with all of our PLA lawyers to focus on delivery of targeted, efficient, and strategic legal advice.

Besides the steering committee, Schulman and Rosenthal created a group of roughly fifteen senior lawyers about equally split between Pfizer and the outside firms that had no formal title but was generally referred to as the "PLA Leadership." This group met regularly at roundtable meetings in the United States and Europe where it made key decisions, addressed the many evolving challenges the PLA faced, and set strategic direction. For example, it took on the difficult task of developing performance metrics for PLA members and a 360-degree performance review process in which both Pfizer and PLA lawyers received feedback twice a year.

Over time, the number and mix of outside firms in the PLA evolved. Most changes were due to shifts in Pfizer's legal needs. But some relationships did not work as intended. Some firms left and new firms replaced them. Senior partners from PLA firms participated in the interviewing and selection process of these new firms.

Rosenthal also introduced operational tools, including an online communications hub, the PLA Exchange, which connected the more than seven hundred Pfizer and PLA lawyers spread around the country. An online "commons," it was a useful tool that not only linked everyone but helped build transparency and trust and encouraged sharing of information and insight. In addition, to manage work flow and any operational issues that came up through the year, senior Pfizer lawyers, called Pfizer Alliance Leaders (PALs), worked closely with designated counterparts, called Firm Relationships Partners, at each PLA firm.

Like de Meo with his design labs at VW and the partners at Pentagram with their biannual partners' meetings, Schulman created opportunities for her legal colleagues to get to know each other and build relationships and trust the old-fashioned way—by facilitating conversation, interaction, and connection. She and her team put in place practices and policies that required all of them to try out new patterns of communication and interaction—to act as if they trusted each other and were part of a community. It wasn't just outside counsel who were initially skeptical about this revolutionary approach; members of the Pfizer legal division were uncertain, too; they had to give up long-standing relationships and learn to work with their new partners in the PLA.

There were PLA-wide "SMART" meetings once or twice a year to review alliance goals and priorities, ensure collective learning, and foster collaboration. There were practice area summits where PLA lawyers involved in the same legal areas met to discuss litigation and share knowledge. And there were monthly continuing legal education courses tailored specifically to Pfizer and PLA lawyers on topics germane to the PLA's work.

In addition, Schulman and Rosenthal encouraged frequent contact and collaboration in the way Pfizer delegated and distributed legal work to PLA firms. In spite of the potential for some inefficiency, they decided very consciously to cross-pollinate tasks so that no firm owned an entire piece of anything.

A different kind of leader

Like Smarr, Schulman eschewed the role of the visionary director. It was a role she could have played—she represented the client, after all—but one she chose, for the most part, to avoid. As one of her senior colleagues at Pfizer said:

> By nature, she is very decisive. [But as] a leader, I think she wants to consciously pull herself back and let the conversation take place, and not jump in too early, because when she does, often because of her intellect and because of her position, the conversation tends to stop and people say, "Yes, we all agree with Amy." She has done a good job of holding back and letting other lawyers have the conversation—even though she may know the answer, and allow that conversation to take place, and then get us to the right place.

Schulman was known for routinely seeking feedback and input about the PLA from her team. Equally important, through her unusual transparency, inclusive style, and obvious desire to learn and improve, she role-modeled, down to small touches, the behaviors, attitudes, and values she wanted all members of the PLA to live by. Not least, she made a habit of sharing credit. Another colleague said, "What she has taught me, and I think my colleagues, is that ... if it's done to you, you do it to others, and so we try to pass it down, and that is give credit where credit is due."

The first four years

Though the PLA continues to be a work in progress as we write this— Schulman still calls it an "uphill climb"—the outcome after the first four years has been a success by almost any measure. Fifteen firms in the PLA were handling over 75 percent of Pfizer's legal work, and Schulman and her colleagues at Pfizer considered the quality of their work to be much higher than that previously produced by individual law firms. They could tell that the PLA firms were investing more in learning about the pharmaceutical industry in general and Pfizer in particular. Though cost cutting was far from the only goal, the fact that Pfizer had reduced its outside legal expenditures by 20 percent was a telling measure.

Rosenthal said of those first few years: "We have successfully litigated mass tort actions and resolved them, successfully fighting these cases with multi-firm teams and experts in many different subject matters collaborating to address incredibly complex problems."

For Schulman, an equally important outcome was that the PLA firms had truly embraced this radical new approach to legal work, in spite of early skepticism. An important sign of this was the unique level of information sharing that was occurring among PLA firms, as explained by one of Schulman's senior colleagues in reference to new firms as they joined the PLA: "The new firms see the PLA firms who are readily willing to share their witness questionnaires and witness notes, or key insights with respect to a particular judge. These are proprietary [pieces of] information that firms have traditionally been less willing to share with other firms."

So strong did the sense of community become, engendered by these and other practices, that the PLA came to *act* in some ways like a real firm. For example, it began, as a group, to develop the next generation of lawyers. For that purpose, it created an Associate Roundtable and a Junior Associate Program.

The Associate Roundtable brought together about fifteen partner-track associates from various member firms and quickly evolved into a network in which associates could seek legal and career advice from each other. Every associate participated in the roundtable for two years and was paired with a Pfizer mentor to help him or her identify developmental opportunities, including the kind of high-profile work critical to building a personal franchise. Members of this group, often paired with their Pfizer mentors, oversee monthly continuing legal education sessions which are conducted live at Pfizer and webcast to all PLA firms. "It's an opportunity for them to show off to a big client," Rosenthal said.

The Junior Associate Program consisted of high-potential lawyers right out of law school (hiring new graduates had not previously been a common practice). Junior Associates rotated assignments between Pfizer and one of the PLA firms and, in their third year, were given the choice to join Pfizer or one of the PLA firms.

In addition, PLA members have joined forces on programs designed to drive change in the legal community and beyond, including a diversity and inclusion initiative (PLA LEAD) that provides person-alized development opportunities for rising minority lawyers at PLA firms and Pfizer. The LEAD program builds skills and profiles of diverse associates at PLA law firms and members of the in-house legal team by providing specifically identified opportunities to engage in meaningful work or initiatives. By sponsoring these individuals, Pfizer gives them the support they need to reach the next levels in their careers. A key suc-cess factor is the way the LEAD program naturally aligns with the PLA's existing structure and strong culture of collaboration. Capitalizing on the collaborative environment within the PLA, the LEAD program provides a broader range of professional opportunities and sponsorship than what might be available in a more traditional one-on-one client-firm relation-ship. Furthermore, the LEAD program leverages the culture of teamwork and existing cross-firm relationships that the PLA already has fostered.

Through these and other similar practices, the PLA became a place where the practice of law was more satisfying for the lawyers in it. It was a place where they were expected and encouraged to do the kind of good work they wanted to do. And, far from least, because of the high level of collaboration, it was a place where each lawyer could learn from talented peers. Like the world-class designers at Pentagram, they chose to join because they were better for being part of that community.

Like Colin Forbes, a founder of Pentagram, Schulman understood that financial rewards were important, but they weren't the glue that could hold a community together through the trials and pressures of innovative problem solving. Even the most senior partners in PLA firms appreciated the opportunities to learn from peers in other firms and broaden their professional networks. With the PLA and the predictable income it repre-sented, they could devote more of their time to what attracted them to law in the first place: the satisfaction of tackling complex strategic problems that demanded huge chunks of ingenuity to solve and the pleasure of coming up with innovative solutions to a client's needs.

In this way, the PLA was becoming a genuine community because it began to connect people at the level of personal identity. It demonstrated what we saw across all the innovative groups we studied: that the innovation process works best in a community where everyone feels able to contribute their slice of genius in solving problems they care about, where their own passions and talents—their personal identities—are aligned with the collective. Schulman was pleased when she learned that PLA firms had decided to take on social issues of common concern through collective pro bono work. It suggested that the members were beginning to feel like a true community.

Schulman's own assessment was this:

> I think four years into it, everybody who participates in it believes in it. We launched this big experiment, and has it worked? The answer is unequivocally yes. Have we learned things along the way that I wish I had known from the beginning that I would do differently? Absolutely. It required a lot of personal conviction. I believed that doing away with the billable hour was the right thing to do, and I was willing to work through the hard issues that came up.

The Lessons of Calit2 and the PLA

Both Smarr and Schulman relied sparingly on top-down interventions and instead worked to connect others and provide opportunities for them to do innovative work. Through their own behavior, they modeled the kind of open, collaborative, inquisitive thinking that innovation requires.

Both also took care to install clear systems of governance and structure. Once purpose and shared values had been clarified, these rules of engagement became critical components of the glue that kept their innovative ecosystems together.

What set them apart from other leaders, however, was that both were careful to create and maintain these systems in transparent and inclusive ways that helped create and reinforce members' sense of community.

Modeling the right mind-set and behavior

Leading an innovative ecosystem requires constant nurturing and tending. The leader has to be prepared to make him- or herself vulnerable and role-model for others the expected values, attitudes, and behaviors so others are willing to take the risk and learn how to behave in new and often unnatural ways.

A colleague said of Schulman:

Amy is so unbelievably different from most law firm partners in that she knows she's not an island. She takes input from everyone, from the lowest member of the team to the highest, because she knows that's what you do if you want the best results. When she gets a compliment, she almost always says, "Well, I couldn't have done it without Loren or Heidi or John." She's really generous; it's like she wants to get credit so she can give it away. She has given me opportunities associates never get. At meetings, I'm often mistaken for a partner because no one else brings along their associates.

The limits of formal authority in creating a community

For all the similarities between Smarr and Schulman as leaders, the settings in which they worked were different in one key aspect. That difference helps illuminate an important point.

The PLA was a collection of outside legal firms chosen by Pfizer that served in a flexible manner that was not prespecified. Whatever the working arrangement between Pfizer and the PLA, no matter how open and inclusive, the company would always be the eight-hundred-pound client in the relationship.

The situation was completely different at Calit2, which truly was a collection of volunteers. To an extent that did not apply to Pfizer and the PLA, Calit2 had to respect the preexisting rights and privileges of the various departments and groups in the two UC universities. Calit2's innovative strength was also a danger. As Smarr said, "We are disruptive in principle." His paradoxical task was to be disruptive without seeming to contradict established roles, status, reputation, or rights and prerogatives. He had to do this through persuasion, without formal authority, by aligning all those groups' own interests and goals with those of Calit2. How he did that was a case study of how to do it without any ability to push people together.

What's noteworthy in Schulman's leadership of the PLA was that, wisely, she exercised her formal power only on rare occasion. She could have used it more extensively, and the outside firms would have had to choose to go along or forgo working for a major national client. But she proceeded in many important ways without relying on that big stick. She knew that regular, blatant use of it would surely undermine the sense of community that was so critical for eliciting the superior innovative work she needed from the PLA firms.

Community building consists not only in *what* the leader does but also in *how* it's done. Every act of the leader—from working with and respecting member organizations to structuring the ecosystem to creating and enforcing the rules that govern it—is done to foster and sustain that fragile but all-important sense of common purpose and shared values.

We've hardly solved the mystery of how to build sustainable ecosystems that can address the increasingly complex problems we face today. The stories of Larry Smarr and Amy Schulman offer inspirational examples of what we think is the next frontier, collective genius 2.0, leading innovative ecosystems.

But our observations of them, combined with what we saw in the many innovative organizations we studied, lead us to two basic conclusions. Without a sense of community—of being pulled together by common purpose, shared values, and clear rules of engagement openly developed—an innovative ecosystem is likely to flounder. Without a leader who understands this and works diligently to build and sustain that sense, the ecosystem will likely remain a mere collection of players who cooperate and coordinate, not a community capable of breakthrough work.

EPILOGUE

WHERE WILL WE FIND TOMORROW'S LEADERS OF INNOVATION?

B y now, the implication of our argument should be clear. Many organizations won't be able to innovate routinely until they revisit their assumptions about leadership. The innovation leader's role differs from the conventional image that many hold of good leadership. Great leaders of innovation, we found, see their role not as take-charge direction setters but primarily as creators of a context in which others are willing and able to make innovation happen.

The question this raises is simple and critical: *where will today's organizations find tomorrow's leaders of innovation?*

Because leaders are more made than born, organizations must identify people with the right stuff for leading innovation and provide them with the experiences and resources needed to develop the required mind-set and skills. Yet, if today's high-potential leaders of innovation don't fit today's popular conception of a good leader, many of them will be invisible to current systems for identifying and developing tomorrow's leaders.

In this final chapter, we will outline what we believe to be the "the right stuff." Then we will profile three leaders who have succeeded not only in setting the stage for others to innovate but also in finding ways to identify and develop those with high potential for leading innovation themselves.

The first of the three is Steve Kloeblen, an executive in business development at IBM, who created a perfect school for innovation leadership as an unintended consequence of his efforts to drive growth. The second is Jacqueline Novogratz, founder of Acumen, who is developing a new generation of leaders able to build and lead innovative ecosystems that span three sectors—business, civil society, and government. The third is Sung-joo Kim at the Sungjoo Group, owner of MCM, a rapidly emerging luxury brand headquartered in Korea, whose mission is to empower and develop the leadership of the marginalized—those whose slices of genius have largely been invisible for too long. Her story literally addresses the question of where tomorrow's leaders will be found.

The Right Stuff

Leadership concerns not only what a person knows and does but also who he or she is.[1] Despite differences in culture, age, and gender, the leaders we studied shared certain personal qualities that allowed them to lead in ways that fostered the growth of innovative communities. They were *idealists, yet pragmatists*. They were *holistic thinkers, yet action-oriented*. They were *generous, yet demanding*. Perhaps most importantly, they were *human, yet resilient*. Just as we stressed the paradoxical nature of the innovation process itself in chapter 2, we focus now on the paradoxical nature of these leaders' traits.

Idealists, yet pragmatists

Our leaders epitomized bold ambition. They eagerly took on complex, difficult problems. They thrived on pushing the boundaries of possibility. But they also understood the need to balance unbounded thinking with levelheadedness. They were fully aware of the persistence and practical steps necessary to overcome inevitable challenges.

Holistic thinkers, yet action oriented

The leaders were holistic or integrative thinkers; they saw problems in all their complexity and enjoyed unraveling them down to their core. They appreciated the intricacies and nuances of a problem. They understood organizational dynamics and thus could balance the tensions built into innovation. Yet they could take action, too. They were inclined to try things, to experiment again and again. They knew that solutions emerged from trial and error, not thought alone.

Generous, yet demanding

For these people, leading for innovation was hard, never-ending work, much of it behind the scenes. If they'd wanted, most of them could have been the star on stage in their own right. Yet they believed in others' slices of genius and let them take the spotlight. That took generosity—the willingness, based on their own sense of personal security, to share power, control, and credit. Many of them were reluctant to be singled out when we talked about what their organizations had accomplished. Instead, they consistently pointed to the individual and collective talents of their colleagues. At the same time, they held people accountable and expected results. They didn't hesitate to change what didn't work or terminate those who ultimately couldn't perform.

Human, yet highly resilient

These leaders were far from perfect. Like all of us, they had anxieties, regrets, and fears. They made mistakes. They had bad days and even bad months when they became self-protective and defensive. Sometimes they lost their way. Yet they were resilient in the face of mistakes and regrets, able to try again and again in the face of disappointment and failure, and capable of coping with uncertainty, complexity, and conflict. Consequently, they brought calm to chaos when others were overwhelmed, disillusioned, or frightened. Most important, they knew they weren't perfect and didn't have the answers. That opened them to seek help and, most of all, to recognize and rely on the slices of genius in all those around them.

Think about what most organizations seek when they try to identify high-potential candidates for a leadership program. How many of them look for candidates with these traits, "idealistic," "a thinker," "generous," "willing to admit imperfections and ask for help"? Yet these same qualities are the ones we most frequently see in leaders of innovation. They are the individuals uniquely willing and able to create a place where others can engage in innovative problem solving.

But Leaders Are More Made Than Born

Selecting the right people is only one part of the equation. The experiences of the following three leaders provide important insights into effective ways not only to identify high-potential candidates for leading innovation but also develop the leadership skills they will need.[2]

Steve Kloeblen at IBM: A school for innovative leadership

Vice president of business development at IBM and a thirty-two-year veteran of the firm, Steve Kloeblen oversaw the acquisition and integration of companies into the IBM fold. Though it was his job to bring outside innovation and talent into the company, he also believed that the people already there were a prime source of innovative ideas for growth.

While attending an executive education course, Kloeblen went to a lecture on business opportunities at the "bottom of the pyramid" (BoP)[3]—the vast numbers of poor around the globe. He was intrigued by what he learned about opportunities in this market for companies with the right products offered in the right way and at the right prices. When he returned to work, he began to do some research, reading and meeting with people working in this fledging field. He became convinced that this market was a significant opportunity for IBM that was aligned with its strategic objective to expand in emerging growth markets. Kloeblen elaborated:

> When Sam Palmisano became CEO, he planned a transformational strategy to focus IBM on higher-value solutions to enable our clients' businesses to succeed. The business could be fueled by innovation and consulting much different than selling computing gear such as personal computers. Sam believed the best way to channel the diverse talent and experience inside of the company was to unite IBMers around a shared purpose. He invited us to join him in collectively articulating IBM's values, using IBM's "jam" technology that enabled a virtual conversation. The idea: return to our early twentieth-century roots while transforming into a globally integrated enterprise. I was really charged by the new values we defined. They were about making innovation that matters for the world and investing in the success of our clients' business. I wanted to be a catalyst that enabled that change.[4]

He wrote an e-mail to a dozen young IBMers he was mentoring, many of them MBAs who had served a rotational stint in business development:

> Hi all, I've been thinking that there are a lot of problems that people in developing nations face that could be solved with IBM's technology ...

Here's what I'm thinking: it could be pretty cool to get a little group together and brainstorm on how IBM can find commercially viable ways to use its technology to address issues that affect the bottom of the pyramid (BoP). I don't mean philanthropy—I'm talking about business development, our business. Obviously, we are never going to serve the poor directly, but our clients do. This could be a nice way to make good on the value of making innovation matter for the world and enable our clients to succeed.

What do you think? Should I set up a conference call for some time soon?

Most of the recipients responded immediately and were so excited that they soon signed on to work on the project in addition to their demanding day jobs. Word spread virally, and in six months, the group, which came to call itself the World Development Initiative (WDI), had grown to more than a hundred volunteers from all over the company. Most were in their twenties and thirties and had worked at IBM for less than five years.

The WDI group held a number of mostly virtual meetings in which it developed a statement of purpose, values, and norms for working together. Its purpose was to "improve the lives of the world's poor by leveraging IBM's leadership in developing innovative and commercially viable technology solutions." The strategic goal was to create a billion dollars in new revenue for IBM, while helping to improve the lives of a billion people.

The WDI was a form of virtual teaming on top of the formal organization that the company encouraged as a way to incubate new ideas aligned with the corporate values to create, as one WDI member said, "innovation that matters for the world." There had previously been, for example, an ad hoc virtual team focused on the environment, as well as groups that emerged around health care and smart energy. Senior management endorsed the WDI and agreed to integrate its findings into the IBM strategy development process.

Kloeblen's role with the WDI was to serve as guide and coach of people's efforts; he mostly "led from behind."[5] He encouraged group members to agree on clear short-term and long-term goals and think through how they should organize their work. In meetings, he typically kept a low profile, made suggestions, and helped them stay focused on the areas and targets they themselves had defined. But he didn't choose the targets they set or what they worked on, and he didn't try to inspire them with stirring speeches. This wasn't his vision they were pursuing. He had simply thrown out an idea, and those interested had volunteered to involve themselves. Focusing on needs that government and philanthropy could not address, they set aggressive one-, three-, and ten-year targets for revenue and profit and for improving the outcome for the poor at the bottom of the pyramid. They each agreed to retain responsibility for these targets as they moved from job to job in IBM. Finally, they divided into teams to explore specific opportunities aligned with their personal passions.

The WDI fast became an extensive global network of strong partnerships inside and outside IBM. As it grew, Kloeblen purposely kept its structure fluid. He encouraged volunteers with interest in a given technology or country to advertise their ideas to the group during its weekly conference call. If there was interest, a new team would coalesce around an idea spontaneously. Some teams formed around solution areas, such as health care and banking. Others concentrated on geographic regions, such as Africa. Still others focused on functional areas, such as marketing, communications, and R&D, and created key infrastructure that supported the overall effort.

Once formed, a team researched the opportunity it hoped to pursue. Usually, one or two members emerged as team leaders. Sometimes, team members were able to do on-site research in places like India and China. Such visits were often eye-opening. For example, two WDI members returned from a trip to India chastened by discovering firsthand how difficult a business plan devised in New York would be to implement in a remote village, given the huge logistical, language, and other barriers. "When you get on the ground," they reported, "you realize your strategy needs to be adapted and you're going to have lots of unforeseen implementation challenges. This is hard work." And, of course, as with all innovative efforts, the teams made missteps and ran into roadblocks and naysayers within their own ranks and in the broader organization. At times like these, Kloeblen would step in and provide protection or candid feedback on what he saw on the part of WDI members as less productive behavior, especially behavior inconsistent with their agreed-upon norms about how they would interact with each other. Kloeben's first choice at these times was to nudge them along with gentle admonitions. When the group violated their values or rules of engagement, he got tough and pointed out the error of their ways. For instance, when they began to marginalize a member whom they found difficult to work with because of her style, not her intentions, Kloeben called them on it and reminded them that inclusion and embracing diversity was what they should stand for.

As they finished their research, teams would prepare business plans and proposals for presentation to appropriate senior management groups. Kloeblen coached them on the political realities of introducing new ideas and on how to develop and present compelling business plans. When their frustration led to unproductive behavior, he would remind them of their goal to raise awareness and garner support for their projects across the company. And sometimes he did step in and provide air cover for them.

Given IBM's traditional products, services, customers, and processes, all this was new territory for WDI members. The challenges at the BoP forced them to seek innovative solutions that were affordable, scalable, and focused on customers' immediate needs, not their wants. Often, they discovered, the market issue was not a lack of consumer buying power but an inability to reach buyers due to inefficient distribution systems. Still, as the group and the various teams learned more, they grew even more convinced that the BoP represented a large, attractive commercial market that aligned with IBM's core competencies and values.

By the end of three years following Kloeblen's initial e-mail, the WDI had grown to over four hundred members from dozens of countries around the world. It included researchers, engineers, salespeople, and marketers and ranged from new hires fresh out of school to old hands who'd joined the company before Kloeblen.

To provide mentors and other resources for WDI members, Kloeblen actively brought external partners and seasoned IBMers into the mix. Frances West, a twenty-five-year IBM veteran and the director of the IBM Human Ability and Accessibility Center, joined the WDI. Among other things, she had helped IBM open the insurance and financial markets and worked on the Shanghai Stock Exchange as the business unit executive of the banking, financial services, securities, and insurance unit for the IBM Greater China Group. Kloeben was excited about West's participation. She could coach the group members on how to negotiate differences and build bridges across cultural divides, talents essential for leading innovation. Thus, the WDI quickly evolved into a network of developmental relationships among both like-minded peers and seniors. For Kloeblen, this was key. "One of the wonderful things about having IBMers from all over the company," he said, "is that the WDI also turned out to be a great networking and peer coaching vehicle. We have people connecting in ways that actually make their day jobs easier."

Projects extended from branchless banking for the masses in India to working with an alliance of African universities to improve infrastructure by leveraging a supercomputer that IBM had donated to the University of Cape Town. WDI members were influential in the formation of an IBM program called the Corporate Service Corps that immersed teams of IBMers in emerging markets, where they worked on a variety of projects for four weeks at a time. A WDI team working with IBM research helped roll out a technical innovation called the "Spoken Web" that allowed illiterate clients in remote Indian villages to connect by voice with commercial trading, employment, and social services. WDI members also participated in a task force for leadership development in emerging markets that reported to the chairman and CEO of IBM.

Most projects initially focused on India and China, but eventually a team formed to explore opportunities in sub-Saharan Africa. Many team members had come from that area and had moved to the United States for education and work opportunities. Their efforts proceeded slowly in the beginning. Appolo Tankeh, now in IBM Finance, recalled with humility and pride the small part he and his WDI colleagues played in establishing IBM as one of the technology companies leading the way in Africa: "At first, it was difficult for us to sell it. Eventually we were able to organize ourselves and we got stronger." The group focused on collecting data about various markets in Africa, particularly in industries like telecommunications, banking, and health care. The Africa team was ecstatic when IBM decided to launch an Africa ThinkPlace Challenge, a three-week open online forum designed to foster global collaboration on innovation opportunities and economic development issues facing Africa. The top ideas generated through this challenge helped shape the long-term agenda for the WDI. In 2010, the members celebrated with their colleagues across IBM, when the company won a $1.3 billion contract with Bharti Airtel to consolidate that mobile operator's sixteen different countries into a single back-end system. From that milestone, IBM went on to open offices in more than twenty of Africa's fifty-four countries, including a major research lab in Nairobi.

Not only did many of its projects turn into real growth opportunities for the company, the WDI also served as a catalyst that influenced IBM's business strategy for emerging markets. But that was far from all it achieved. As he saw how WDI was evolving and what members were doing, Kloeblen realized that he had also uncovered one of the best ways to identify tomorrow's leaders of innovation. It couldn't have been simpler or more intuitive: to find and develop leaders of innovation, create a setting in which potential leaders can make themselves visible and let them go at it; leadership development happens through real experience with real consequences.

If IBM managers had selected people to develop the different business opportunities the WDI came up with from their pool of seasoned executives or officially identified pool of high-potential candidates, would the makeup of the teams have been the same? Kloeblen had a cadre of top-notch mentees, so there surely would have been some overlap. Would those people have had the drive, passion, and persistence to develop communities of compatriots willing and able to find new solutions to new challenges? Perhaps, but probably not.

Most company leadership development programs are based on a planned trajectory: people are selected to participate at specific stages in their careers as they move up the hierarchy. Kloeblen's program, in contrast, was "come one, come all." Its voluntary nature was perhaps the program's most significant feature. "It wasn't my initial intention," said Kloeblen, "but I soon realized that I was also creating an excellent leadership development crucible."

Kloeblen encouraged people to do what he did when he started the WDI: volunteer to take the lead. Many did, and for them it was an opportunity to self-select and then to learn how to collaborate and do innovative problem solving with others worldwide. Their experience—learning to accomplish real work with a diverse group of peers on a team that had no formal boss—differed vastly from the early career experience of working on a project team at, say, a global consulting firm or bank.

WDI participants had to figure out how to manage diversity of expertise, thought, and cultures across multiple stakeholders. The problems they took on required bold original thinking. They had, of course, plenty of opportunities to develop holistic thinking and engage in discovery-driven learning. They had to devise integrative solutions, because their passionate colleagues wouldn't compromise or be dominated. Without traditional carrots or sticks to influence others, they all had to learn how to build a sense of community around shared purpose, values, and rules of engagement that bound them together and guided their individual and collective actions. They had to develop the patience and resilience required to weather the inevitable disappointment of not seeing their proposals funded in the end. As one WDI member said:

Where I shared with my peers a commonality in the purpose and intent for this work, the synergy and partnership I was able to drive was exceptional. There was passion, creativity, and innovation. Where the personal drivers were divergent, it became more of a process and less about the optimal outcome.

Without diminishing the value of all the innovative ideas the WDI developed, we suspect that its greatest "product" was a new generation of skilled and seasoned leaders of innovation now applying their skills across IBM. Over a dozen WDI members went on to key roles and executive positions where they are practicing and disseminating the leadership lessons they learned in the WDI—for example, as heads of operations in Kenya, Nigeria, and Senegal; as the head of strategy for IBM's emerging growth market unit; as an IBM Fellow (one of IBM's highest honors); as marketing analyst for the company's Smarter Planet initiative; as the program director for the IBM Corporate Service Corps; and as the director for IBM business supporting people with disabilities.

For us, the lesson of the WDI is clear: to find tomorrow's leaders of innovation, don't just rely on formalized leadership development systems like programs for high-potential candidates. Instead, give people the opportunity to reveal themselves and then to discover and develop the leadership skills they need to fulfill their personal passions by unleashing and harnessing them to drive innovation.

Jacqueline Novogratz of Acumen: Developing leaders who can build innovative ecosystems

As a young woman, Jacqueline Novogratz believed that she was "singlehandedly going to save the world." But her first trip to Africa changed her mind. She discovered that "people don't want to be saved but want to solve their own problems, make their own decisions." Refusing to see the poor as passive individuals waiting for handouts, she began to envision how business models might be used to create effective, sustainable systems where governments or charity alone had failed.[6]

In 2001, Novogratz founded Acumen to identify, invest in, strengthen, and scale early-stage enterprises that provided low-income consumers with access to health care, water, housing, education, alternative energy, and agricultural inputs. Using venture capital investing as a model, Acumen raised money for investment from individuals, foundations, and corporations and operated under the innovative model of "patient capital," a term and idea Novogratz coined. Patient capital meant long-term, high-risk debt or equity investments backed by philanthropy, with the goal of maximizing social, not financial, returns.

Acumen was clear about where it would invest. "We were looking for ventures with visionary leaders," Novogratz said, "who were using business approaches to solve big social problems. Their enterprises had to demonstrate the likelihood of financial sustainability and hold the promise of reaching a million customers over time." Like Kloeblen at IBM, she saw that bridging the gap between what philanthropy and the marketplace could accomplish at the BoP was one way to tackle such intractable problems as poverty.

From the start, however, finding good candidates proved difficult. For one thing, Acumen's mission required leaders who fell outside the typical mold. It relied on individuals who could manage nonprofits or public-sector organizations, but who also had needed business and operational skills. Acumen was also seeking leaders who could think and collaborate beyond traditional systems, work with longer time horizons, and succeed in spite of limited resources.

Few individuals could meet these standards, and so in 2007, Novogratz created the Global Fellows Program, a yearlong training program aimed at building a corps of leaders for the sector at the intersection between business and society. Eight years later, seventy-five individuals from twenty-four countries had already participated in the program. Acumen sought applications from talented young professionals with a broad range of backgrounds and experiences. Many applicants were star performers from early in their careers, but Acumen was looking for more than a record of achievement. Successful candidates had to demonstrate moral imagination, which meant, according to Novogratz, "the humility to see the world as it is, and the audacity to envision the world for what it could be."

After a rigorous selection process, the first annual program brought together ten Fellows who, among other criteria, had "demonstrated courage and willingness to take risks; generosity to share ideas, knowledge, and credit; and ability to build relationships across lines of difference." Character, not just competence or content, was emphasized. It's no coincidence that Novogratz and her colleagues were looking for individuals who had what we identified above as the right stuff for leading innovation. Some of them had earned MBAs from elite institutions while others had grown up in the slums of East Africa.

The Fellows spent their first two months going through intensive training in Acumen's New York City office. The goal was twofold: first, to impart important knowledge and skills in finance, operations, and marketing as they applied to low-income markets; and, second, to help Fellows reflect deeply on their moral imagination—their values, assumptions, and aspirations concerning human nature, leadership, and society.

They heard the personal stories and perspectives of leaders, such as Tim Brown, CEO of IDEO, who discussed design thinking. A well-known spoken-word poet performed for them. They read the works of philosophers like Rousseau and leaders like Gandhi and Martin Luther King Jr. as a means of enriching their own ideas about leadership and community. The training included several retreats and exercises. For example, the "everyday barriers" exercise helped individuals appreciate the perspective of the poor. Fellows spent a day in the city with five dollars and a subway card and no cellphone. Then, they were asked to do an assessment and redesign of city services.

The two months in New York also served to turn the group into a learning community where Fellows could absorb one another's diverse experiences and build relationships of trust as the foundation for the long-term community. Following the two months of leadership training, each Fellow spent the following nine months working with one of Acumen's portfolio companies. It was a necessary way to put their learning into practice. Blair Miller, who designed and led Acumen's leadership programs for four years, said:

> It was critical for the Fellows to understand the challenges of what it takes to apply their learning in some of the most challenging environments in the world. Without this application, the training is incomplete. We strived to build the type of leader who can walk into pristine rooms of the largest global financial institutions and run the numbers, and then a day later sit on the ground in the slum and learn from one of the poorest people in the world. They have to hold that tension and build from that place. This is not only an academic exercise; it must be developed through practice.

Novogratz and Miller were pleased with the work the Global Fellows did after they completed the program. A few joined Acumen while others created their own social enterprise ventures in various parts of the world. One alum launched a company that built housing and provided first-time mortgages for low-income Pakistanis. Another founded a talent management company aimed at placing creative people in companies across the Middle East. Recognizing a hunger among people living in poverty to access knowledge, share ideas, and hold conversations about innovation, one Fellow started a book club in a Nairobi slum. After his fellowship year, he continued this effort by working with local communities to host TEDx-style talks in the slums.[7]

"You invest in these Fellows," Miller said "... and allow them to see the good, bad, and ugly of what works and what doesn't work in this field. We provide them with the network, training, and support to process these experiences. As a result, we are seeing them create new innovations across industries and sectors, leveraging the tools of business to create social change."

When the number of applicants for fellowship reached a thousand, Novogratz and Miller began to think about how to scale the program. Instead of simply increasing the number of Fellows, they decided to create regional, locally embedded leadership programs. Taking such an approach would force them to focus on identifying local talent and create regional eco-systems of skilled social enterprise leaders and their organizations. Acumen created Regional Fellows programs in the areas where it operates to support individuals actively working on social initiatives and provide an outlet for training, networking, and connection. The regional programs showed social entrepreneurs in emerging markets that they weren't alone. Alums served as global role models, living examples that social entrepreneurship is a viable path for people.

When the first regional program was launched in East Africa in 2011, the group included two people born and raised and still living in the slums, the granddaughter of a former president of Kenya, and a Harvard MBA. This kind of diversity was particularly remarkable and part of the program's power, because in so many countries around the world, Miller said, race, tribe, and different castes rarely interact on an equal playing field, let alone collaborate. The program was built to bring together people who never would have met, to collaborate and learn from one another to build more inclusive communities, nations, and societies.

In 2013, the East Africa Regional Fellows program was in its third year, the Pakistan Regional Fellows were selecting their second class, the India Regional Fellows program was launched, and the West Africa program was set to launch in the coming years. In addition, the curriculum was placed online for anyone to access and was being used by thousands of people across the world.

Another important outcome of regional programs was that the Fellows gained extensive cross-sector experience empathizing with, speaking the language of, and collaborating with individuals across the private, public, and social sectors. Finding innovative solutions to the vexing problems of poverty required such "tri-sector athletes" who were able to persevere and succeed in spite of the overwhelming odds against them.[8]

As we write this, Acumen has invested more than $80 million in South Asian and African companies and created more than sixty thousand jobs. Based on its experience with its Fellows programs, Acumen changed its mission statement to say, "Acumen invests in companies, leaders, and ideas that are changing the way the world tackles poverty," in recognition of how core leadership is to its mission. And the programs' successes have shown the value of a regional approach to developing leaders. Providing a critical mass of promising individuals with leadership tools that cut across sectors can create global ecosystems of innovation leaders. Not only does Acumen create a cadre of leaders able to operate and innovate at the bottom of the pyramid, it also builds, in Miller's words, "huge communities of interconnected leaders that can become architects for the sector." Novogratz and her colleagues realize that finding sustainable solutions to vexing and intractable problems requires leaders who know how to build innovative ecosystems, not just organizations.

Sung-joo Kim at Sung joo Group and MCM Products AG:
Leave no slices of genius behind

We have argued that leading innovation is different from the conventional image many hold of great leadership. Too often, such behavior as taking the lead in meetings, being tough-minded about people, or appearing to know everything and being the smartest guy in the room are still considered indicators of leadership potential. Ironically, these behaviors represent traits that are likely to stifle others' ability and willingness to create new and useful breakthroughs.

Effective innovation leaders, in contrast, are sensitive to the demands of the situation and display those conventional qualities only selectively. Because their behavior or way of approaching problems and working with groups seldom fit the profile of a stereotypical high-potential leader, they risk becoming what we call "stylistic invisibles."

Besides such stylistic invisibles, there are also "demographic invisibles" who are frequently overlooked altogether. These are people who could become leaders of innovation but, because of preconceived notions about their gender, ethnicity, nationality, class, or even age, are neglected. Often, they're invisible because of *explicit* limitations—lack of political rights in apartheid South Africa, say, or the absence of outlets for entrepreneurial flair in former Communist countries. In addition, *implicit* limitations may also deny certain people the opportunity to grow into leadership roles in both emerging and developed economies. These invisibles don't have equal access to the tools—the social networks, the fast-track training courses, the stretch assignments—that could prepare them for positions of authority and influence.

In order to overcome these biases, managers need to identify new criteria for selecting high-potential leaders of innovation—to look hard at the individual slices of genius within their organizations or nations and to value different kinds of personal characteristics and behaviors.

One of the leaders we studied, Sung-joo Kim, chair and chief visionary officer of a global luxury products group headquartered in Korea, attributes the unlikely success of her organization to her mission-driven approach. Thanks to her commitment to develop and empower marginalized people, she has been able to build an innovative global team able to compete with the behemoths in her industry.

Growing up with strict, traditional parents in one of Korea's richest families, Kim was expected to marry well and never work. Her ambition and high performance in school were frowned upon. However, she had her own plans. She applied to college in the United States without her family's knowledge. When Amherst College accepted her, she finagled her father into letting her attend by asking his permission in public, where, to save face, he reluctantly agreed. When she completed her studies, she refused to return home and accept the prospect of an arranged marriage. Instead, she remained in America and married, a decision that led her family to disown her. She took a position as a project manager for Korean promotions at Bloomingdale's, a job that served as a crash course in luxury retailing with an icon of the industry, Marvin Traub.

Despite falling out with her family, Kim agreed to help a few years later when a joint venture between an American manufacturer and her father's company began to fail. Casting aside any bad feeling, she led the negotiations to a deal that was satisfactory to all, undeterred by operating as a young Asian woman in an all-male setting. Afterward, her father sought to reward her and agreed to a business loan.

Kim's plan was to create a company that would offer women world-wide a new kind of luxury that symbolized the "freedom and empowerment of women." As she said:

> There's this image that women with expensive bags are either concubines or rich men's wives. They're passive and they are what many luxury companies target. I wanted to define a twenty-first-century luxury ... for the stylish working woman who had multiple identities and craved luxurious, high-quality products that could help her live a better life. These women were wealthy—but their money was their own. Beautiful, functional goods could empower them to live better lives.

In 1990, Kim launched the Sungjoo Group, a retailer of luxury fashion that, under her leadership as chair and CEO, pioneered the luxury goods industry in Korea. She paid back her father's initial investment with interest and, within a few years, grew the company into a billion-dollar fashion enterprise catering to the economically powerful woman. Despite ups and downs—the Asian financial crisis in the late 1990s left Sungjoo Group on the verge of bankruptcy for a time—Kim managed to secure exclusive licensing deals with such European retailers as Marks & Spencer and such luxury companies as Gucci, Yves Saint Laurent, Sonia Rykiel, and MCM Products AG, a German brand known for "precision, practicality, and quality craftsmanship." At the time, MCM was a megabrand, a favorite of supermodels and sophisticates. Infused with Kim's "Asian know-how," MCM became the Group's crown jewel.[9]

As a result of poor management from the German team, MCM lost its allure in every market except Korea. In 2005, Kim took the bold and strategic move of acquiring MCM and moving its headquarters to Seoul. Her aim was to grow MCM back into a global luxury brand that appealed to the values and needs of women worldwide.

Kim understood that Asia—in particular, China—was the future of all luxury brand companies. As she and her colleagues were aware, the Asian luxury brand customers were younger than those in the West. They were technologically sophisticated and fast becoming what Kim called "global nomads." Her global strategy was to create a portfolio of MCM products with a common theme but customized for local markets.

Kim recognized the significant obstacles she faced. For one, the luxury leather goods and accessories market was dominated by well-established Western brands. But formidable competitors were only one of her challenges. Business culture in South Korea was male dominated, patriarchal, and often corrupt. Top positions and fast-track opportunities went to members of an old boys' club, and women were entirely resented in the corporate sphere. "Women are second-class citizens in business in Korea," Kim said. "They serve tea to bosses. And in home life, they should be quiet wives and act as if they know nothing. I believed the only way Korea could strengthen its global competitiveness was by waking up its women and equipping them with world-class capabilities."

From the time she founded her company, Kim made a point of building an inclusive, welcoming culture. She hired Korean women like herself, many of them single mothers. By the time Sungjoo Group acquired MCM, 90 percent of its two hundred employees were women, and many of its products were made in 190 home-based artisan facilities in South Korea that were run by women, not standard practice in her country.

Kim carried on her mission of empowerment as she assembled teams for the global relaunch of MCM. Women were appointed at every level, including as managers of global offices in the United States, United Kingdom, Europe, and China. "In our societies in different degrees," Kim said, "women face different kinds of challenges and even discrimination, so that's why when I enter new markets, the women often think it's amazing to be appointed to run these businesses." But because they have faced so much adversity, she said, "I find they often have developed what I call the 'emotional quotient' required to do great global work."

She steered away from prima donna designers, instead selecting young, up-and-coming designers who demonstrated a willingness to collaborate. She also rewarded the loyalty of employees who had been with Sungjoo Group from the start, even if they didn't speak English or have experience outside Korea. "I showed my team—men and women, it doesn't matter—that I treat them fairly. I promote them. I support them," she commented.

Korea's hierarchical culture was another impediment, and Kim knew she would need to lead differently in order for her team to compete globally.

"When I started my company," she recalled, "even my male colleagues came and stood by my desk and bowed at ninety degrees." She believed that horizontal communication channels would be needed for her team to compete. "I put chairs in front of my desk. While looking through materials, I asked 'How's your family, your sons and daughters?' I made everyone feel at home."

Kim also installed a rich intranet, much like the one we saw at HCL, that gave everyone in the company a voice. For the majority of Kim's employees, this level of openness and access to the CEO was unprecedented. She said, "People were so used to patriarchal society that they were not only amazed, they were confused. They didn't know how to deal with me at first. Now they see how beneficial it is; that a horizontal, communicative culture helps them to be more globalized."

As MCM's global launch got under way, negotiating differences in language, culture, and artistic opinion proved to be a challenge. However, Kim viewed experiences to work with diverse others as development crucibles, and she grasped every opportunity to bring her teams together. For many employees, it was their first time abroad. One young manager described how much she learned from her interactions with teams of young and seasoned managers across Europe and the United States, even though the work wasn't always easy. In addition, because of MCM's small size, the pace of growth, and its global footprint, the managers were all learning how to do more than their formal jobs asked of them, something not usually required in larger companies with significant resources. As we saw at IBM, these kinds of stretch assignments provide people with the opportunity to learn how to collaborate and innovate together.

In meetings, Kim encouraged open debate and even conflict. For example, at a meeting of design teams in Seoul, a European designer dismissed a heavily logoed prototype of a bag in favor of a sportier look. "He came in and saw this bag we'd worked on," said one of the Korean designers.

> ... he pulled it to the floor and said, "I don't like this." So I picked
> it up and said, "This is the most important bag in our brand." He
> put it down again, and I picked it up. Right then, Sung-joo came
> into the showroom and decided to leave the subject for us to decide.

We decided it would sell, but only in Korea. So sometimes we agree
and sometimes not. Sometimes a bag we only intro in Korea then
goes global. Still, how to communicate and collaborate with the
global team was very hard. But Sung-joo kept saying we need to share
both sides because that is how we could come up with very pure,
original concepts.

Kim's teams delivered results. Competing against luxury giants like Louis Vuitton and Prada, MCM's gross revenue grew from $100 million to $400 million over six years. And its product range grew tenfold, with stylish multifunctional handbags and backpacks becoming the company's signature products. With growth into new markets, MCM's global head of sales and merchandising, Carol Fok, met the challenge of addressing consumers' unique needs and values across regions. Working collaboratively with merchandisers, Fok succeeded in ensuring that MCM's brand image remained consistent, despite the company's launch of regionally customized product lines.

Another Korean woman, Kris Lee, appointed to head global marketing, was tasked with anticipating the lifestyle needs of the next generation of global consumers. To engage younger buyers—the key demographic in most emerging markets with their young populations—Lee led the launch of a strategic initiative called the Blogger Ambassador Program, a collective of fashion bloggers selected within each of MCM's key regions to represent the brand's products online. For example, the Program provided a platform where young Asian women in different countries could begin to define what luxury meant to them, given their specific cultural experiences and who they wanted to be.

MCM's R&D teams were breaking new ground as well. Most luxury products in the marketplace were produced using high percentages of polyvinyl chloride (PVC) materials, which are hazardous to the environment, but Kim challenged her teams with the vision to create a quality line of sustainable luxury products. By experimenting with ecoconscious synthetics and natural fibers like palm leaves and rice paper, MCM decreased its percentage of revenue from goods made of PVC materials to under 50 percent. The company also began to build partnerships with women in small villages in Indonesia and devastated communities such as Fukushima, Japan. Together, with the help of MCM, the women in

Japan began testing new ways of "upcycling" existing handbag materials into unique new products that would appeal to the growing ranks of luxury consumers concerned with making the world a better place. While Kim's hope for a new sustainable luxury was a forward-looking vision, MCM was on track to lead the way.

Kim has been named by many business and media groups as one of the most powerful and influential women in Asia. In a speech at the United Nations, she acknowledged that her life's work was just beginning—work that required both a sense of urgency and patience—and she admitted that not everyone was onboard with this initiative yet. Given the pace at which the business was growing, the competition for funds and other resources was fierce. She was quick to remind her listeners that when she started her company, composed predominantly of Korean women, and set a goal of building a billion-dollar fashion enterprise, everyone told her she was crazy. The team was excited when in 2013, during Golden Week—a vacation week when affluent Chinese traditionally travel abroad and shop— MCM was the number-one seller of handbags in the $7 billion Korean duty-free market.

Stretch assignments like the ones Kim made available to her colleagues might appear to someone from the West merely part and parcel of any decent enterprise. In actuality, these opportunities would have been unavailable to her team if Kim had chosen to lead by the status quo. As one team leader said, "It's not just the evolution of a brand image. It's the actual tangible, visible evolution of people."

Kim's story reminds us that emerging markets—not developed markets alone—will increasingly become the engines driving global innovation. Moreover, as organizations become more global, they will create greater opportunity and greater need for developing talent in young markets. Yet in some cultural or political contexts, traditional notions of leadership, cultural values, and rules of engagement are inconsistent with the innovative process.

After years of researching emerging markets, we have found many extraordinary individuals like Kim, who are willing and able to lead differently despite complicated external factors. Limited resources and rapid growth will only continue to create problems that need creative solutions. There's a long way to go, to be sure. If more global businesses hope to create and sustain innovative environments in the future, they can learn from Kim's example: by equipping people—even seemingly ordinary individuals—with leadership capabilities, they can unlock extraordinary innovations.

Postscript

When we started our journey we asked, why are some organizations able to innovate again and again, while others hardly innovate at all? We believe that leadership is a key piece of the puzzle, and we hope we have shed some light on what leaders of innovation actually do.

The leaders we studied would be the first to admit they are by no means perfect and are still learning, but they are at the forefront of creating collective genius. Delving deep into their worlds, we showed you who they are, what they do, and how they think. Regardless of the specifics of the innovation challenges they faced, the leaders we profiled in this book create environments in which the unique *slices of genius* in their organizations are rendered into a single work of *collective genius*.

They fostered *willingness* to innovate by creating real communities whose members were bound by a mutual compelling purpose supported by shared values and rules of engagement. And they fostered the *ability* to innovate by making sure their organizations possessed the three capabilities of innovative groups: creative abrasion, creative agility, and creative resolution.

We wrote *Collective Genius* to provide both inspiration and practical guidance for those who want more innovation from the organizations they lead. In that spirit, we close with the hope that, if you are one of those leaders— or aspiring to be one—we've encouraged you to examine your own mind-set and practices. Do you cling to the idea that you the leader are the one who sets vision and drives your people to pursue new and useful solutions? Or do you see yourself as someone who creates a place that elicits people's slices of genius and turns them into collective genius?

Leading innovation begins with this kind of self-reflection. We hope the leaders you have met in this book have emboldened you to take the next step on your own journey to creating collective genius.

NOTES

Introduction

1. There are some notable exceptions, including Jeff Dyer, Hal Gregersen, and Clayton M. Christensen, *The Innovator's DNA: Mastering the Five Skills of Disruptive Innovators* (Boston: Harvard Business Review Press, 2011); Teresa M. Amabile and Mukti Khaire, "Creativity and the Role of the Leader," *Harvard Business Review*, October 2008, 100–109; Eric von Hippel, *Democratizing Innovation* (Cambridge, MA: MIT Press, 2005); Byron Reeves, Thomas W. Malone, and Tony O'Driscoll, "Leadership's Online Labs," *Harvard Business Review*, May 2008, 58–66; Brian Uzzi and Jarrett Spiro, "Collaboration and Creativity: The Small World Problem," *American Journal of Sociology* 111, no. 2 (2005): 447–504; and Deborah Ancona and Henrik Bresman, *X-Teams: How to Build Teams That Lead, Innovate, and Succeed* (Boston: Harvard Business School Press, 2007).

2. Our research took us deep inside the worlds of these leaders and the organizations they led. Our approach was ethnographic in nature; we wanted to see and experience the worlds of the individuals we studied through their eyes, as they experience them. Data collection involved interviews and observations of daily life in the leaders' organizations. In conducting interviews, we found the following useful: Robert Weiss, *Learning from Strangers: The Art and Method of Qualitative Interview Studies* (New York: Free Press, 1994); and Howard S. Becker, *Tricks of the Trade: How to Think About Your Research While You're Doing It* (Chicago: University of Chicago Press, 1998). For collecting observational data and writing ethnographic field notes, we drew on R. Emerson, R. Fretz, and L. Shaw, *Writing Ethnographic Fieldnotes* (Chicago: University of Chicago Press, 1995). Our analysis

occurred in parallel with data collection. We found several scholars' work useful in guiding our analysis, including John Lofland, David A. Snow, Leon Anderson, and Lyn H. Lofland, *Analyzing Social Settings: A Guide to Qualitative Observation and Analysis* (Boston: Cengage Learning, 2005); Kathy Charmaz, *Constructing Grounded Theory: A Practical Guide through Qualitative Analysis* (Thousand Oaks, CA: Sage Publications, 2010); and Ann Langley, "Strategies for Theorizing from Process Data," *Academy of Management Review* 24, no. 4 (1999): 691–710. When writing the stories of those we studied, we were inspired by J. Van Maanen, *Tales of the Field: On Writing Ethnography* (Chicago: University of Chicago Press, 2011); Karen Golden-Biddle and Karen Locke, "Appealing work: An investigation of how ethnographic texts convince," *Organization Science* 4, no. 4 (1993): 595–616; and Karen Locke and Karen Golden-Biddle, "Constructing Opportunities for Contribution: Structuring Intertextual Coherence and 'Problematizing' in Organizational Studies," *Academy of Management Journal* 40, no. 5 (1997): 1023–1062. Throughout our research journey, data collection and analysis occurred in parallel. Our approach was inductive, even abductive; we asked not what "must" be but what "may" be. See Karen Locke, Karen Golden-Biddle, and Martha S. Feldman, "Making Doubt Generative: Rethinking the Role of Doubt in the Research Process," *Organization Science* 19, no. 6 (2008): 907–918. See also Lotte Bailyn, "Research as a Cognitive Process: Implications for Data Analysis," *Quality and Quantity* 11, no. 2 (1977): 97–117. Given our methodology, we cannot prove that leadership matters for innovation, but we believe that our findings are suggestive of its importance and offer promising avenues for future research.

3. We clearly stand on the shoulders of extensive research on leading innovation. We are an interdisciplinary team and have introduced each other to the classic works in our respective fields. Our perspective has been shaped not only by relevant research in the social sciences, but also by writings on agile software engineering, architecture, and urban planning. While the lion's share of the work on innovation is macro in scope, our research looks at the connection between the micro level (the leader) and this macro view. To gain more insight into the intellectual foundations of this work, see, for example, Kim B. Clark and Rebecca Henderson, "Architectural Innovation: The Reconfiguration of Existing Product Technologies and the Failure of Established Firms," *Administrative Science Quarterly* 35, no. 1 (1990): 9–30; Clayton M. Christensen, *The Innovator's Dilemma: When New Technologies Cause Great Firms to Fail* (Boston: Harvard Business School Press, 1997); Clayton M. Christensen and Michael E. Raynor, *The Innovator's Solution: Creating and Sustaining Successful Growth* (Boston: Harvard Business School Press, 2003); Gary Hamel and C. K. Prahalad, *Competing for the Future* (Boston: Harvard Business School Press, 1994); James I. Cash, Michael J. Earl, and Robert Morison, "Teaming Up to Crack Innovation and Enterprise Integration," *Harvard Business Review*, November 2008, 90–100; Eric von Hippel, *The Sources of Innovation* (New York: Oxford University Press, 1988); Rosabeth Moss Kanter, *The Change Masters: Innovation for Productivity in the American Corporation* (New York: Simon & Schuster, 1983);

Nicholas Negroponte, "Creating a Culture of Ideas," *Technology Review*, February 2003, 34–35; C. K. Prahalad and M. S. Krishnan, *The New Age of Innovation: Driving Co-created Value through Global Networks* (New York: McGraw-Hill, 2008); Michael Schrage, *Serious Play: How the World's Best Companies Simulate to Innovate* (Boston: Harvard Business School Press, 2000); and Michael Tushman and Charles A. O'Reilly, *Winning through Innovation: A Practical Guide to Leading Organizational Change and Renewal* (Boston: Harvard Business School Press, 2002).

Chapter 1

1. See, for example, Karen Paik, *To Infinity and Beyond!: The Story of Pixar Animation Studios* (San Francisco: Chronicle Books, 2007); David A. Price, *The Pixar Touch: The Making of a Company* (New York: Alfred A. Knopf, 2008); and Ed Catmull, "How Pixar Fosters Collective Creativity," *Harvard Business Review*, September 2008, 64–72.

2. Catmull, "How Pixar Fosters Collective Creativity," 72.

3. Catmull, "How Pixar Fosters Collective Creativity," 66.

4. See, for example, Peter F. Drucker, "The Discipline of Innovation," *Harvard Business Review*, August 2002, 95–103; Mehrdad Baghai and James Quigley, *As One: Individual Action, Collective Power* (New York: Penguin, 2011); Warren G. Bennis and Patricia Ward Biederman, *Organizing Genius: The Secret of Creative Collaboration* (Reading, MA: Addison-Wesley, 1997); J. Richard Hackman, *Collaborative Intelligence: Using Teams to Solve Hard Problems* (San Francisco: Berrett-Koehler, 2011); and Keith Sawyer, *Group Genius: The Creative Power of Collaboration* (New York: Basic Books, 2007), 5, 8–9. For a cultural and historical look at the key relationships and social contexts of some of the most creative people of our time, see Howard Gardner, *Creating Minds: An Anatomy of Creativity Seen through the Lives of Freud, Einstein, Picasso, Stravinsky, Eliot, Graham, and Gandhi* (New York: Basic Books, 1993); Howard Gardner, *Extraordinary Minds: Portraits of Four Exceptional Individuals and an Examination of Our Own Extraordinariness* (New York: Basic Books, 1998); and Vera John-Steiner, *Creative Collaboration* (New York: Oxford University Press, 2000). Other works on creative people include Mihaly Csikszentmihalyi, *Creativity: Flow and the Psychology of Discovery and Invention* (New York: HarperCollins, 1996); and Jacob Getzels and Mihaly Csikszentmihalyi, *The Creative Vision: A Longitudinal Study of Problem Finding in Art* (New York: Wiley, 1976). In addition, the research of Teresa Amabile and Dorothy Leonard-Barton has been especially influential on our thinking. In particular, see Teresa Amabile, *The Social Psychology of Creativity* (New York: Springer-Verlag, 1983); Teresa Amabile, *Creativity in Context: Update to the Social Psychology of Creativity* (Boulder, CO: Westview Press, 1996); Teresa Amabile, Sigal G. Barsade, Jennifer S. Mueller, and Barry M. Shaw, "Affect and Creativity at Work," *Administrative Science Quarterly* 50, no. 3 (2005): 367–403;

and Dorothy Leonard-Barton, *Wellsprings of Knowledge: Building and Sustaining the Sources of Innovation* (Boston: Harvard Business School Press, 1995). There are many other works that explore the creative process and organizational life. See, for example, John Kao, *Jamming: The Art and Discipline of Business Creativity* (New York: Collins Business, 1997); R. Keith Sawyer, *Explaining Creativity: The Science of Human Innovation* (New York: Oxford University Press, 2006); and Robert Sutton and Andrew Hargadon, "Brainstorming Groups in Context: Effectiveness in a Product Design Firm," *Administrative Science Quarterly* 41, no. 4 (1996): 685–718.

5. For an in-depth look at Edison's life, see, for example, Neil Baldwin, *Edison: Inventing the Century* (Chicago: University of Chicago Press, 2001).

6. See, for example, Tim Brown, "Design Thinking," *Harvard Business Review*, June 2008, 84–92; Tom Kelley and Jonathan Littman, *The Art of Innovation: Lessons in Creativity from IDEO, America's Leading Design Firm* (New York: Doubleday, 2001); Rita Gunther McGrath and Ian C. MacMillan, *Discovery-Driven Growth: A Breakthrough Process to Reduce Risk and Seize Opportunity* (Boston: Harvard Business Press, 2009); Colin Raney and Ryan Jacoby, "Decisions by Design: Stop Deciding, Start Designing," *Rotman Magazine*, Winter 2010, 31–39; Michael Schrage, *Serious Play: How the World's Best Companies Simulate to Innovate* (Boston: Harvard Business School Press, 2000); and Roberto Verganti, *Design-Driven Innovation: Changing the Rules of Competition by Radically Innovating What Things Mean* (Boston: Harvard Business Press, 2009). Stefan Thomke's work is useful for understanding the process and importance of what we call creative agility. See Stefan Thomke, "Enlightened Experimentation: The New Imperative for Innovation," *Harvard Business Review*, February 2001, 66–75. See also Stefan Thomke and Eric von Hippel, "Customers as Innovators: A New Way to Create Value," *Harvard Business Review*, April 2002, 74–81. The work on process innovation is also helpful. See Gary P. Pisano, *The Development Factory: Unlocking the Potential of Process Innovation* (Boston: Harvard Business School Press, 1997).

7. See, for example, Roger Martin, *The Opposable Mind: How Successful Leaders Win through Integrative Thinking* (Boston: Harvard Business School Press, 2007), 4; Roger Martin, *The Design of Business: Why Design Thinking Is the Next Competitive Advantage* (Boston: Harvard Business Press, 2009); Pauline Graham, ed., *Mary Parker Follett—Prophet of Management: A Celebration of Writings from the 1920s* (Boston: Harvard Business School Press, 1995), 20; and Mary Parker Follett, *Creative Experience* (Bristol: Thoemmes Press, 2001).

8. Quoted in Mihaly Csikszentmihalyi and J. W. Getzels, "Discovery-Oriented Behavior and the Originality of Creative Products: A Study with Artists," *Journal of Personality and Social Psychology* 19, no. 1 (1971): 47–52.

9. Boris Groysberg, Jeffrey T. Polzer, and Hillary Anger Elfenbein, "Too Many Cooks Spoil the Broth: How High Status Individuals Decrease Group Effectiveness," *Organization Science* 22, no. 3 (May-June 2011): 722–737.

10. As Pixar has scaled its business and begun to produce more than one feature film at a time, this practice has had to be reviewed. Whatever future credits include, the intention remains the same: to be as inclusive as possible.

Chapter 2

1. For other examples of a discussion of the paradoxes of management, see, for example, Wendy K. Smith and Marianne W. Lewis, "Toward a Theory of Paradox: A Dynamic Equilibrium Model of Organizing," *Academy of Management Review* 36, no. 2 (2011): 381–403; David L. Bradford and Allan R. Cohen, *Managing for Excellence: The Guide to Developing High Performance in Contemporary Organizations* (New York: John Wiley, 1984); and Kenwyn K. Smith and David N. Berg, *Paradoxes of Group Life: Understanding Conflict, Paralysis, and Movement in Group Dynamics* (San Francisco: Jossey-Bass, 1987).

2. For research on the importance of psychological safety and the effects of too little support, see Amy Edmondson, "Psychological Safety and Learning Behavior in Work Teams," *Administrative Science Quarterly* 44, no. 2 (1999): 350–383. Also useful is Edmondson's article on organizations that foster "execution-as-learning." See Amy Edmondson, "The Competitive Imperative of Learning," *Harvard Business Review*, July–August 2008, 60–67. For research on groupthink and the effects of too much support, see Irving L. Janis, *Groupthink: Psychological Studies of Policy Decisions and Fiascoes* (Boston: Houghton Mifflin, 1982).

3. See, for example, Amy C. Edmondson, "Strategies for Learning from Failure," *Harvard Business Review*, April 2011, 48–55.

4. To learn more about doing effective postmortems, see, for example, David A. Garvin, *Learning in Action: A Guide to Putting the Learning Organization to Work* (Boston: Harvard Business School Press, 2000); Peter M. Senge, *The Fifth Discipline: The Art and Practice of the Learning Organization* (New York: Doubleday/Currency, 2006); and Francesca Gino and Gary P. Pisano, "Why Leaders Don't Learn from Success," *Harvard Business Review*, April 2011, 68–74.

5. See, for example, Nitin Nohria and J. D. Berkley, "From Structure to Structuring: A Pragmatic Perspective on Organizational Design," working paper 96-053, Harvard Business School, Boston, 1996. For other insights into structuring, see Lowell L. Bryan and Claudia Joyce, *Mobilizing Minds: Creating Wealth from Talent in the 21st Century Organization* (New York: McGraw-Hill, 2007); Anne S. Miner, Paula Bassoff, and Christine Moorman, "Organizational Improvisation and Learning: A Field Study," *Administrative Science Quarterly* 46, no. 2 (2001): 304–337; and Clay Shirky, *Here Comes Everybody: The Power of Organizing without Organizations* (New York: Penguin, 2008). See also Alistair Cockburn and Jim Highsmith, "Agile Software Development: The Business of Innovation,"

Computer 34, no. 9 (2001): 121, which argues that "organizations are complex adaptive systems. A complex adaptive system is one in which decentralized, independent individuals interact in self-organizing ways, guided by a set of simple, generative rules, to create innovative, emergent results." Cockburn and Highsmith define generative rules as, "a minimum set of things you must do under all situations to generate appropriate practices for special situations."

6. Tad Friend, "Second Act Twist," *The New Yorker,* October 17, 2011, 62–71.

Chapter 3

1. There is no one best way to lead. For more work on leadership, see, for example, John P. Kotter, *Leading Change* (Boston: Harvard Business School Press, 1999); John P. Kotter, *John P. Kotter On What Leaders Really Do* (Boston: Harvard Business School Press, 1999); and John P. Kotter and Dan S. Cohen, *The Heart of Change: Real-Life Stories of How People Change Their Organizations* (Boston: Harvard Business School Press, 2002). See also, Warren Bennis and Burt Nanus, *Leaders: The Strategies for Taking Charge* (New York: HarperBusiness, 1997). Kotter and Bennis both make the distinction between leadership and management. Leadership is about coping with change: setting direction, aligning people, and motivating and inspiring. Management is about coping with complexity: planning and budgeting, organizing and staffing, controlling, and problem solving. They both found that many companies lack agility and the capacity to adapt to new competitive environments because they are overmanaged and underled—a very important observation. Note that their work was focused on change, not innovation; these are related but different phenomena. This book is about leading innovation.

2. For more on Vineet Nayar and HCL, see Linda A. Hill, Tarun Khanna, and Emily A. Stecker, "HCL Technologies (A)," Case 9-408-004 (Boston: Harvard Business School, 2008); and Linda A. Hill et al., "HCL Technologies (B)," Case 9-408-006 (Boston: Harvard Business School, 2008). See also Vineet Nayar, *Employees First, Customers Second: Turning Conventional Management Upside Down* (Boston: Harvard Business Press, 2010).

3. N. Mayes, "HCL Technologies Captures $330 million DSG Deal," *Computer Business Review,* January 23, 2006.

4. Barry Rubenstein, "Why HCL Technologies is Disruptive and Bears Watching," *IDC,* November 2006.

5. "Hungry Tiger, Dancing Elephant: How India Is Changing IBM's World," *The Economist,* April 4, 2007.

6. We are looking specifically at leading innovation. It should be noted that others have espoused some of the ideas here with regard to leadership in general, given

today's knowledge economy. See, for, example, Nitin Nohria and Rakesh Khurana, eds., *Handbook of Leadership Theory and Practice: An HBS Centennial Colloquium on Advancing Leadership* (Boston: Harvard Business School Press, 2010); and John Hagel III, John Seely Brown, and Lang Davison, *The Power of Pull: How Small Moves, Smartly Made, Can Set Big Things in Motion* (New York: Basic Books, 2010). For more on how companies attract and develop world-class talent, see Claudio Fernández-Aráoz, *Great People Decisions: Why They Matter So Much, Why They Are So Hard, and How You can Master Them* (Hoboken, NJ: Wiley, 2007). For more work on "stars," see Robert Kelley and Janet Caplan, "How Bell Labs Creates Star Performers," *Harvard Business Review*, July-August 1992, 128–139. For understanding the mechanisms at play in shaping experience, see B. Joseph Pine II and James Gilmore, *The Experience Economy: Work Is Theatre and Every Business a Stage* (Boston: Harvard Business School Press, 1999). For more on intrinsic motivation and on the effective leadership of teams, see, for example, J. Richard Hackman, *Leading Teams: Setting the Stage for Great Performances* (Boston: Harvard Business School Press, 2002); and Daniel Pink, *Drive: The Surprising Truth About What Motivates Us* (New York: Riverhead, 2009). For more on the ingredients of positive workplace energy and how these lead to innovation, see Lynda Gratton, *Hot Spots: Why Some Teams, Workplaces and Organizations Buzz with Energy—and Others Don't* (New York: Berrett-Koehler, 2007). For an insightful perspective on how work and the workforce are changing, see James O'Toole, Edward Lawler, and Susan Meisinger, *The New American Workplace* (New York: Palgrave Macmillan, 2007). For more on management innovation, see Gary Hamel, "The Why, What, and How of Management Innovation," *Harvard Business Review*, February 2006, 72–84.

Chapter 4

1. To learn more about Luca de Meo and Volkswagen, see Linda A. Hill and Dana M. Teppert, "Luca de Meo at Volkswagen Group," Case 8-413-124 (Boston: Harvard Business School, 2013). See also Luca de Meo, *Da 0 a 500: Storie Vissute, Idee e Consigli da Uno Dei Manager Più Dinamici Della Nuova Generazione* (Venice, Italy: Marsilio, 2010).

2. Joann Muller, "The Best Laid Plan," *Forbes*, April 17, 2013, 91–100.

3. "VW Conquers the World," *The Economist*, July 7, 2012, 59–60.

4. "VW Conquers the World," 60. Its exact statement was: "Last year [2011] ... as Toyota struggled with the aftermath of Japan's tsunami and GM floundered in Europe, VW reached its goal seven years early ..., if you do not count Subaru, Toyota's distant affiliate, or GM's Wuling joint venture in China, which mainly makes Chinese-branded cars."

5. Muller, "The Best Laid Plan."

6. See, for example, Peter Block, *Community: The Structure of Belonging* (San Francisco: Berrett-Koehler, 2008), 24. The literature regarding social movement and community building is also helpful in this regard. See, for example, Gerald F. Davis, Doug McAdam, W. Richard Scott, and Mayer N. Zald, eds., *Social Movements and Organization Theory* (London: Cambridge University Press, 2005); Doug McAdam and David A. Snow, *Social Movements: Readings on Their Emergence, Mobilization, and Dynamics* (Los Angeles: Roxbury Publishing Company, 1997); and Rosabeth Moss Kanter, *Commitment and Community: Communes and Utopias in Sociological Perspective* (Boston: Harvard University Press, 1972). See also John Pepper, *What Really Matters: Service, Leadership, People, and Values* (New Haven, CT: Yale University Press, 2007).

7. For more work on the importance of purpose, see, for example, Doug A. Ready and Emily Truelove, "The Power of Collective Ambition," *Harvard Business Review*, December 2011, 94–102; Joel Podolny, Rakesh Khurana, and Mary Hill-Popper, "Revisiting the Meaning of Leadership," *Research in Organizational Behavior* 26, no. 1 (2005): 1–36; John Henry Clippinger, *A Crowd of One: The Future of Individual Identity* (New York: PublicAffairs, 2007); and Sumantra Ghoshal and Christopher A. Bartlett, *The Individualized Corporation: A Fundamentally New Approach to Management* (New York: HarperBusiness, 1997), chap. 8–9. For more on community building and social capital, see, for example, Robert Putnam, "Bowling Alone: America's Declining Social Capital," *Journal of Democracy* 6, no. 1 (1995): 65–78; Henry Mintzberg, "Rebuilding Companies As Communities," *Harvard Business Review*, July 2009, 140–143; and Gerben S. van der Vegt and J. Stuart Bunderson, "Learning and Performance in Multidisciplinary Teams: The Importance of Collective Team Identification," *Academy of Management Journal* 48, no. 3 (2005): 532–547.

8. See, for example, Peter Block's description of how "transformation hinges on changing the structure of how we engage with each other" in *Community: The Structure of Belonging*, 25. In the spirit of structuring, leaders of innovation are always prepared to adapt the structure as necessary, so they watch what patterns of interaction emerge, reflect, and then course-correct (or recalibrate) when necessary. In so doing, they seem to rely on biological models when making structure decisions. Many put in place a few simple principles from which they hope a complex social system conducive to innovation will emerge.

Chapter 5

1. For more about Kit Hinrichs and Pentagram, see Linda A. Hill and Emily A. Stecker, "Kit Hinrichs at Pentagram (A)," Case 9-408-127 (Boston: Harvard Business School, 2008); and Linda A. Hill and Emily A. Stecker, "Kit Hinrichs at Pentagram (B)," Supplement 9-408-128 (Boston: Harvard Business School, 2008).

2. Bruce Sterling, "Look Right, Work Right," *Profile: Pentagram Design*, edited by Susan Yelavich (London: Phaidon, 2004), 162.

3. Emily Barker, "The Pentagram Papers," *Inc.* 21, no. 12 (September 1999).

4. Rick Poynor, "The Idea of Pentagram," *Profile: Pentagram Design*, edited by Susan Yelavich (London: Phaidon, 2004), 20–21.

5. Poynor, "The Idea of Pentagram," 27.

6. Poynor, "The Idea of Pentagram," 20.

7. Members of true communities share values. The importance of values and their associated rules of engagement have been discussed by many who looked at the relationship between culture and organizational outcomes. See, for example, Jennifer A. Chatman and Sandra A. Cha, "Leading by Leveraging Culture," *California Management Review*, July 1993, 104–111; Edgar Schein, *Organizational Culture and Leadership: A Dynamic View* (San Francisco: Jossey-Bass, 1985); Robert Simons, *Levers of Control: How Managers Use Innovative Control Systems to Drive Strategic Renewal* (Boston: Harvard Business School Press, 1995); and James L. Heskett, *The Culture Cycle: How to Shape the Unseen Force That Transforms Performance* (Upper Saddle River, NJ: FT Press, 2012).

8. Randall Rothenberg, "Global Warming: The Multinational Interdisciplining of Pentagram Design," *Pentagram Book Five* (New York: Monacelli Press, 1999), 12.

9. Pentagram Partners and Delphine Hirasuna, *The Pentagram Papers* (San Francisco: Chronicle Books, 2006), 13.

10. There are many definitions of trust. This definition is what emerged from our analysis of the data, and it differs somewhat from the notion of trust discussed in *Being the Boss,* in which we argue that a leader's intentions (or character) and judgment (or competence) form the basis for trust. See Linda A. Hill and Kent Lineback, *Being the Boss: The Three Imperatives for Becoming a Great Leader* (Boston: Harvard Business Review Press, 2011).

11. Pentagram Partners and Delphine Hirasuna, *The Pentagram Papers* (San Francisco: Chronicle Books, 2006), 13.

Chapter 6

1. The term "creative abrasion" was first used by Jerry Hirshberg in *The Creative Priority: Driving Innovative Business in the Real World* (New York: HarperBusiness, 1998). Dorothy Leonard's work on creative abrasion has been especially helpful to us as well. See, for example, Dorothy Leonard and Walter Swap, *When Sparks*

Fly: Igniting Creativity in Groups (Boston: Harvard Business School Press, 1999). We also drew on Keith Sawyer's *Group Genius: The Creative Power of Collaboration* (New York: Basic Books, 2007).

2. Frank Lewis Dyer and Thomas Commerford Martin, *Edison, His Life and Inventions* (New York: Harper Brothers, 1929), chap. XXIV.

3. See, for example, Jane Magruder Watkins and Bernard J. Mohr, *Appreciative Inquiry: Change at the Speed of Imagination* (San Francisco: Jossey-Bass/Pfeiffer, 2001); John Child, "Commentary on Constructive Conflict," *Mary Parker Follet—Prophet of Management: A Celebration of Writings from the 1920s*, ed. Pauline Graham (Boston: Harvard Business School Press, 1995), 87–95; and Kathleen M. Eisenhardt, Jean L. Kahwajy, and L. J. Bourgeois III, "How Management Teams Can Have a Good Fight," *Harvard Business Review*, July-August 1997, 77–85.

4. Our research has been influenced by David Thomas and Robin Ely's work on leveraging diversity. See Robin Ely and David Thomas, "Cultural Diversity at Work: The Moderating Effects of Work Group Perspectives on Diversity," *Administrative Science Quarterly* 46 (June 2001): 229–273. Another interesting perspective comes from Scott Page. See Scott E. Page, *The Difference: How the Power of Diversity Creates Better Groups, Firms, Schools, and Societies* (Princeton, NJ: Princeton University Press, 2008). See also Richard Florida, *The Rise of the Creative Class: And How It's Transforming Work, Leisure, Community, and Everyday Life* (New York: Basic Books, 2002), 8, 15; and Frans Johansson, *The Medici Effect: Breakthrough Insights at the Intersection of Ideas, Concepts, and Cultures* (Boston: Harvard Business School Press, 2004).

5. See Page, *The Difference*.

6. Quoted in Mark Stefik and Barbara Stefik, *Breakthrough: Stories and Strategies of Radical Innovation* (Cambridge, MA: MIT Press, 2004), 169–170.

7. Florida, *The Rise of the Creative Class*, 227.

8. See Karen A. Jehn. "A Multimethod Examination of the Benefits and Detriments of Intragroup Conflict," *Administrative Science Quarterly* 40, no. 2 (June 1995): 256–282.

9. Amy C. Edmondson, "Psychological Safety and Learning Behavior in Work Teams," *Administrative Science Quarterly* 44, no. 2 (1999): 350–383.

10. For insights into the impact of context (physical space) on innovation and the role of space on patterns of interaction, see, for example, Christopher Alexander, Sara Ishikawa, and Murray Silverstein, *A Pattern Language: Towns, Buildings, Construction* (New York: Oxford University Press, 1977); and Stewart Brand, *How Buildings Learn: What Happens After They're Built* (New York: Viking, 1994).

Chapter 7

1. For more about Meg Whitman, Philipp Justus, and eBay Germany, see Linda A. Hill and Maria T. Farkas, "Meg Whitman at eBay Inc., (A)" Case 9-401-024 (Boston: Harvard Business School, 2000); Linda A. Hill and Maria T. Farkas, "Meg Whitman and eBay Germany," Case 9-402-006 (Boston: Harvard Business School, 2001); Linda A. Hill and Maria T. Farkas, "Philipp Justus at eBay Germany (A)," Case 9-402-007 (Boston: Harvard Business School, 2002); Linda A. Hill and Maria T. Farkas, "Philipp Justus at eBay Germany (B)," Case 9-402-015 (Boston: Harvard Business School, 2001); and Linda A. Hill and Emily A. Stecker, "Philipp Justus at eBay Germany (C)," Case 9-409-029 (Boston: Harvard Business School, 2008).

2. Prudential Equity Group, LLC, Company Report on eBay, Inc., January 8, 2007.

3. Credit Suisse Equity Research Report on eBay, January 18, 2012.

4. See Stefan Thomke, "Enlightened Experimentation: The New Imperative for Innovation," *Harvard Business Review*, February 2011, 66–75; Stefan Thomke and Eric von Hippel, "Customers as Innovators: A New Way to Create Value," *Harvard Business Review*, April 2002, 74–81. See also Neil Baldwin, *Edison: Inventing the Century* (Chicago: University of Chicago Press, 2001), 73–74, 83; Tom Kelley and Jonathan Littman, *The Art of Innovation: Lessons in Creativity from IDEO, America's Leading Design Firm* (New York: Doubleday, 2001), 232.

5. For example, see Edison's "cut and try" method, as documented in Baldwin, *Edison*, 73–75.

6. See, for example, Shona L. Brown and Kathleen M. Eisenhardt, "The Art of Continuous Change: Linking Complexity Theory and Time-Paced Evolution in Relentlessly Shifting Organizations," *Administrative Science Quarterly* 42, no. 1 (March 1997): 1–34.

Chapter 8

1. For more about Bill Coughran and Google's infrastructure group, see Linda A. Hill and Emily A. Stecker, "Systems Infrastructure at Google (A)," Case 9-410-110 (Boston: Harvard Business School, 2010); and Linda A. Hill and Emily A. Stecker, "Systems Infrastructure at Google (B)," Case 9-410-111 (Boston: Harvard Business School, 2010).

2. See Thomas R. Eisenmann and Kerry Herman, "Google Inc.," Case 9-806-105 (Boston: Harvard Business School, 2010), 4.

3. See Chad Bartley and Steve Weinstein, "High growth in search creates opportunities for niche players," Pacific Crest Securities, November 4, 2003, 11.

4. Coughran was working on what is referred to as a "wicked problem." Urban planner and designer Horst Rittel, upon finding that traditional planning and problem-solving methods were inadequate for the ill-structured problems he often encountered in city planning, used this term to describe those problems that, among other things, cannot really be understood until they are solved. For this definition and more information on what Rittel defines as wicked problems, see his work as discussed in Jeffrey Conklin, *Dialogue Mapping: Building Shared Understanding of Wicked Problems* (Hoboken, NJ: Wiley, 2006). For more on wicked problems, see also John Camillus, "Strategy as a Wicked Problem," *Harvard Business Review*, May 2008, 98–106.

5. See Mary Parker Follett, *Creative Experience* (Bristol: Thoemmes Press, 2001). Follett discusses the importance of not settling for choice A or B, but, rather, creating an innovative third way that combines elements of and improves on both A and B. An integrative solution is an approach that solves a conflict by accommodating the real demands of all the parties involved. The result is often represented more aptly as a mosaic rather than a melting pot of the varied talents and perspectives of those involved.

6. See Roger Martin, *The Opposable Mind: How Successful Leaders Win through Integrative Thinking* (Boston: Harvard Business School Press, 2007). See also Roger Martin, "How Successful Leaders Think," *Harvard Business Review*, June 2007, 60–67.

7. See Ronald A. Heifetz and Marty Linsky, *Leadership on the Line: Staying Alive through the Dangers of Leading* (Boston: Harvard Business School Press, 2002), 13–20. Although Heifetz and Linsky do not write about innovation specifically, they do discuss how leaders must sometimes disappoint followers' expectations.

8. The structure of innovative companies we have studied seems to fit what Karl Weick found in his work presented in *The Social Psychology of Organizing*. He described the structures as "loosely coupled" or network-like organizations formed of relatively autonomous building blocks (smaller units) that were brought together, disassembled, or reconfigured as necessary. See Karl Weick, *The Social Psychology of Organizing* (New York: McGraw-Hill, 1969).

9. Eric Schmidt and Hal Varian, "Google: Ten Golden Rules," *Newsweek*, spec. ed., December 2005, 42–46.

10. For more, see Eric von Hippel, *Democratizing Innovation* (Cambridge, MA: MIT Press, 2005); and Clay Shirky, *Here Comes Everybody: The Power of Organizing without Organizations* (New York: Penguin, 2008). See also Peter Skarzynski

and Rowan Gibson, *Innovation to the Core: A Blueprint for Transforming the Way Your Company Innovates* (Boston: Harvard Business Press, 2008), 264–265; and Harold J. Leavitt, *Top Down: Why Hierarchies Are Here to Stay and How to Manage Them More Effectively* (Boston: Harvard Business School Press, 2005).

Chapter 9

1. In understanding such ecosystems, we found several streams of work particularly useful. Benkler is useful for understanding how modes of production are changing. See Yochai Benkler, *The Wealth of Networks: How Social Production Transforms Markets and Freedom* (New Haven, CT: Yale University Press, 2006); Thomas W. Malone, Robert Laubacher, and Michael S. Scott Morton, eds., *Inventing Organizations of the 21st Century* (Cambridge, MA: MIT Press, 2003); and Gary P. Pisano and Roberto Verganti, "Which Kind of Collaboration Is Right for You?" *Harvard Business Review*, December 2008, 78–86. Von Hippel's work is useful in this regard, too. See Carliss Y. Baldwin and Eric von Hippel, "Modeling a Paradigm Shift: From Producer Innovation to User and Open Collaborative Innovation," *Organization Science* 22, no. 6 (December 2011): 1399–1417. See also Eric von Hippel, *Democratizing Innovation* (Cambridge, MA: MIT Press, 2005). Marco Iansiti's work demonstrates the complexity of the networks in which today's organizations must operate. See Marco Iansiti and Roy Levien, *The Keystone Advantage: What the New Dynamics of Business Ecosystems Mean for Strategy, Innovation, and Sustainability* (Boston: Harvard Business School, 2004). See also Andrew King and Karim R. Lakhani, "Using Open Innovation to Identify the Best Ideas," *MIT Sloan Management Review* 55, no. 1 (Fall 2013): 41–48; and Kevin J. Boudreau and Karim R. Lakhani, "Using the Crowd as an Innovation Partner," *Harvard Business Review*, April 2013, 60–69.

2. See, for example, Karim R. Lakhani, Hila Lifshitz-Assaf, and Michael Tushman, "Open Innovation and Organizational Boundaries: Task Decomposition, Knowledge Distribution and the Locus of Innovation," *Handbook of Economic Organization: Integrating Economic and Organization Theory*, edited by Anna Grandori (Northampton, MA: Edward Elgar Publishing, 2013), 355–382.

3. See Chesbrough's work on open innovation. Henry William Chesbrough, *Open Innovation: The New Imperative for Creating and Profiting from Technology* (Boston: Harvard Business School Press, 2003).

4. See, for example, the 2013 IBM study of C-suite executives, "The Customer-Activated Enterprise: Insights from the Global C-suite Study," October 2013.

5. Governor Gray Davis, "State of the State Address," Sacramento, CA, January 5, 2000.

6. For more on Calit2, see Linda A. Hill and Alison Berkley Wagonfeld, "Calit2: A UC San Diego, UC Irvine Partnership," Case 9-411-105 (Boston: Harvard Business School, 2011).

7. KAUST was the first higher education opportunity in Saudi Arabia to include women, who made up 15 percent of its inaugural class. For the visualization facilities, see http://kvl.kaust.edu/sa/Pages/Showcase.aspx.

8. For a recent book on how Bell Labs operated, see Jon Gertner, *The Idea Factory: Bell Labs and the Great Age of American Innovation* (New York: Penguin Press, 2012).

9. Those who bridge gaps, as Smarr did well, are called brokers. Brokers occupy structural positions that enable them to link pairs of otherwise unconnected actors. The literature on brokerage is extensive. For an introduction, see Ronald Burt, *Structural Holes* (Boston: Harvard Business School Press, 1992). For a discussion of how value is derived from "weak" ties, see Mark S. Granovetter, "The Strength of Weak Ties," *American Journal of Sociology* 78, no. 6 (May 1973): 1360–1380. We also found Hargadon and Sutton's study of technology brokering at IDEO to be useful. See Andrew Hargadon and Robert I. Sutton, "Technology Brokering and Innovation in a Product Development Firm," *Administrative Science Quarterly* 42, no. 4 (December 1997): 716–749.

10. A colleague, Boris Groysberg, introduced us to Schulman as one of the most collaborative innovative leaders he had ever met. For more about Schulman and DLA Piper, see Boris Groysberg, Victoria W. Winston, and Shirley M. Spence, "Leadership in Law: Amy Schulman at DLA Piper," Case 9-407-033 (Boston: Harvard Business School, 2008); and Boris Groysberg, L. Kevin Kelly, and Bryan MacDonald, "The New Path to the C-Suite," *Harvard Business Review*, March 2011, 60–68.

Epilogue

1. See, for example, Jeff Dyer, Hal Gregersen, and Clayton M. Christensen, *The Innovator's DNA: Mastering the Five Skills of Disruptive Innovators* (Boston: Harvard Business Review Press, 2011); Scott Snook, "Be, Know, Do: Forming Character the West Point Way," *Compass: A Journal of Leadership* 1, no. 2 (Spring 2004): 16–19, 38; Morgan W. McCall Jr., *High Flyers: Developing the Next Generation of Leaders* (Boston: Harvard Business Review Press, 1998); and Deborah Ancona, Thomas W. Malone, Wanda J. Orlikowski, and Peter M. Senge, "In Praise of the Incomplete Leader," *Harvard Business Review*, February 2007, 92–100.

2. See, for example, Linda A. Hill, *Becoming a Manager: How New Managers Master the Challenges of Leadership*, 2nd ed. (Boston: Harvard Business School Press, 2003); Morgan W. McCall Jr. and Michael M. Lombardo, *The Lessons of Experience* (Lexington, MA: Lexington Books, 1988); and Warren G. Bennis and Thomas Robert, "Crucibles of Leadership," *Harvard Business Review*, September 2002, 39–45.

3. See, for example, C. K. Prahalad, *The Fortune at the Bottom of the Pyramid: Eradicating Poverty through Profits*, 5th anniv. ed. (Upper Saddle River, NJ: Pearson Education, 2010). It may also be useful to read C. K. Prahalad and M. S. Krishnan, *The New Age of Innovation: Driving Co-created Value Through Global Networks* (New York: McGraw-Hill, 2008). See also Vijay Govindarajan and Chris Trimble, *Reverse Innovation: Create Far from Home, Win Everywhere* (Boston: Harvard Business Review Press, 2012); and Richard T. Pascale, Jerry Sternin, and Monique Sternin, *The Power of Positive Deviance: How Unlikely Innovators Solve the World's Toughest Problems* (Boston: Harvard Business Press, 2010).

4. Sam Palmisano, CEO of IBM, provides an apt example of a leader who understands the importance of community and a sense of shared purpose and values in an organization's ability to innovate. For more about Palmisano's focus on values at IBM, see Samuel J. Palmisano, "Leading Change When Business Is Good," *Harvard Business Review*, December 2004, 60–70.

5. Some have noted that while Western conceptions of leaders tend to focus on leading from the front ("tribalizing"), Eastern views often focus on leaders leading from behind ("trailing the group"). The latter may be more in line with our own research on the leaders of innovation. See Tanya Menon, Jessica Sim, Jeanne Ho-Ying Fu, Chi-yue Chiu, and Ying-yi Hong, "Blazing the Trail Versus Trailing the Group: Culture and Perceptions of the Leader's Position," *Organizational Behavior and Human Decision Processes* 113, no. 1 (2010): 51–61. For more about leading from behind, see Nelson Mandela, *Long Walk to Freedom: The Autobiography of Nelson Mandela* (London: Little, Brown & Company, 1995), 22.

6. For more about Jacqueline Novogratz, see Novogratz, *The Blue Sweater: Bridging the Gap Between Rich and Poor in an Interconnected World* (New York: Rodale, 2009).

7. "Created in the spirit of TED's mission, 'ideas worth spreading,' the TEDx program," as described on the official TED website, "is designed to give communities, organizations and individuals the opportunity to stimulate dialogue through TED-like experiences at the local level." See http://www.ted.com/tedx.

8. For more on "tri-sector athletes," see, for example, Nick Lovegrove and Matthew Thomas, "Triple-Strength Leadership," *Harvard Business Review*, September 2013, 46–56.

9. For more about Kim's life, which could be made into a blockbuster movie, see her autobiography (published in Korean). Sung-joo Kim, *Wake Up Call: A Beautiful Outcast* (Seoul: Random House JoongAng, 2000).

SELECTED BIBLIOGRAPHY

For the complete bibliography, visit hbr.org/books/collective-genius. The selected references listed below are publications we recommend to readers who would like to learn more about the topics raised in a particular chapter.

Introduction

Amabile, Teresa M., and Mukti Khaire. "Creativity and the Role of the Leader." *Harvard Business Review*, October 2008, 100–109.

Christensen, Clayton M. *The Innovator's Dilemma: When New Technologies Cause Great Firms to Fail.* Boston: Harvard Business School Press, 1997.

Christensen, Clayton M., and Michael E. Raynor. *The Innovator's Solution: Creating and Sustaining Successful Growth.* Boston: Harvard Business School Press, 2003.

Dyer, Jeff, Hal Gregersen, and Clayton M. Christensen. *The Innovator's DNA: Mastering the Five Skills of Disruptive Innovators.* Boston: Harvard Business Review Press, 2011.

Govindarajan, Vijay, and Chris Trimble. *Ten Rules for Strategic Innovators: From Idea to Execution.* Boston: Harvard Business School Press, 2005.

Hamel, Gary, and C. K. Prahalad. *Competing for the Future.* Boston: Harvard Business School Press, 1994.

Hargadon, Andrew. *How Breakthroughs Happen: The Surprising Truth About How Companies Innovate.* Boston: Harvard Business School Press, 2003.

Henderson, Rebecca, and Richard G. Newell, eds. *Accelerating Energy Innovation: Insights from Multiple Sectors.* National Bureau of Economic Research Conference Report. Chicago: University of Chicago Press, 2011.

Mui, Chunka, and Paul B. Carroll. *The New Killer Apps: How Large Companies Can Out-Innovate Start-Ups.* Cornerloft Press. Printed in Charleston by CreateSpace, 2013.

Reeves, Byron, Thomas W. Malone, and Tony O'Driscoll. "Leadership's Online Labs." *Harvard Business Review,* May 2008, 58–66.

Tushman, Michael, and Charles A. O'Reilly. *Winning through Innovation: A Practical Guide to Leading Organizational Change and Renewal.* Boston: Harvard Business School Press, 2002.

Tushman, Michael L., Wendy K. Smith, and Andy Binns. "The Ambidextrous CEO." *Harvard Business Review,* June 2011, 74–80.

Chapter 1

Amabile, Teresa, Sigal G. Barsade, Jennifer S. Mueller, and Barry M. Staw. "Affect and Creativity at Work." *Administrative Science Quarterly* 50, no. 3 (2005): 367–403.

Amabile, Teresa, and Steven Kramer. *The Progress Principle: Using Small Wins to Ignite Joy, Engagement, and Creativity at Work.* Boston: Harvard Business Review Press, 2011.

Brown, John Seely. *Seeing Differently: Insights on Innovation.* Boston: Harvard Business School Press, 1997.

Brown, Tim. *Change by Design: How Design Thinking Transforms Organizations and Inspires Innovation.* New York: HarperCollins, 2009.

———. "Design Thinking." *Harvard Business Review,* June 2008, 84–92.

Catmull, Ed, and Amy Wallace. *Creativity, Inc.: Overcoming the Unseen Forces That Stand in the Way of True Inspiration.* New York: Random House, 2014.

Catmull, Ed. "How Pixar Fosters Collective Creativity." *Harvard Business Review,* September 2008, 64–72.

Csikszentmihalyi, Mihaly. *Creativity: Flow and the Psychology of Discovery and Invention.* New York: HarperCollins, 1996.

Downes, Larry, and Paul Nunes. *Big-Bang Disruption: Strategy in the Age of Devastating Innovation.* New York: Penguin, 2014.

Drucker, Peter F. "The Discipline of Innovation." *Harvard Business Review,* August 2002, 95–103.

Gardner, Howard. *Creating Minds: An Anatomy of Creativity Seen through the Lives of Freud, Einstein, Picasso, Stravinsky, Eliot, Graham, and Gandhi.* New York: Basic Books, 1993.

Graham, Pauline, ed. *Mary Parker Follett—Prophet of Management: A Celebration of Writings from the 1920s.* Boston: Harvard Business School Press, 1995.

Hagel, John III, and John Seely Brown. *The Only Sustainable Edge: Why Business Strategy Depends on Productive Friction and Dynamic Specialization.* Boston: Harvard Business School Press, 2005.

Isaacson, Walter. "The Real Leadership Lessons of Steve Jobs." *Harvard Business Review,* April 2012, 92–102.

Leonard-Barton, Dorothy. *Wellsprings of Knowledge: Building and Sustaining the Sources of Innovation.* Boston: Harvard Business School Press, 1995.

Sawyer, R. Keith. *Group Genius: The Creative Power of Collaboration.* New York: Basic Books, 2007.

Chapter 2

Baghai, Mehrdad, and James Quigley. *As One: Individual Action, Collective Power.* New York: Penguin, 2011.

Bennis, Warren G., and Patricia Ward Biederman. *Organizing Genius: The Secret of Creative Collaboration.* Reading, MA: Addison-Wesley, 1997.

Clippinger, John Henry. *A Crowd of One: The Future of Individual Identity.* New York: PublicAffairs, 2007.

Deci, Edward L., and Richard M. Ryan. *Intrinsic Motivation and Self-Determination in Human Behavior.* New York: Plenum, 1985.

Edmondson, Amy C. "Psychological Safety and Learning Behavior in Work Teams." *Administrative Science Quarterly* 44, no. 2 (1999): 350–383.

Edmondson, Amy C., and Edgar H. Schein. *Teaming: How Organizations Learn, Innovate, and Compete in the Knowledge Economy.* San Francisco: Jossey-Bass, 2012.

Follett, Mary Parker. *Creative Experience.* Bristol: Thoemmes Press, 2001.

Graham, Pauline. "Mary Parker Follett (1868–1993): A Pioneering Life." In *Mary Parker Follett—Prophet of Management: A Celebration of Writings from the 1920s,* edited by Pauline Graham, 11–32. Boston: Harvard Business School Press, 1995.

Groysberg, Boris, Jeffrey T. Polzer, and Hillary Anger Elfenbein. "Too Many Cooks Spoil the Broth: How High Status Individuals Decrease Group Effectiveness." *Organization Science* 22, no. 3 (May–June 2011): 722–737.

Hackman, J. Richard. *Collaborative Intelligence: Using Teams to Solve Hard Problems*. San Francisco: Berrett-Koehler, 2011.

Hagel, John III, John Seely Brown, and Lang Davison. *The Power of Pull: How Small Moves, Smartly Made, Can Set Big Things in Motion*. New York: Basic Books, 2010.

John-Steiner, Vera. *Creative Collaboration*. New York: Oxford University Press, 2000.

Kelley, Tom, and David Kelley. *Creative Confidence: Unleashing the Creative Potential Within Us All*. New York: Crown Publishing, 2013.

Leavitt, Harold J. *Top Down: Why Hierarchies Are Here to Stay and How to Manage Them More Effectively*. Boston: Harvard Business School Press, 2005.

Paik, Karen. *To Infinity and Beyond!: The Story of Pixar Animation Studios*. San Francisco: Chronicle Books, 2007.

Pink, Daniel. *Drive: The Surprising Truth About What Motivates Us*. New York: Riverhead, 2009.

Pisano, Gary P., and Roberto Verganti. "Which Kind of Collaboration Is Right for You?" *Harvard Business Review*, December 2008, 78–86.

Sawyer, R. Keith. *Group Genius: The Creative Power of Collaboration*. New York: Basic Books, 2007.

Senge, Peter M. *The Fifth Discipline: The Art and Practice of the Learning Organization*. New York: Doubleday/Currency, 2006.

Shirky, Clay. *Here Comes Everybody: The Power of Organizing Without Organizations*. New York: Penguin, 2008.

Smith, Kenwyn K., and David N. Berg. *Paradoxes of Group Life: Understanding Conflict, Paralysis, and Movement in Group Dynamics*. San Francisco: Jossey-Bass, 1987.

Smith, Wendy K., and Marianne W. Lewis. "Toward a Theory of Paradox: A Dynamic Equilibrium Model of Organizing." *Academy of Management Review* 36, no. 2 (2011): 381–403.

Sutton, Robert I. *Weird Ideas That Work: How to Build a Creative Company*. New York: Free Press, 2007.

Uzzi, Brian, and Jarrett Spiro. "Collaboration and Creativity: The Small World Problem." *American Journal of Sociology* 111, no. 2 (2005): 447–504.

Weick, Karl. *The Social Psychology of Organizing*. Reading, MA: Addison-Wesley, 1979.

Chapter 3

Cappelli, Peter. *The India Way: How India's Top Business Leaders Are Revolutionizing Management*. Boston: Harvard Business School Press, 2010.

Fernández-Aráoz, Claudio. *Great People Decisions: Why They Matter So Much, Why They Are So Hard, and How You Can Master Them.* Hoboken, NJ: Wiley, 2007.

Hackman, J. Richard, and Greg R. Oldham. "Motivation through the Design of Work: Test of a Theory." *Organizational Behavior and Human Performance* 16, no. 2 (1976): 250–279.

Hagel, John III, John Seely Brown, and Lang Davison. *The Power of Pull: How Small Moves, Smartly Made, Can Set Big Things in Motion.* New York: Basic Books, 2010.

Hamel, Gary. *The Future of Management.* Boston: Harvard Business School Press, 2007.

———. "The Why, What, and How of Management Innovation." *Harvard Business Review*, February 2006, 72–84.

Hill, Linda A., Tarun Khanna, and Emily A. Stecker. "HCL Technologies (A)." Case 9-408-004. Boston: Harvard Business School, 2008.

———. "HCL Technologies (B)." Case 9-408-006, Boston: Harvard Business School, 2008.

Kotter, John P. *John P. Kotter On What Leaders Really Do.* Boston: Harvard Business School Press, 1999.

———. "Accelerate!" *Harvard Business Review*, November 2012, 44–58.

Lafley, A. G., and Ram Charan. *The Game-Changer: How Every Leader Can Drive Everyday Innovation.* London: Profile Books, 2008.

Leonard, Dorothy, Gavin Barton, and Michelle Barton. "Make Yourself an Expert: How to Pull Knowledge from the Smartest People around You." *Harvard Business Review*, April 2013, 127–131.

Morieux, Yves. "Smart Rules: Six Ways to Get People to Solve Problems without You." *Harvard Business Review*, September 2011, 78–86.

Nayar, Vineet. *Employees First, Customers Second: Turning Conventional Management Upside Down.* Boston: Harvard Business Press, 2010.

Chapter 4

Block, Peter. *Community: The Structure of Belonging.* San Francisco: Berrett-Koehler, 2008.

Burt, Ronald. *Structural Holes.* Boston: Harvard Business School Press, 1992.

Clippinger, John Henry. *A Crowd of One: The Future of Individual Identity.* New York: PublicAffairs, 2007.

De Meo, Luca. *Da 0 a 500: Storie Vissute, Idee e Consigli da Uno Dei Manager Piu Dinamici Della Nuova Generazione.* Venice, Italy: Marsilio 2010.

Gratton, Lynda. *Living Strategy: Putting People at the Heart of Corporate Purpose.* London: Prentice Hall, 2000.

Heifetz, Ronald A., and Martin Linsky. *Leadership on the Line: Staying Alive through the Dangers of Leading.* Boston: Harvard Business School Press, 2002.

Heskett, James L. *The Culture Cycle: How to Shape the Unseen Force That Transforms Performance.* Upper Saddle River, NJ: FT Press, 2012.

Hill, Linda A., and Dana M. Teppert. "Luca de Meo at Volkswagen Group." Case 8-413-124 Boston: Harvard Business School, 2013.

Kanter, Rosabeth Moss. *Commitment and Community: Communes and Utopias in Sociological Perspective.* Boston: Harvard University Press, 1972.

Nayar, Vineet. *Employees First, Customers Second: Turning Conventional Management Upside Down.* Boston: Harvard Business Press, 2010.

Nohria, Nitin, and Rakesh Khurana, eds. *Handbook of Leadership Theory and Practice: An HBS Centennial Colloquium on Advancing Leadership.* Boston: Harvard Business School Press, 2010.

Pepper, John. *What Really Matters: Service, Leadership, People, and Values.* New Haven, CT: Yale University Press, 2007.

Podolny, Joel, Rakesh Khurana, and Mary Hill-Popper. "Revisiting the Meaning of Leadership." *Research in Organizational Behavior* 26, no. 1 (2005): 1–36.

Ready, Doug A., and Emily Truelove. "The Power of Collective Ambition." *Harvard Business Review*, December 2011, 94–102.

Sutton, Robert I. *Weird Ideas That Work: How to Build a Creative Company.* New York: Free Press, 2007.

Ulrich, David, and Wendy Ulrich. *The Why of Work: How Great Leaders Build Abundant Organizations That Win.* Maidenhead, UK: McGraw-Hill, 2010.

Vegt, Gerben S. van der, and J. Stuart Bunderson. "Learning and Performance in Multidisciplinary Teams: The Importance of Collective Team Identification." *Academy of Management Journal* 48, no. 3 (2005): 532–547.

Chapter 5

Chatman, Jennifer A., and Sandra A. Cha. "Leading by Leveraging Culture." *California Management Review*, July 1993, 104–111.

Gibbs, David, ed. *Pentagram: The Compendium.* London: Phaidon, 1993.

Heskett, James L. *The Culture Cycle: How to Shape the Unseen Force That Transforms Performance.* Upper Saddle River, NJ: FT Press, 2012.

Hill, Linda A., and Kent Lineback. *Being the Boss: The 3 Imperatives for Becoming a Great Leader.* Boston: Harvard Business Review Press, 2011.

Hill, Linda A., and Emily A. Stecker. "Kit Hinrichs at Pentagram (A)." Case 9-408-127. Boston: Harvard Business School, 2008.

———. "Kit Hinrichs at Pentagram (B)." Supplement 9-408-128. Boston: Harvard Business School, 2008.

Pentagram Partners and Delphine Hirasuna. *The Pentagram Papers.* San Francisco: Chronicle Books, 2006.

Schein, Edgar. *Organizational Culture and Leadership: A Dynamic View.* San Francisco: Jossey-Bass, 1985.

Simons, Robert. *Levers of Control: How Managers Use Innovative Control Systems to Drive Strategic Renewal.* Boston: Harvard Business School Press, 1995.

Thomas, Douglas, and John Seely Brown. *A New Culture of Learning: Cultivating the Imagination for a World of Constant Change.* Printed in Charleston by CreateSpace, 2011.

Yelavich, Susan, ed. *Profile: Pentagram Design.* London: Phaidon, 2004.

Chapter 6

Brand, Stewart. *How Buildings Learn: What Happens After They're Built.* New York: Viking, 1994.

Edmondson, Amy C. "Psychological Safety and Learning Behavior in Work Teams." *Administrative Science Quarterly* 44, no. 2 (1999): 350–383.

Eisenhardt, Kathleen M., Jean L. Kahwajy, and L. J. Bourgeois III. "How Management Teams Can Have a Good Fight." *Harvard Business Review*, July-August 1997, 77–85.

Ely, Robin, and David Thomas. "Cultural Diversity at Work: The Moderating Effects of Work Group Perspectives on Diversity *Administrative Science Quarterly* 46, no. 2 (June 2001): 229–273.

Florida, Richard. *Cities and the Creative Class.* London: Routledge, 2005.

———. *The Rise of the Creative Class: And How It's Transforming Work, Leisure, Community and Everyday Life.* New York: Basic Books, 2002.

Johansson, Frans. *The Medici Effect: Breakthrough Insights at the Intersection of Ideas, Concepts, and Cultures.* Boston: Harvard Business School Press, 2004.

Leonard, Dorothy, and Walter Swap. *Deep Smarts: How to Cultivate and Transfer Enduring Business Wisdom.* Boston: Harvard Business School Press, 2005.

————. *When Sparks Fly: Igniting Creativity in Groups.* Boston: Harvard Business School Press, 1999.

Page, Scott E. *The Difference: How the Power of Diversity Creates Better Groups, Firms, Schools, and Societies.* Princeton, NJ: Princeton University Press, 2008.

Pisano, Gary P. *The Development Factory: Unlocking the Potential of Process Innovation.* Boston: Harvard Business School Press, 1997.

Sawyer, R. Keith. *Group Genius: The Creative Power of Collaboration.* New York: Basic Books, 2007.

Simons, Tony L., and Randall S. Peterson. "Task Conflict and Relationship Conflict in Top Management Teams: The Pivotal Role of Intragroup Trust." *Journal of Applied Psychology* 85, no. 1 (February 2000): 102–111.

Watkins, Jane Magruder, and Bernard J. Mohr. *Appreciative Inquiry: Change at the Speed of Imagination.* San Francisco: Jossey-Bass/Pfeiffer, 2001.

Chapter 7

Edmondson, Amy C. "Strategies for Learning from Failure." *Harvard Business Review,* April 2011, 48–55.

Garvin, David A. "How Google Sold Its Engineers on Management." *Harvard Buisness Review,* December 2013, 74–82.

————. *Learning in Action: A Guide to Putting the Learning Organization to Work.* Boston: Harvard Business School Press, 2000.

Garvin, David A., Alison Berkley Wagonfeld, and Liz Kind. "Google's Project Oxygen: Do Managers Matter?" Case 9-313-110. Boston: Harvard Business School, 2013.

Gino, Francesca, and Gary P. Pisano. "Why Leaders Don't Learn from Success." *Harvard Business Review,* April 2011, 68–74.

Hill, Linda A., and Maria T. Farkas. "Meg Whitman and eBay Germany." Case 9-402-006. Boston: Harvard Business School, 2001.

————. "Meg Whitman at eBay Inc. (A)." Case 9-401-024. Boston: Harvard Business School, 2000.

————. "Philipp Justus at eBay Germany (A)." Case 9-402-007. Boston: Harvard Business School, 2002.

————. "Philipp Justus at eBay Germany (B)." Case 402-015. Boston: Harvard Business School, 2001.

Hill, Linda A., and Emily A. Stecker. "Philipp Justus at eBay Germany (C)." Case 9-409-029. Boston: Harvard Business School, 2008.

Kelley, Tom, and Jonathan Littman. *The Art of Innovation: Lessons in Creativity from IDEO, America's Leading Design Firm*. New York: Doubleday, 2001.

Martin, Roger. *The Design of Business: Why Design Thinking Is the Next Competitive Advantage*. Boston: Harvard Business Press, 2009.

McGrath, Rita Gunther, and Ian C. MacMillan. *Discovery-Driven Growth: A Breakthrough Process to Reduce Risk and Seize Opportunity*. Boston: Harvard Business School Press, 2009.

Omidyar, Pierre. "How I Did It: EBay's Founder on Innovating the Business Model of Social Change." *Harvard Business Review*, September 2011, 41–44.

Raney, Colin, and Ryan Jacoby. "Decisions by Design: Stop Deciding, Start Designing." *Rotman Magazine*, Winter 2010, 31–39.

Schrage, Michael. *Serious Play: How the World's Best Companies Simulate to Innovate*. Boston: Harvard Business School Press, 2000.

Senge, Peter M. *The Fifth Discipline: The Art and Practice of the Learning Organization*. New York: Doubleday/Currency, 2006.

Thomke, Stefan. "Enlightened Experimentation: The New Imperative for Innovation." *Harvard Business Review*, February 2001, 66–75.

Thomke, Stefan, and Eric von Hippel. "Customers as Innovators: A New Way to Create Value." *Harvard Business Review*, April 2002, 74–81.

Thomke, Stefan H. *Experimentation Matters: Unlocking the Potential of New Technologies for Innovation*. Boston: Harvard Business School Press, 2003.

Chapter 8

Camillus, John. "Strategy as a Wicked Problem." *Harvard Business Review*, May 2008, 98–106.

Follett, Mary Parker. *Creative Experience*. Bristol: Thoemmes Press, 2001.

Gertner, Jon. *The Idea Factory: Bell Labs and the Great Age of American Innovation*. New York: Penguin Press, 2012.

Heifetz, Ronald A., and Martin Linsky. *Leadership on the Line: Staying Alive through the Dangers of Leading*. Boston: Harvard Business School Press, 2002.

Hill, Linda A., and Emily A. Stecker. "Systems Infrastructure at Google (A)." Case 9-410-110. Boston: Harvard Business School, 2010.

———. "Systems Infrastructure at Google (B)." Case 9-410-111. Boston: Harvard Business School, 2010.

Martin, Roger. "How Successful Leaders Think." *Harvard Business Review*, June 2007, 60–67.

———. *The Opposable Mind: How Successful Leaders Win Through Integrative Thinking.* Boston: Harvard Business School Press, 2007.

Skarzynski, Peter, and Rowan Gibson. *Innovation to the Core: A Blueprint for Transforming the Way Your Company Innovates.* Boston: Harvard Business Press, 2008.

Weick, Karl. *The Social Psychology of Organizing.* New York: McGraw-Hill, 1969.

Chapter 9

Benkler, Yochai. *The Wealth of Networks: How Social Production Transforms Markets and Freedom.* New Haven, CT: Yale University Press, 2006.

Boudreau, Kevin J., and Karim R. Lakhani. "Using the Crowd as an Innovation Partner." *Harvard Business Review*, April 2013, 60–69.

Burt, Ronald. *Structural Holes.* Boston: Harvard Business School Press, 1992.

Chesbrough, Henry William. *Open Innovation: The New Imperative for Creating and Profiting from Technology.* Boston: Harvard Business School Press, 2003.

Gertner, Jon. *The Idea Factory: Bell Labs and the Great Age of American Innovation.* New York: Penguin Press, 2012.

Groysberg, Boris, Victoria W. Winston, and Shirley M. Spence. "Leadership in Law: Amy Schulman at DLA Piper." Case 9-407-033. Boston: Harvard Business School, 2008.

Groysberg, Boris, L. Kevin Kelly, and Bryan MacDonald. "The New Path to the C-Suite." *Harvard Business Review*, March 2011, 60–68.

Hill, Linda A., and Alison Berkley Wagonfeld. "Calit2: A UC San Diego, UC Irvine Partnership." Case 9-411-105. Boston: Harvard Business School, 2011.

Hippel, Eric von. *Democratizing Innovation.* Cambridge, MA: MIT Press, 2005.

Huston, Larry, and Nabil Sakkab. "Connect and Develop: Inside Procter & Gamble's New Model for Innovation." *Harvard Business Review*, March 2006, 58–66.

Iansiti, Marco, and Roy Levien. *The Keystone Advantage: What the New Dynamics of Business Ecosystems Mean for Strategy, Innovation, and Sustainability.* Boston: Harvard Business School, 2004.

IBM. "The Customer-Activated Enterprise: Insights from the Global C-Suite Study." Armonk, NY: IBM, October 2013.

King, Andrew, and Karim R. Lakhani. "Using Open Innovation to Identify the Best Ideas." *MIT Sloan Management Review* 55, no. 1 (Fall 2013): 41–48.

Lakhani, Karim R., Hila Lifshitz-Assaf, and Michael Tushman. "Open Innovation and Organization Boundries: Task Decomposition, Knowledge Distribution and the Locus of Innovation." In *Handbook of Economic Organization: Integrating Economic and Organization Theory*, edited by Anna Grandori, 355–382. Northampton, MA: Edward Elgar Publishing, 2013.

Martin, Roger, and James Milway. "User-Driven Innovation: Putting an End to Inventing in the Dark." *Rotman Magazine*, Fall 2012, 5–9.

Pisano, Gary P., and Roberto Verganti. "Which Kind of Collaboration Is Right for You?" *Harvard Business Review*, December 2008, 78–86.

Prahalad, C. K., and M. S. Krishnan. *The New Age of Innovation: Driving Co-created Value Through Global Networks*. New York: McGraw-Hill, 2008.

Shirky, Clay. *Here Comes Everybody: The Power of Organizing Without Organizations*. New York: Penguin, 2008.

Surowiecki, James. *The Wisdom of Crowds*. New York: Anchor Books, 2005.

Wenger, Etienne C., and William M. Snyder. "Communities of Practice: The Organizational Frontier." *Harvard Business Review*, January 2000, 139–145.

Epilogue

Ancona, Deborah, Thomas W. Malone, Wanda J. Orlikowski, and Peter M. Senge. "In Praise of the Incomplete Leader." *Harvard Business Review*, February 2007, 92–100.

Bennis, Warren G., and Thomas Robert. "Crucibles of Leadership." *Harvard Business Review*, September 2002, 39–45.

Christensen, Clayton M., Heiner Bauman, Rudy Ruggles, and Thomas M. Sadtler. "Disruptive Innovation for Social Change." *Harvard Business Review*, December 2006, 94–101.

Dyer, Jeffrey H., Hal B. Gregersen, and Clayton M. Christensen. *The Innovator's DNA: Mastering the Five Skills of Disruptive Innovators*. Boston: Harvard Business Review Press, 2011.

Govindarajan, Vijay, and Chris Trimble. *Reverse Innovation: Create Far from Home, Win Everywhere*. Boston: Harvard Business Review Press, 2012.

Groysberg, Boris, Victoria W. Winston, and Shirley M. Spence. "Leadership in Law: Amy Schulman at DLA Piper." Case 9-407-033. Boston: Harvard Business School, 2008.

Groysberg, Boris, L. Kevin Kelly, and Bryan MacDonald. "The New Path to the C-Suite." *Harvard Business Review*, March 2011, 60–68.

Hill, Linda A. *Becoming a Manager: How New Managers Master the Challenges of Leadership.* 2nd ed. Boston: Harvard Business School Press, 2003.

Hill, Linda A., and Kent Lineback. *Being the Boss: The 3 Imperatives for Becoming a Great Leader.* Boston: Harvard Business Review Press, 2011.

IBM. "The Enterprise of the Future: Global CEO Study." Armonk, NY: IBM, 2008.

Kao, John J. *Innovation Nation: How America Is Losing Its Innovation Edge, Why It Matters, and What We Can Do to Get It Back.* New York: Free Press, 2007.

Kim, Sung-joo. *Wake Up Call: A Beautiful Outcast.* Seoul: Random House JoongAng, 2000.

Lovegrove, Nick, and Matthew Thomas. "Triple-Strength Leadership." *Harvard Business Review*, September 2013, 46–56.

Mandela, Nelson. *Long Walk to Freedom: The Autobiography of Nelson Mandela.* London: Little, Brown & Company, 1995.

McCall, Morgan W. Jr. *High Flyers: Developing the Next Generation of Leaders.* Boston: Harvard Business Review Press, 1998.

McCall, Morgan W. Jr., and Michael M. Lombardo. *The Lessons of Experience.* Lexington, MA: Lexington Books, 1988.

McGonagill, Grady, and Tina Doerffer. *Leadership and Web 2.0: The Leadership Implications of the Evolving Web.* Gütersloh: Varlag Bertelsmann Stiftung, 2011.

Negroponte, Nicholas. *Being Digital.* New York: Alfred A. Knopf, 1995.

Novogratz, Jacqueline. *The Blue Sweater: Bridging the Gap Between Rich and Poor in an Interconnected World.* New York: Rodale, 2009.

Palmisano, Samuel J. "Leading Change When Business Is Good." *Harvard Business Review*, December 2004, 60–70.

Pascale, Richard T., Jerry Sternin, and Monique Sternin. *The Power of Positive Deviance: How Unlikely Innovators Solve the World's Toughest Problems.* Boston: Harvard Business Press, 2010.

Prahalad, C. K. *The Fortune at the Bottom of the Pyramid: Eradicating Poverty through Profits.* 5th anniversary ed. Upper Saddle River, NJ: Pearson Education, 2010.

Reeves, Byron, Thomas W. Malone, and Tony O'Driscoll. "Leadership's Online Labs." *Harvard Business Review*, May 2008, 58–66.

Senge, Peter M. *The Necessary Revolution: How Individuals and Organizations Are Working Together to Create a Sustainable World*. New York: Crown Publishing, 2008.

Snook, Scott. "Be, Know, Do: Forming Character the West Point Way." *Compass: A Journal of Leadership* 1, no. 2 (Spring 2004): 16–19, 38.

Washburn, Nathan T., and B. Tom Hunsaker. "Finding Great Ideas in Emerging Markets." *Harvard Business Review*, September 2011, 115–120.

INDEX

ABOUT THE AUTHORS

LINDA A. HILL

Linda A. Hill is the Wallace Brett Donham Professor of Business Administration at Harvard Business School. She is the faculty chair of the Leadership Initiative and has chaired numerous HBS Executive Education programs, including the Young Presidents' Organization Presidents' Seminar and the High Potentials Leadership Program.

Hill's consulting and executive education activities have been in the areas of leadership development, talent management, leading change and innovation, implementing global strategies, and managing cross-organizational relationships. She has worked with organizations worldwide, including General Electric, Reed Elsevier, Accenture, Pfizer, IBM, MasterCard, Mitsubishi, Morgan Stanley, the National Bank of Kuwait, AREVA, and the *Economist*.

Hill is the coauthor, with Kent Lineback, of *Being the Boss: The 3 Imperatives for Becoming a Great Leader*, which the *Wall Street Journal* named one of "Five Best Business Books to Read for Your Career in 2011." Hill is also the author of *Becoming a Manager: How New Managers Master the Challenges of Leadership* (2nd Edition), as well as course modules, award-winning multimedia management development programs, and numerous *HBR* articles. In 2013 she was named by Thinkers50 as one of the top ten management thinkers in the world.

Hill is currently a member of the boards of State Street Corporation, Eaton Corporation, and Harvard Business Publishing. She is a trustee of The Bridgespan Group and the Art Center College of Design, an adviser for the Nelson Mandela Children's Fund USA, and a special representative to the Board of Trustees of Bryn Mawr College. She is also on the advisory board of the Aspen Institute Business and Society Program.

Hill holds a PhD in behavioral sciences and an MA in educational psychology, both from the University of Chicago. She received a BA *summa cum laude* in psychology from Bryn Mawr College.

GREG BRANDEAU

Greg Brandeau is President and Chief Operating Officer of Maker Media. Previously he served as Chief Technology Officer for The Walt Disney Studios.

Prior to that, Brandeau was Senior Vice President of Technology for Pixar and Disney Animation Studios. He joined Pixar in 1996 as the studio's Director of Technology. After five successful years, during which he was promoted to Vice President, he left the studio to broaden his expertise within other areas of technology. He returned to Pixar in 2004 and was promoted to Senior Vice President in 2006. In that role, Brandeau was responsible for providing, maintaining, and continually adapting the systems and technology used in creating computer-animated feature films that put Pixar on the cutting edge of filmmaking.

Among his other career milestones, Brandeau served as Chief Information Officer for the biotechnology start-up company, Perlegen Sciences. His résumé also includes a variety of senior-level positions in Silicon Valley, including Director of Operations at NeXT.

Brandeau earned BS and MS degrees in electrical engineering from MIT. After serving in the US Air Force, he continued his education at Duke University's Fuqua School of Business, where he received an MBA.

EMILY TRUELOVE

Emily Truelove is a researcher with a decade of experience studying leadership, innovation, and organizational change in firms around the world. She is currently a PhD student in Organization Studies at MIT Sloan School of Management.

Truelove has presented her research in settings ranging from the International Design Forum in Dubai to London Business School to the Greater Boston Executive Program at MIT Sloan. She has published in outlets including *Harvard Business Review* and *Business Strategy Review*.

Previously, Truelove was a research associate at Harvard Business School and coauthored more than a dozen case studies on leadership, culture, and organizational change. She was also a researcher at ICEDR, a consortium of global companies focused on global talent management. Truelove has lived and worked in Malaysia and South Africa. She holds a master's degree in Human Development and Psychology from Harvard's Graduate School of Education and a degree in English from Johns Hopkins University.

KENT LINEBACK

Kent Lineback has authored, coauthored, or collaborated with business leaders and thinkers on fifteen books, including two bestsellers. He has coauthored four *Harvard Business Review* articles as well as articles in other business journals, such as the *European Business Review*, and blogs for harvardbusiness.org, fortune.com, and IBM. *Collective Genius* is his second collaboration with Linda Hill. They also coauthored *Being the Boss: The 3 Imperatives for Becoming a Great Leader*, which reviewers hailed as a "modern management classic" and "the manager's bible." A major online/ blended learning program based on *Being the Boss* is currently available from Harvard Business Publishing.

Lineback also coaches and speaks to executives and their teams as they face strategic opportunities and challenges so difficult they can succeed only by rising above their current capabilities.

Prior to his current work as a writer and coach, Lineback spent more than twenty-five years as a leader, executive, and manager in private, public, not-for-profit, and governmental organizations, where he wrestled with diverse challenges: creating a new organization, growing an internal start-up, and piloting an ongoing $250 million business through a fundamental rethinking of its strategy.

Lineback holds a BA from Harvard College and an MBA from Boston College.